WESTMAR COLLEGE I

W9-CBQ-126

Religious Education and Theology

Religious Education and Theology

Edited by

NORMA H. THOMPSON

Religious Education Press
Birmingham Alabama

BV
1464
.R44

Copyright © 1982 by Religious Education Press
All rights reserved

No part of this publication may be reproduced, stored in a retrieval system, or transmitted, in any form or by any means, electronic, photocopying, recording, or otherwise, without the prior written permission of the publisher.

Library of Congress Cataloging in Publication Data
Main entry under title:

Religious education and theology.

    Includes bibliographical references and index.
    1. Christian education (Theology)—Addresses, essays, lectures. I. Thompson, Norma H.
BV1464.R44   207   81-17852
ISBN 0-89135-029-2   AACR2

Religious Education Press, Inc.
1531 Wellington Road
Birmingham, Alabama 35209
10 9 8 7 6 5 4 3 2

Religious Education Press publishes books exclusively in religious education and in areas closely related to religious education. It is committed to enhancing and professionalizing religious education through the publication of serious, significant, and scholarly works.

PUBLISHER TO THE PROFESSION

100289

To William Paul Thompson

who has shared with me in
intellectual pursuits as
well as in the diverse
experiences of married life

Contents

Preface

Religious education has been subject to many fads during the years in which I have been involved in it. But one of the recurring issues, which has taken on almost faddish proportions at certain points in the history of the field, is the role of theology as it relates to the educational process. At times the scholars working at this issue were theologians; at other times they were religious educators. But the issue was never resolved except for the individuals and the groups with which they were working. Other persons saw the relationship between theology and religious education differently. As time went on, it became clear that there are diverse approaches to the problem. Out of my fascination and confusion, the idea was born to bring together essays from religious educators who were addressing this specific question. All of these persons have written on this subject and have presented distinctive points of view.

The essays in this collection are original for this work and have not been previously published. I am grateful for the willingness of these scholars to participate in this endeavor to provide a basic framework for discussion of this subject and for discerning those areas in which there may be agreement and those areas in which religious educators widely disagree. No attempt was made to present all the possible approaches to the role of theology in religious education, but rather to present the thinking of a few of the persons who are working on religious education theory and whose written works give evidence of some resolution of the problems involved. In particular, I acknowledge my gratitude that one of the essayists, James Michael Lee, is also the publisher. His help has been of immense value to me.

Contributions have been sought from Protestants and Roman Catholics. Since my purpose was to present different approaches, there is no "grand design" in the order of presentation. However, it was not my purpose to show Protestant as opposed to Roman Catholic positions, so contributions from leaders of these two faiths are interwoven in the volume. Also, there seemed no need to distinguish contributions from Protestants of evangelical theological persuasion from those of more liberal backgrounds nor to separate the representative of the emerging liberation theologies (in this case, black theology) from the more traditional theological orientations, although the nature of the essay itself sets it apart somewhat. What has been done in ordering the essays, therefore, is to begin with Randolph Crump Miller's placement of theology in the background of religious education, a view in which theology certainly does influence the educational process. From that perspective the volume moves to Gabriel Moran's "From Obstacle to Modest Contributor," in which he sees theology as supplying a part of the content of religious education but offering nothing directly to the method, structure, and institutional form of religious education. The next two articles take a radically different stand. Olivia Pearl Stokes agrees that theology does influence content and the educational process, but she presents a radical theology. James Michael Lee confines his discussion to religious instruction rather than the total work of religious education and adopts a social-science approach, because it is social science which provides an appropriate macrotheory for religious instruction. The final two articles have in common reference to intentional socialization in a community of Christian faith, although Richards uses the term *Christian education,* and Westerhoff calls this *process catechesis.*

NORMA H. THOMPSON

Chapter 1

The Role of Theology in Religious Education: An Introduction

NORMA H. THOMPSON

Theology is a term which has assumed primary importance in the Western world, especially in the Christian West. As "Queen of the Sciences" it ruled over intellectual and religious life for centuries, until comparatively recent times. In particular, theology has assumed the pinnacle role in nations in which Christianity was the major, and often the established, religion. As a result, chairs in theology were set up in European universities, and in the United States most of the early universities originated in order to train the clergy. The courses offered in such universities were almost totally related to theology, Bible, and the languages of the biblical period.

In nations where other religions than Christianity have prevailed, it appears that religious philosophy, or religious thought, has permeated all aspects of society. The ultimate questions of the meaning of life have been expounded, but theology as a "study of God" issuing in doctrine, or dogma, seems foreign to such countries. Even Judaism, which has been closely aligned to Christianity throughout the past two thousand years and which has been influenced by Christian modes in the nations where most of the Jews lived, has never developed theology as Christian scholars have. Some usage of the term, theology, is evident among Jewish scholars, but for the most part these leaders prefer the term *religious thought*.

Perhaps it is because theology in Christian circles has so often

1

issued in dogma that it has been able to assume a position of primary importance in the West; perhaps it is because of the link to the rationalism which has flowered in the West culminating in the Enlightenment. For whatever reasons, theology retains a position of importance which is almost awesome in the churches in the Western world. At the same time, theology has been dethroned in the secular world, and increasingly it appears less and less relevant to the affairs of society and even to the meaning of life for indivduals.

THE CONCERN FOR THEOLOGY IN RELIGIOUS EDUCATION

With theology holding such a dominant place in the churches, it is small wonder that the role of theology in religious education has been and continues to be one of the major issues. Early within the history of the Christian Church, at least by the middle of the third century, a statement had developed to which the Christian gave assent at the time of his baptism,[1] and the catechumenate was devised for instructing adult converts. In the period 325 to 450 the catechumenate reached its peak in development, and a somewhat closed system emerged in which the confession of faith with its attendant theological considerations was an important element. Lewis J. Sherrill summarized the Christian tradition in the ancient church as "the 'rule' of faith, its measure and standard; as such, it inevitably remained at the focus of thought and teaching in the ancient church."[2]

The "rule" of faith has continued to play a central role in Christianity until the present time. With the origin of the "religious education movement" in the early part of the twentieth century the issue was intentionally raised and answers sought. From time to time the issue has become a "hot" one. A few points in the history of

1. Lewis J. Sherrill, *The Rise of Christian Education* (New York: The Macmillan Co., 1944), p. 176.
2. Ibid., pp. 207–208.

the religious education movement give evidence of the tensions related to the role of theology in the religious education process.

No adequate history traces the relation of theology to religious education. Such a work would provide an excellent resource for the study of this field, but it remains for the future. Randolph Crump Miller, in the first essay in this volume, provides a historical background covering the period 1934 to 1950 for his own approach to the issue, and similar treatments can be found in other books and articles. In this chapter, I am not attempting to write a history of the problem, but only to highlight the controversy which has developed with respect to theology and religious education and which continues to be evident in the approaches of scholars working on the edges of the discipline.

The early years of the Religious Education Association, founded in 1903, were devoted to relating the exciting developments in education and psychology to religious education. A liberal theology formed the background in this effort, but it was not clearly enunciated. Thus, when the crisis theologies of Europe, particularly those represented by the theological works of Karl Barth and Emil Brunner, began to make an impact in the United States and tensions were rising among religious educators, members of the Religious Education Association, under the leadership of George Albert Coe, stated that "progressive religious education needs a theology, that it does not have one, and that the discovery of an adequate theology is one of our most pressing needs."[3]

An adequate theology was never developed for progressive religious education as a framework for the educational task in the main stream of Protestant Christianity. Sophia Lyons Fahs did later respond to the challenge of the neo-Reformation theologies with her work, entitled *Today's Children and Yesterday's Heritage*,[4] in which she asserted that "It matters what we believe," and in which she

3. Minutes of the Annual Meeting of the Religious Education Association, 1937, *Religious Education*, XXXIV (October-December, 1939), p. 194.
4. Sophia L. Fahs, *Today's Children and Yesterday's Heritage* (Boston: Beacon Press, 1952).

developed a system of religious thought compatible with both liberal theology and educational theory. But by that time the major
denominations (the United Presbyterian Church in the USA, the
Episcopal Church, the United Church of Christ, and others) were
already creating new curricula influenced by the crisis theologies,
and the International Council of Religious Education (later the
National Council of the Churches of Christ in the USA) had called
together denominational representatives for a complete rethinking
of the field and had issued a report in which the theological impact
was clearly evident.[5] As a result of these denominational efforts and
the ensuing curricular resources, Fahs' approach was never influential among the major denominations. As would be expected, it
became the position paper for the liberal churches, the Unitarian
and Universalist denominations.

At the turning point in this movement, roughly 1940, Harrison
Elliott fought hard to retain a concept of theology and the education
process as interacting in such a fashion that each is retesting, reinterpreting, and restructuring the other.[6] He was concerned about the
growing demand in Protestant Christianity for historical formulations. In his work, entitled *Can Religious Education Be Christian?* he
observed:

> It seems abundantly clear that these critics of a modern educa-
> tional approach to the work of the churches are reaffirming the
> historic Protestant viewpoint that there is a true interpretation of
> the Christian religion which has the authority of divine revela-
> tion, and are reemphasizing the function of religious education as
> furnishing an improved methodology for mediating this au-
> thoritative interpretation to children, young people, and adults.[7]

5. International Council of Religious Education, *A Study of Christian Education*
(Chicago: Committee on the Study of Christian Education, ICRE, 1947),
Mimeographed.

6. Harrison S. Elliott, *Can Religious Education Be Christian?* (New York: The
Macmillan Co., 1940).

7. Ibid., p. 79.

He believed that historic doctrines and traditions of the church do have a place in Christian education, but they become in his thinking resources by means of which each individual, each group, each generation must work out its own personal convictions. In this approach "there is no assumption that what a person believes makes no difference, if only he believes it hard enough to live by it."[8] For Elliott, beliefs "determine the emphasis and the direction of life and are of crucial importance. But it is beliefs that are one's own and not those which have been authoritatively accepted which are dynamic."[9]

Nevertheless, the tide was against Elliott's reinterpreting and restructuring of theology, the church, and the education process, as evidenced by such works as H. Shelton Smith's *Faith and Nurture*[10] in which he attacked Elliott's position ferociously, making sharp criticisms of prevailing liberal theology. He rejected particularly such concepts as divine immanence, growth, the goodness of human beings, and the historical Jesus. His discussion did not deal so much with the place of theology, but rather with the type of theology which should undergird religious education. After rejecting liberalism, he made his case for the "new currents in theological thought,"[11] with more emphasis placed upon what the church is teaching and less upon how it teaches. Elmer G. Homrighausen[12] had made a similar criticism in 1938 and 1939, and others followed suit during the next several years.

With the battle lines fairly well drawn between Elliott and Smith at the beginning of the period of emphasis upon theological reevaluation, later educators tended to range on the one side or the other.

---

8. Ibid., p. 88.

9. Ibid.

10. H. Shelton Smith, *Faith and Nurture* (New York: C. Scribner's Sons, 1941).

11. Ibid.

12. Elmer G. Homrighausen, "The Real Problem of Religious Education," *Religious Education* XXXIV (January-March, 1939), pp. 10–17; and "The Minister and Religious Education," *Christian Education,* (April, 1939).

In 1943 William Clayton Bower reemphasized the role of theology as a creative one in which the church is constantly reconstructing the meaning of the Christian gospel in the light of its own experience.

> Theology is most truly understood as the intellectual reflection of the church upon Christian experience and as the attempt to organize these interpretations into a logically consistent system of thought. . . . There are still depths and heights of meaning in the Christian gospel which no age in the past has exhausted and which our own age will not exhaust. It is in this movement of the forward-moving present that God always has been and is now creatively at work.[13]

By 1944 the controversy had assumed sufficient magnitude to become of pressing concern to the leaders in the International Council of Religious Education. That organization projected a study in which theological and educational foundations of Christian education were specified as a major area of exploration. The report of this study, although it did not take a radical position with regard to the place of theology (this outcome would be anticipated in an organization representing many denominations), did assume a much more definite theological position than at any time in the previous history of the Council.

In speaking of the change in attitude of the International Council, Bower and Hayward stated that: "Prior to 1937 the Council had not felt the need of attempting to state its theological position. . . . In the middle thirties, there was a general feeling in the Council that the time had come for comprehensive restudy of its entire program, from both the standpoint of practical operation and that of basic thinking."[14]

The restudy of the thirties mentioned by Bower and Hayward

    13. William Clayton Bower, *Christ and Christian Education* (New York & Nashville: Abingdon Press, 1943), pp. 72–73.
    14. William Clayton Bower and Percy Hayward, *Protestantism Faces Its Educational Task Together* (Appleton, Wisconsin: C. C. Nelson Pub. Co., 1949), pp. 52–53.

resulted in the issue in 1940 of *Christian Education Today,* a statement of philosophy of education in which a partially formulated theological position was assumed, especially apparent in the statement of objectives.[15] No section of this report dealt specifically with theology. However, when the later study (projected in 1944 and issued as *A Study of Christian Education* in 1947)[16] was undertaken, a full section on the theological and educational foundations of Christian education was included. Bower and Hayward commented that the section on "Theological and Educational Foundations" carried further the concern for theology which was only beginning to become evident in the earlier document, *Christian Education Today.* They observed that this inclusion of a section on theological foundations "marks a change in the approach to theology in that it commits itself to much more specifically theological positions than the earlier document does. In this the committee felt that its report was more in keeping with the present situation in theology."[17]

This document attempted to synthesize the liberal and neo-Reformation views. Bower and Hayward commented that "the difficulty of achieving such a synthesis arises from the fact that two widely different systems of theological thought, each based upon fundamentally different presuppositions, lie side by side in the report as they do in the constituency of the Council."[18]

The reemphasis upon theology was evident in the new "Faith and Life" curriculum of the United Presbyterian Church in the U.S.A., first published in 1948, as seen in the concern for doctrine in the *Prospectus* for the first year's publications.

Doctrinal emphases in this new curriculum should be clearly understood. Nowhere in it will there be found a set of dogmatic

15. *Christian Education Today, A Statement of Basic Philosophy* (Chicago: International Council of Religious Education, 1940).

16. *A Study of Christian Education* (Chicago: International Council of Religious Education, 1947). Mimeographed.

17. Bower and Hayward, pp. 59–60.

18. Ibid.

propositions such as might be found in a textbook of systematic theology. Children and youth cannot take over a ready-made body of truth from other people. They must wrestle with each aspect of truth in the light of their experience until they make it their own and until it becomes a part of their lives. Each child and each young person must learn to know what the Christian faith is. At each level of growth he must be confronted with certain aspects of it. This is doctrine.[19]

It will be noted that there is some ambiguity in this statement. On the one hand, it appears that pupils are not to be given a set of dogmatic propositions, and on the other hand, they are to be confronted with certain aspects of the Christian faith at every level of growth. This may indicate some uncertainty in the minds of the writers of curriculum as to the place of doctrine, or theology, in the teaching process. It may also indicate that the conflict between a revealed theology and an experience-centered curriculum had not been entirely resolved in the Presbyterian religious educational circles responsible for curriculum. Nevertheless, it clearly shows the concern for doctrine.

It was in 1950 that this concern found its most eloquent verbal expression. After struggling for some time to discover the "clue" to Christian education, Randolph Crump Miller at last concluded that the clue lies in a rediscovery of theology. "The major task of Christian education today is to discover and impart the relevance of Christian truth. The one missing topic in most educational schemes today is theology, and in theology properly interpreted lies the answer to most of the pressing educational problems of the day."[20] Since Miller has presented that insight in some detail in his chapter entitled, "Theology in the Background," and since he has put a major emphasis upon this issue throughout the intervening years, it is sufficient here to note that Miller's "clue" became a sort of rally-

19. Presbyterian Church in the U.S.A., *Christian Faith and Life, A Program for Church and Home* (Philadelphia: Board of Christian Education, 1948), p. 9.

20. Randolph Crump Miller, *The Clue to Christian Education* (New York: Scribner's Sons, 1950), p.4.

ing point for the new direction in religious education. He stated it thus:

> The clue to Christian education is the rediscovery of a relevant theology which will bridge the gap between content and method, providing the background and perspective of Christian truth by which the best methods and content will be used as tools to bring the learners into the right relationship with the living God who is revealed to us in Jesus Christ, using the guidance of parents and the fellowship of life in the church as the environment in which Christian nurture will take place.[21]

Other religious educators emphasized theology over the next several years. D. Campbell Wyckoff and Lewis J. Sherrill were among these educators, though there appears to be some difference in their approaches. For Wyckoff theology seemed to be rooted in a systematic statement of the Christian faith. "We are teachers of theology. The most profound questions with which we have to deal are summed up in the systematic statement of our faith. We teach in order to develop an awareness of certain theological questions and to make clear those propositions through which the church seeks to answer them. We teach about God, his nature, and his relationship to his universe and to man."[22] Sherrill, on the other hand, did not establish certain elements or essentials of the Christian faith, but he believed theology was important as a dynamic quality within the experience of encountering God and human beings in the Christian community. In such experiences, theological meaning is adapted to the individual person. He called this a "two-way communication in which the meaning of the symbols is developed in the dialogue going on between the interacting selves."[23]

In 1958 Allen O. Miller wrote his *Invitation to Theology,* designed

---

21. Ibid., p. 15.
22. D. Campbell Wyckoff, *The Task of Christian Education* (Philadelphia: Westminster Press, 1955), p.58.
23. Lewis J. Sherrill, *The Gift of Power* (New York: The Macmillan Co., 1955), p. 180.

as a course of theological instruction for parents, teachers, and
pastors engaged in Christian education in which he stated his intention as twofold: 1) "To help Christian parents and teachers to understand the church's teaching about God and man, and the meaning of
our existence as members of the church of Jesus Christ," and 2) "to
invite parents and teachers to accept the role of lay theologian."

By this time the concern for theology had moved away from
attempts to formulate particular truths, as the theology to be communicated, and toward a dynamic process in which a biblical theology (that is, the biblical picture of God, human beings, and the
universe) is communicated in experience, particularly in one's relationships with other human beings and with God. This, said
Sherrill, usually takes palce within the Christian community,"[24]
and it has an added dimension because of this fact, but it may take
place in any relationship between human beings or between persons
and God. Robert Koenig described this process of what might be
termed "theologizing" as the attempt of persons "to put into words
their understanding of God's working—as it affects their lives."[25]
This process of "theologizing" had considerable kinship to the reconstructive and re-creative role of theology of the liberal religious
educators and, indeed, the idea that theology and the educational
process are somehow in dialogue with each other, influencing and
affecting directions, has continued in the literature and will be found
in most of the essays in this volume. The primary difference between
the theologizing of this period and the reconstructing and reinterpreting of the liberal period, as I see it, lies in the use of biblical
theology, or the traditional theology of the church, as the criterion
for the interpretation of experience among the later religious
educators. This approach was stated by Miller thus: "The task of
Christian education is to provide opportunities for the right kind of
relationships and to interpret all relationships within the framework
of the revelation of God in Christ."[26] For the earlier religious

24. Ibid., p. 82.
25. Robert Koenig, "Theological Foundations of Christian Education,"
Church School Worker (February, 1956), p. 18.
26. Randolph Crump Miller, *Education for Christian Living* (Englewood Cliffs,
New Jersey: Prentice-Hall, 1956), p. 12.

educators, as I understand them, although Christian education was rooted in the Christian tradition and all reconstructive activity was in the stream of that tradition, there was no thought that this tradition, or the Bible, or an interpretation of the Bible, should become authoritative for the understanding of the experience.

While religious educators were working through these questions, we moved into the period of the sixties with its social unrest, its questions of the relevance of the church and religion to the problems of the world, the rise of liberation theologies (which emphasized the process of theologizing in light of not only one's individual experience, but also in relation to the experience of one's race, sex, or economic and social status), and the development within Roman Catholicism of religious education as a field. The movement to replace religious education staff in the denominations and local churches with community organizers or other social action personnel and the virtual equating of religious education and social action resulted in even greater theologizing as the "popular" approach to the role of theology in religious education. C. Ellis Nelson's "Is Church Education Something Particular?"[27] discusses the relation between social action and church education and concludes that social action is an appropriate work of the church, that it may be education if reflected upon, but the educational task of the church with respect to the problems of society is "to help church members develop a mentality for social justice." Among other movements of this period, currents of process thought (as developed into process theology) had their impact upon the educational endeavor, and these currents are still growing, it seems. Miller, though continuing to maintain that his concept of theology as the "clue" to Christian education is valid, has gradually developed that theology along process lines, as found in his more recent works.[28]

The impact of developments within Roman Catholic education

27. C. Ellis Nelson, "Is Church Education Something Particular?" *Religious Education* LXVII (January–February, 1972).

28. See Randolph Crump Miller, *The American Spirit in Theology* (Philadelphia: Pilgrim Press, 1974); *This We Can Believe* (New York: Hawthorn-Seabury, 1976); *The Theory of Christian Education Practice* (Birmingham: Religious Education Press, 1980).

during the past fifteen years has, I believe, been a vitalizing force in the entire field. James Michael Lee states that "by the seventies much of the American Catholic Church had come to the realization that religious education is not synonymous with Catholic schooling or with CCD."[29] He further states that "the growth of a distinct field of religious education within American Catholicism has enabled Catholic religious educationists and educators to engage in a depth of ecumenical dialogue and shared activities with Protestants which the very structure, rationale, and preservation orientation of a separate Catholic school system all but precluded."[30] From this time on the streams of Protestant and Roman Catholic religious education have so merged that the problems of the one are in the main the problems of the other; the leaders speak and write for both groups; the approaches to theology and religious education are not related specifically to the branch of Christianity in which one participates, but rather to the educational, sociological, and theological issues confronting the field.

In this process, however, two or three persons and movements should be seen as instrumental in bringing Roman Catholic religious education to a broader concept. First, as Lee points out, "there had never been an American Catholic religious education theorist of outstanding calibre" until the mid-fifties.[31] Religious education practice in America was derived from European theorists, among whom were Josef Andreas Jungmann, who was perhaps the most influential religious education theorist in Europe during this century and who "triggered in postwar European and American Catholic circles an emphasis on the kerygmatic character of religious education."[32] The kerygmatic emphasis highlighted salvation history with its concern for biblical theology and fidelity to the resurrection event. Among European Catholics who influenced both European

29. James Michael Lee, "Roman Catholic Religious Education," in Marvin J. Taylor, Ed., *Foundations for Christian Education in an Era of Change* (Nashville: Abingdon Press, 1976), p. 249.
30. Ibid., p. 250.
31. Ibid., p. 251.
32. Ibid., p. 252.

and American religious education leaders with this approach were Johannes Hofinger[33] and Marcel van Caster.[34]

The similarity between the salvation history approach to religious education and the biblical theological approach of Protestantism provided a common meeting ground. Abetted by the Second Vatican Council and the ecumenical dialogues arising out of that Council, the voices of several American Roman Catholic religious educators began to be heard. In the mid-fifties Gerard Sloyan was among the first of the Catholic educators to make an impact upon Protestant religious education. Gabriel Moran's work on the theology of revelation, revelation and catechetics, reexamination of priorities, and the education of adults[35] began a series of studies on the relation of revelation to religious education which was continued and which is reflected in the essay written by Moran for this work. James Michael Lee called for a "social-science approach" to religious education, which has forced Catholics and Protestants alike to reexamine their theories of religious education, especially the relation of educational practice to the traditional formulations of Christian faith.

Many more scholars, books, and events could be cited to highlight some of the points in the history of the religious education movement when the question of the role of theology has created tensions, brought forth creative leadership, or developed diverse approaches to the problem. As yet there is little Jewish participation in the discussion, but an occasional article by Eugene Borowitz, such as "Beyond Immanence,"[36] exhibits his interest and suggests

33. Johannes Hofinger, *The Art of Teaching Christian Doctrine,* rev. ed. (Notre Dame, Indiana: University of Notre Dame Press, 1962).

34. Marcel van Caster, *The Structure of Catechetics,* trans. Edward J. Dirkswager, Jr., et al (New York: Herder and Herder, 1965).

35. Gabriel Moran, *Theology of Revelation* (New York: Herder and Herder, 1966); *Design for Religion* (New York: Herder and Herder, 1971); *The Present Revelation* (New York: Herder and Herder, 1972); *Vision and Tactics: Toward an Adult Church* (New York: Herder and Herder, 1968); *Education Toward Adulthood* (New York: Paulist Press, 1979).

36. Eugene Borowitz, "Beyond Immanence," *Religious Education* 75 (July–August, 1980), pp. 387–408.

that other Jewish scholars may also be drawn into the explorations of this issue.

ISSUES IN THE ROLE OF THEOLOGY IN THE EDUCATIONAL PROCESS

The historical materials and the points of conflict or tension suggest several issues related to the role of theology in the process of religious education. Among these issues are: 1) Does theology determine (or influence) decisions regarding the content of religious education? How does theology affect methodology, objectives, curriculum, and administration in religious education? 2) Do the problems of communication prohibit or impede discussion of the issues in depth? The problems include differing usages of the terms: religious education, Christian education, church education, Christian nurture, catechetics, and catechesis. These terms relate to the educational task, but there is an equally diverse set of meanings for theological terms: God, church, salvation, redemption, revelation, liberation. 3) Does the educational process itself have a creative role to play in religious education; that is, as the process goes forward, is reconstruction and reinterpretation of the basic concepts of the faith a natural outcome of that process? What is the result of the interaction of theology and the educational process? 4) What is the impact of a growing pluralism in religion on the question of the role of theology? Is this a problem for Christian groups only, or is it applicable to the religious educational theories of all religions? Is it possible to come to an adequate resolution of this issue which is acceptable for all faiths?

Most of these issues will be reflected in the articles which follow. Some attempts are made to resolve one or more of the issues; recognition is given of the existence of such issues in several of the essays. They are presented here in an attempt to provide a systematic framework for examining the question, and they may be useful in following the development of the various approaches. They are not, therefore, developed in depth at this point, but some comments on one of them are in order.

Gabriel Moran, among other religious educators, has worked at the problem of communication and has attempted to define religious education in a distinctive manner, as different from Christian education, Jewish education, catechesis, and the other terms mentioned. John Westerhoff has adopted the Roman Catholic term, catechesis, as the most adequate term for the Christian faith community. The reader, however, will find that several of the terms mentioned above are used by the writers in this volume. They are used with different meanings, and often they are used interchangeably. I personally find it difficult to avoid using some of the terms interchangeably. My initial contacts with the field of religious education came at a period in its history when the term *religious education,* was used almost exclusively. Only later did the more restricted terms come into usage. I have mentally woven all of these terms into the broader term, religious education, and it is only when I intend to speak specifically to some point regarding Jewish education, Christian education, education as related to the church, or the nurturing process that I turn to these terms to express my meanings. Behind my usage is undoubtedly an assumption that there is a commonality in religious education which cuts across faiths, but at some points it seems advantageous to speak specifically to some aspect of one of those faiths or to the nature of the educational process.

Further, there is an emotional component to the language one uses which arises out of one's personal history. For persons who have worked for many years using a particular term, and that term has summed up their vocational commitments, no other term can replace that one about which meanings have developed except with great difficulty and much conscious effort. For Protestants, for example, the terms, catechesis and catechetics, are not part of their vocabulary, except as historical terms, so most Protestant religious educators do not follow John Westerhoff in his use of the term catechesis, even if intellectually they follow his reasoning. On the other hand, Roman Catholics have used this term, as well as catechetics, for so long that is not natural for them to shift easily to such terms as Christian education or Christian nurture. Nevertheless, a growing number of Catholics are using these terms, suggesting that if a common vocabulary can be developed religious educators might not only adopt it, but also find communication greatly facilitated.

In closing this introductory chapter and pointing toward the approaches presented by the several authors, we return to the basic question of the role of theology in the religious educational process. As stated by a contemporary religious educator, Padriac O'Hare:

> There may be several points at which theology and education are related, but at least at a functional level, theological reflection provides the religious educator with systematic investigation of the meanings and shared symbols of the religious community. As such—and despite polemic against undue influence of theology on education—it is indispensable throughout the education act, and most especially at that preeducational moment in which the teacher seeks to know her/his own mind; what to value; what to transmit.[37]

---

37. Padraic O'Hare, "Religious Education: Neo-Orthodox Influence and Empirical Corrective," *Religious Education* LXX (November–December, 1978), p. 627.

Chapter 2

Theology in the Background

RANDOLPH CRUMP MILLER

In 1934, H. Shelton Smith published in *Religious Education* an article entitled "Let Religious Educators Reckon with the Barthians." No one among the established religious educators, such as George Albert Coe, William Clayton Bower, Adelaide Case, and Harrison Elliott, had the slightest idea of responding to this challenge, and although Smith published "Is Religious Naturalism Enough?" in 1936 and "Theological Reconstruction in Religious Education" in *Christendom* in 1939, nothing resulted until Harrison Elliott published his *Can Religious Education Be Christian?* in 1940.

What was at stake was the theological understanding of religious education. Mainline religious educators, attuned to the Religious Education Association and the International Council of Religious Education, had been working with the unquestioned presuppositions of liberal theology, sometimes based on the tradition going back to Horace Bushnell and sometimes on the naturalism of the University of Chicago, but chiefly on the thought of George Albert Coe. Smith did not reject the liberal spirit or method, but he disputed some of the findings of the liberal theologians who were strongly influencing religious education. With his understanding of the history of religious thinking in the United States, Smith made his points against what he thought of as extreme positions. Although his 1934 article focused on the Barthian position, what Smith was striving for might be called a liberal orthodoxy.

Rather than move toward an exclusive emphasis on transcendence, Smith criticized the educators' stress on immanence. Bushnell, for example, according to Smith, was eager to insist on immanence as long as naturalism did not take over. Bushnell could see the supernatural in the natural and therefore could keep the balance between immanence and transcendence, although Smith doubted the success of this effort. Other liberals, however, were not as careful about the limits of immanence and moved toward a more thoroughgoing doctrine of immanence at the expense of transcendence.

Liberals had the idea that people and history were going somewhere, and therefore emphasized the idea of growth. The concept of growth was essential to Bushnell's theory of nurture and moral progress. Human beings could grow toward the kingdom of God! Henry Nelson Wieman and Walter Marshall Horton called their jointly authored book *The Growth of Religion* (1938). Wieman's naturalism interpreted God as present in the here and now as a creative synthesis. Smith did not think much of this position. When growth is tied in with the theory of evolution, or the psychology of human development, it becomes a major element in the theory of education. The combination of growth and evolution "brought modern education and liberal Christianity into fruitful cooperation."[1]

The emphasis on the divinity of human beings, a basic element in Channing's theology, was widespread among all liberals. If students were allowed to unfold their higher values and to work for understanding, love and justice would prevail. Human goodness could lead to perfection. We can have faith in the future, said Bushnell, because human goodness will overcome evil. There is an upward movement that is indicated by the findings of evolution and by the techniques of modern science. With a high value placed on human beings, the concept of sin dropped from normal usage among the educators. The paradox of being a child of God and a sinner at the same time was emptied of meaning.

1. *Faith and Nurture* (New York: Scribners, 1941), p. 14.

There has been a consistent treatment of Jesus as a human and historical figure, a view strongly held by the liberals, at least from the time of Bushnell. It has rooted the Christology of the liberals in humanity, and sometimes it has seemed that Jesus is simply an example. Bushnell, however, placed his Christology within the framework of vicarious sacrifice. No penal theory is adequate, but an understanding of God's love is sufficient. The principle of vicarious sacrifice is evident in all human beings and is different only in degree, yet Christ "differs from us, not in degree, but in kind," according to Bushnell.[2] The liberal educators, however, usually failed to make this final claim.

The social-gospel movement pointed to an earthly kingdom, which was to be fulfilled by human achievement and obedience to God's will. Adelaide T. Case in 1924 wrote: "In general, the [liberals] affirm the desirability and the possibility of operating the political unit, whether large or small, upon the humanitarian principles of Jesus—with (a) the absence of economic strife, (b) no race or class privilege, (c) participation in government of all those not physically or mentally incompetent, and (d) the ruling motive of aggression replaced by that of mutual service."[3] Smith believed that such an appeal to "the humanitarian principles of Jesus" was unrealistic, for it failed to recognize both the limitations of human creativity and the elements of sin in all human endeavors.

Smith wrote that "the theological roots of contemporary liberal religious education run far back into the history of American Christianity."[4] Smith was calling for a theological reconstruction. He was aware of the challenge of neo-orthodoxy and he was accused of deserting the liberal camp, but he wanted a continuing of the critical, liberal, and realistic spirit in the reconstruction of theology to meet the current needs, which in turn would lead to a reconstruction of religious education theory and practice. Unfortunately,

2. *God in Christ* (Hartford: Brown & Parsons, 1849), p. 75.
3. *Liberal Christianity and Religious Education* (New York: Macmillan, 1924), p.48.
4. "Theological Reconstruction in Religious Education," *Christendom* IV, No. 4 (Autumn, 1939), p. 565.

Smith never carried out publicly his theory of reconstruction, but he did make an indelible impression with his critique of the theological base that had been in the ascendency with George Albert Coe, John L. Childs, William Clayton Bower, John Dewey, and others.[5]

THE RESPONSE

What set off Smith's disavowal of liberal religious education was a 1931 book by John L. Childs, *Education and the Philosophy of Experimentalism,*[6] which was based on an empirical naturalism. It turned Smith back to a study of the history of theology in America and to a reevaluation of his religious education theory. The first reactions to his new views were negative. There were discussions in *The International Journal of Religious Education* and *Religion in Life* featuring mainline religious educators who supported liberal views and some theologians who had been influenced by European neo-orthodoxy.

Prior to the publication of *Faith and Nurture,* Harrison Elliott had written *Can Religious Education Be Christian?*,[7] a revision of his doctoral dissertation at Yale. Elliott had two goals: One was a presentation of the liberal viewpoint that protected education as a source of knowledge as well as learning; this was the theme in response to the question, can religious education be Christian? When understood in this way, of course it could, for the educational process led to a Christian world view. The second goal was an attack on neo-orthodoxy, especially Emil Brunner's position. Elliott sensed, quite rightly, that the whole movement was a threat to religious education and its theological underpinnings as he had known it. His book was a thoroughgoing and responsible defense of his position, a "last hurrah" for the liberal period.

5. See two articles by McMurray S. Richey, "Toward the Renewal of Faith and Nurture," *The Duke Divinity School Bulletin,* May, 1963, pp. 127–141, and, Spring 1964, pp. 102–113.
6. New York: Century Co., 1931.
7. New York: Macmillan, 1940.

At first the move away from liberalism was theological. Georgia Harkness wrote an article on "Theology in Religious Education" in 1941.[8] The next year, Elmer Homrighausen wrote on "The New Emphasis in Religious Education."[9] H. Shelton Smith, William Clayton Bower, and Henry Pitney Van Dusen discussed "Issues in Religious Education" for the Winter 1942-43 issue of *Religion in Life,* directly reflecting the Smith-Elliott conflict. Dewey had become the scapegoat for some of this theological analysis, for Dewey's *A Common Faith* hardly provided a theological base satisfactory to the churches. Yet Dewey's methods worked, and the question of the relation of content and method needed to be faced. In a 1943 volume, I put it this way:

> So it happened that just at the time when the better teachers in Church schools became used to modern methods and materials and had turned from the old content-centered approach, religious educators came up against the whole problem of content. This is the major task of religious educators today, for until the connection between the Christian tradition and the philosophy of modern education is made clear, there can be no satisfactory solution to the problem. In brief, the problem is this: Someone has to make a Christian out of John Dewey! By this I mean we must show how the fundamental insights of progressive education can be made consistent with the Christian way of life and belief.[10]

It is possible to work out a theology that finds the methods of John Dewey congenial. Thus there can be dialogue between the disciplines of theology and education, to the mutual benefit of both, illustrating that how one thinks theologically influences one's educational theory, as with H. Shelton Smith, and how one thinks educationally influences one's theological development, as with

---

8. *Journal of Religion* XXI, 2 (April, 1941).
9. *Christendom* VII, 1 (Winter, 1942).
10. Randolph C. Miller and Henry H. Shires, eds., *Christianity and the Contemporary Scene* (New York: Morehouse-Gorham Co., 1943), p. 197.

Harrison Elliott. But this was only the beginning of a massive effort in rethinking and restructuring the field.

In 1944, the International Council of Religious Education got into the act by forming a committee to work on the many problems facing Protestant Christian education. The task was too important to be left to professional educators. Others were enlisted. Some of the participants were Edwin E. Aubrey, John C. Bennett, Clarence T. Craig, F. Ernest Johnson, Wayne K. Clymer, and Theodore O. Wedel. Among the educators were Harrison Elliott and H. Shelton Smith, Grace Loucks Elliott, Samuel L. Hamilton, Mary Alice Jones, Gerald E. Knoff, Lewis J. Sherrill, and Luther A. Weigle. Paul H. Vieth, of Yale, was the editor of the final report, which appeared in 1947. The report stressed the interrelationships between our knowledge of the nature of human beings, our understanding of the faith which the church professes, and the principles of education which define how learning takes place.[11] It worked out the implications for educational practice and a program for Christian education in the church. *The Church and Christian Education* was an important intermediate step pointing in a positive direction and paving the way for later developments in the 1950s.

THE CLUE

It had become clear to me that theology was a key factor in understanding religious education. New ferment was already raising the level of interest in the church's educational endeavor. The Presbyterians were talking in the late 1940s about a radical new curriculum. I can remember cornering Eugene Carson Blake after his attendance at Presbyterian curriculum meetings to find out what was happening. At the same time I was exposed to the working of the Episcopalians as we explored a variety of theories of curriculum building that led to the *Seabury Series*. We found that we were

---

11. Paul H. Vieth, ed., *The Church and Christian Education* (St. Louis: Bethany Press, 1947), p. 52.

reading theology and that we were exposing our editors to theology as well as to age-group characteristics. Vesper O. Ward became editor-in-chief and proposed a program that included Martin Buber's "I-thou" relationship, the latest on group dynamics from Bethel, Maine, and an interpretation of a theology or language of relationships from Reuel Howe. Ward later withdrew from the program because of disagreements over the place of existentialism in the curriculum, but the impact of his thinking was not lost.[12] It was within this context that I wrote *The Clue to Christian Education* (1950).

In spite of H. Shelton Smith's negative critique and of Harrison Elliott's reassertion of the liberal tradition, in spite of the recovery of the biblical tradition, and in spite of the new endeavors in curriculum construction, no one was doing theology as a basis for Christian education. We were still in the battle between content and method, and I attempted to make the solution more relevant by insisting that *"the center of the curriculum is a twofold relationship between God and the learner. The curriculum is both God-centered and experience-centered. Theology must be prior to the curriculum!* Theology is 'truth-about-God-in-relation-to-man.' "[13]

This was the first breakthrough in my thinking. It resolved some problems, and it provided a context in which other problems could be resolved. It made clear that God is involved in the educational process, and that we had better come to some conclusions about the nature of God prior to forming a curriculum. This was a demand on the curriculum makers, but ultimately it was a demand on the teachers as well.

Obviously I had my own theology, but my point was that each educator had to have a theology (not necessarily mine). Later I was to spell out a biblical theology, a theology of the church, and a process theology, all built around an understanding of the language

12. See John M. Gessell, in Kendig B. Cully, ed., *The Episcopal Church and Education* (New York: Morehouse-Barlow, 1966), pp. 22–31; Reuel Howe, *Man's Need and God's Action* (New York: Seabury Press, 1953).

13. *The Clue to Christian Education* (New York: Charles Scribner & Son, 1950), p. 5.

of relationships which made possible an understanding of the slogan that resulted from this approach. The slogan for Christian education was this: *"Theology in the background: faith and grace [or grace and faith] in the foreground."*[14] The emphasis is on having a background guide for the process, but the *foreground* is the human response to God and God's response to us. For grace is God's offering of love in relationship, and faith is the human response of trust and commitment. This grace-faith relationship is an experience that we cannot create, but which we are empowered to offer to others when we have known it for ourselves. The writings of the relationship theology cohorts turn on this experience of grace and faith which is the heart of the Christian experience.

"For by grace you have been saved through faith; and this is not your own doing, it is the gift of God—not because of works, lest any one should boast" (Eph. 2:8–9, RSV). This passage indicates that we begin with a consideration of what God has done and is doing, especially of what God has done in and through Jesus Christ. It is the free gift of God to creation, providing sources of strength, enlightenment, and freedom to seek and to do God's will. We understand ourselves better through the concept of grace. "Our talents differ with the grace that is given us" (Rom. 12:6,M). "By the grace of God, I am what I am" (I Cor. 15:10, RSV). Grace is essentially a source of power. It is inescapably associated with the Cross, and it points beyond suffering to glory.

This grace is persuasive rather than irresistible. It is the product of love rather than coercion. It is a gracious personal relationship which we are free to reject. God's grace saves our freedom, and therefore is both moral and religious. John Oman writes that "grace is precisely grace because, *though wholly concerned with moral goodness, it does not at all depend on how moral we are."*[15] One meaning of grace is summarized in this prayer:

14. Ibid., p. 7. See change in word order in my *Christian Nurture and the Church* (New York: Charles Scribner & Son, 1961), p. 33 and note. For a recent treatment of the place of faith, see Thomas H. Groome, *Christian Religious Education* (San Francisco: Harper & Row, 1980), pp. 56–81.

15. John Oman, *Grace and Personality* (Cambridge: at the University Press, 1917; New York: Association Press, 1961), p. 164.

Give them grace, we pray thee, to stand fast in the faith, to obey they Word, and to abide in thy love; that, being made strong by thy Holy Spirit, they may resist temptation and overcome evil, and may rejoice in the life that now is, and dwell with thee in the life that is to come.[16]

The response to the gift of grace is faith, trust, commitment. This is a free act, and involves a change in the one who trusts. It is a decision to commit oneself completely to God, to obey God's will, and to look on the world as under God's sovereignty. It centers in Jesus Christ because of what God has done through him. The choice is influenced by other people, as well as by events, but it remains a free act.

This factor of free choice has not always been recognized, but when grace and faith are in the foreground in our thinking about Christian education, understood properly because theology is in the background, the question of decision becomes central. This is the evangelical element in Christian education. Unless the educational system of the church brings boys and girls, women and men, to the brink of the abyss, where they made a decision for Christ and are saved, or else fall back and end up in the abyss, it is not a Christian system of education. Education at this point is evangelical. It does not matter when this occurs, and it may be long postponed, but the opportunity for decision must be part of the educational process.

The author of Ephesians spells this out: "Of this gospel I was made a minister according to the gift of God's grace which was given me by the working of his power. To me, though I am the very least of all the saints, this grace was given, to preach to the Gentiles the unsearchable riches of Christ"(Eph. 3:7–8, RSV). The grace was given, says the writer, for ministry, to offer the unsearchable riches of Christ. By implication, if not directly, this was a universal ministry given to all believers.

Theodore Wedel makes much of the change that comes when the author says, "I *therefore,* a prisoner of the Lord, beg you to lead a life

16. John Wallace Suter, ed., *The Book of English Collects* (New York: Harper & Row, 1949), No. 397, p. 235.

worthy of the calling to which you have been called" (Eph. 4:1, RSV). Because of all that God has done, as recorded in the first three chapters, because we are saved by grace through faith, *therefore,* in thanksgiving, we are to fulfill our ministries.[17] These ministries vary according to the specific gifts we have received, but in any case we are to be equipped and "to equip God's people for work in his service" (Eph. 4:12,NEB). Thus we will be free from any kind of immorality, for we will be children of light.

When grace and faith are in the foreground of Christian education, the dynamics of the relationships will lead to action. We are to "walk in love" and guard against all kinds of moral decay. We can use the present opportunity to the full, avoiding the sins of pagans and others, using our brains to discern God's will in every situation. Christians gather to sing psalms, hymns, and songs, making music in their hearts and giving thanks to God. This is our hope.

HOW THEOLOGY AFFECTS EDUCATION

Sara Little, in *The Role of the Bible in Contemporary Christian Education,*[18] develops the thesis that the theory of revelation is the key to theology and its impact on educational theory and practice. She demonstrates this by a careful survey of the theological bases and educational applications of James Smart, Randolph Miller, and Lewis J. Sherrill. In each case, there is an interpretation of revelation that distinguishes one from the other. Smart, generally, supports a Barthian approach that centers all revelation in the Bible, and therefore in the Trinity as the outcome of the biblical record. This leads unhesitatingly to an emphasis on the church as the locale of education, and on faith alone as its distinguishing mark. The center of the revelation is the content which must be passed on to the learners. Smart is convinced that "if we would let God's truth loose among us, unchained and undistorted, we should soon see the

17. *Interpreter's Bible* (Nashville: Abingdon Press, 1953), X, 681–683.
18. Richmond: John Knox Press, 1961.

changes coming about, both in the Church and in the world, which we so much desire."[19] To achieve this, the educational approach must be related to a sound theology based on the Word of God. This takes place in the church, an implication made necessary by the doctrine of the Trinity. Smart writes, "Our goal must be no lesser goal than that which Jesus and the apostles had before them. We teach so that through our teaching God may work in the hearts of those whom we teach to make them disciples wholly committed to his gospel, with an understanding of it, and with a personal faith that will enable them to bear convincing witness to it in word and action in the midst of an unbelieving world. . . . God may bring into being a Church whose glory will be the fullness with which God indwells it in his love and truth and power, and whose all-embracing aim will be to serve Jesus Christ as an earthly body through which he may continue his redemption of the world."[20] "It is God who educates,"[21] and this is an ongoing process. The Bible is essential, for through it the student discovers what God has been doing for people throughout history.

Lewis J. Sherrill also begins with revelation, on which the Christian community is based. He sees the possibility of dialogue between his doctrine of revelation and his theory of Christian education in which each pole enriches the other. He says that one of the simplest ways to express the concept of revelation is as confrontation, which means that "God as infinite Personal Being faces man as a finite personal being."[22] It is God's "*Self*-disclosure," and the recipients are human beings. The media of revelation include physical nature, human nature, events in history, and Jesus Christ. We appropriate the meaning of these media so that our lives are illuminated. Such "revelation is redemptive in nature."[23] It occurs primarily within the Christian fellowship.

19. *What a Man Can Believe* (Philadelphia: Westminster Press, 1943), p. 7.
20. James Smart, *The Teaching Ministry of the Church* (Philadelphia: Westminster Press, 1954), p. 107.
21. Ibid., p. 168.
22. Lewis J. Sherrill, *The Gift of Power* (New York: Macmillan, 1955), p. 69.
23. Ibid., p. 78.

The view of Christian education which results from this interpretation of revelation is different from that of Smart. Rather than deal with content, it centers on "changes which take place in persons."[24] What happens to persons depends on the nature of the educating society, which is the Christian community, on the intentions of the learners, and on the objectives. This is summarized by Sherrill as follows: "*Christian education is the attempt, ordinarily by members of the Christian community, to participate in and to guide the changes which take place in persons in their relationship with God, with the church, with other persons, with the physical world, and with oneself.*"[25]

In an approach similar to that of Paul Tillich, but with the overtones of personalism expressed by Herbert Farmer and Reuel Howe, Sherrill works out a predicament and theme correspondence. Human beings have the capacity for wholeness, but they stand under the threat of anxiety which can undermine selfhood. Only as genuine two-way communication is developed can education deal with the human predicament in a manner that is freeing. Biblical symbols stand at the center of this kind of communication. The dynamics of this approach to Christian education are expressed in becoming new persons. Relationships are prior to symbols, and therefore "the themes of revelation lend themselves to communication from person to person in nonverbal ways." They can be "communicated to the very young before they are old enough to understand words, indeed, from the beginning of life."[26] This sounds very much like Reuel Howe or Horace Bushnell rather than like Paul Tillich.

What becomes clear in these brief condensations of the positions of Smart and Sherrill is that theology is crucial to their educational theory and practice. Smart was the general editor of the Presbyterian *Christian Faith and Life Series.* Although Sherrill had no direct influence on any series, he was a consultant on the Southern Presbyterian *Covenant Life Series.* My own *The Clue to Christian Education* was

24. Ibid., p. 79.
25. Ibid., p. 82. Sherrill's italics.
26. Ibid., p. 179.

written in conjunction with my service on the editorial board that led to the *Seabury Series*. At least two other books that were theologically oriented, Reuel Howe's *Man's Need and God's Action*[27] and David Hunter's *Christian Education As Engagement,*[28] were written to express the theological basis for the *Seabury Series*.

Sara Little's study of Smart, Miller, and Sherrill makes clear that there are differences in educational theory and practice because of previous cleavages in theological thinking. She suggests that there are two poles of thought about the Bible. The first position puts the emphasis on the content of the Bible as the dynamic element in the Bible message. It places revelation squarely within the Bible, and this content has the power to transform persons. The Bible, therefore, is always relevant without our making it so. This reflects the thinking of Karl Barth and James Smart. The second pole emphasizes the process by which God reveals himself. It turns on the acts of God in the Bible and elsewhere. Revelation is a continuing activity of God. William Temple and Emil Brunner have held this position, and it has been activated in the educational theory of Miller and to some extent Sherrill. Within this second area, says Sara Little, there is an emphasis on "the language of relationships, which is as decisive a language as that of words."[29] The *koinonia* is a community of persons in relationship with each other and with God. Within this community there may be experiences of grace to which the response is faith or commitment. It may be a question of a disclosure or insight into the understanding of God at work, and this is followed by a new or renewed act of faith. Although this approach makes use of the experience-centered curriculum, it avoids the lack of structure of that curriculum and provides a more consistent sense of meaning because of its theological root.

Remember, however, that this position was developed in the 1950s, and that Little's book was published in 1961. Much has happened in the past twenty years to throw such conclusions as those

27. New York: Seabury Press, 1953.
28. New York: Seabury Press, 1963.
29. *The Role of the Bible in Contemporary Christian Education,* p. 159.

of Smart, Miller, and Sherrill in doubt. By 1976, Sara Little wrote that we were "between" theologies.[30] The great theologians of the previous period has passed from the scene. Theology was being done, but none had captured the interest or imagination of great numbers of educators. Iris Cully wrote that process theology was "a theology for the space age,"[31] and conservative theologians were refining their tools and making social and political applications of their educational procedures. There were "special interest" theologies of blacks and other minorities, of the oppressed, of women, and of the ecologists, but these did not capture the whole picture of the condition of the world.

There are two questions facing religious education theorists today: (1) What theology can provide the background for religious education? (2) What should be the relation between theology and education? Sara Little, in dealing with the second question, lists five possibilities: theology as content, theology as norm, theology as irrelevant, "doing" theology as educating, and dialogue between theology and education.[32] Unless it is decided that theology is irrelevant, one must take up theology as one activity among others. The least the educator can do is to select a theological position as a basis for developing both theory and practice. Norma Thompson, writing on a similar question, also lists five possibilities: theology behind the curriculum, a social science approach, theology and religious education as two complementary languages, an ecumenical approach, and theologizing.[33] Within this framework, she questions the need to insist on *Christian* education as distinguished from business education or health education. She is also aware of the

30. "Theology and Religious Education," in Marvin J. Taylor, ed., *Foundations for Christian Education in an Era of Change* (Nashville: Abingdon Press, 1976), pp. 33–35.

31. Iris V. Cully, *Change, Conflict, and Self-Determination* (Philadelphia: Westminster Press, 1972), p. 81.

32. See Sara Little, "Theology and Religious Education," in Taylor, *Foundations for Christian Education*, pp. 31-33.

33. See Norma Thompson, "Current Issues in Religious Education," *Religious Education* LXXIII, No. 6 (November-December, 1978), pp. 613–618.

variety of religious expressions which a particular theology cannot include. The situation is fluid and needs restructuring which relates the traditional symbols to both history and to the world of today.

TOWARD A POSITION FOR TODAY

My own position, which has been established since 1943 but which has been consistently modified since then, is that theology stands behind the curriculum but also that theology and educational theory must be in conversation, with both elements having equal status. This was best expressed in 1943 in terms of a theology that could make use of John Dewey's education theory. In my *Education for Christian Living*,[34] I tried to bring subject matter and method together by quoting Dewey: "Method means that arrangement of subject matter which makes it most effective in use. Never is method something outside of the material. . . . It is simply an effective treatment of material."[35] The subject matter may or may not be derived from theology. It may come from knowledge of the past, of current ways of solving problems, of lesson materials and resources, and of one's own way of achieving results. The purpose of method is to make a student think, and the act of thinking is facing real problems with the resources of the person and the community. Marc Belth describes education in a similar way as that which "deals with the relationship between concepts and powers nurtured in learners, and with the methods of creating concepts as the inventions of intelligence, in whatever fields these methods come to be employed."[36] This is not simply using education as a rational exercise, however, for the human person is more than a thinking machine, and attitudes and feelings are essential elements in all activity.

A particular theology stands in the background for every educator. It may not be clearly articulated or at the forefront of one's

34. Englewood Cliffs: Prentice Hall, rev. ed., 1963, p. 168.
35. John Dewey, *Democracy and Education* (New York:Macmillan), p. 194.
36. Marc Belth, *Education as a Discipline* (Boston: Allyn & Bacon, 1965), p. 7.

consciousness, but the implications become evident upon analysis. What one assumes about the nature of God or the value of human beings becomes evident as various educational problems are faced. We have seen that James Smart held a particular view that worked itself out in his educational theory and carried over into a series of curriculum materials for the Presbyterian Church. William Temple's view of revelation led indirectly to the creation of the *Seabury Series,* although other factors, such as Martin Buber's view of the value of persons in the I-Thou relationship, was also influential. The confrontation in the light of predicament and theme was essential in Lewis Sherrill's view. But if Sara Little and Norma Thompson are right, these views do not carry much weight today, and we need a new look at the possibilities.

One possibility is that process theology, arising from A. N. Whitehead's philosophy of organism, may provide a background for Christian educational theory or practice.[37] There is a large bibliography of interpretations of this theology, but little has been done to apply it to educational theory. It should be noted, however, that Temple made use of the insights of process philosophy in his *Nature, Man and God,* and that his interpretation of revelation is consistent with an organismic view of the cosmos and with the I-thou emphasis of Martin Buber.

One starting point is the organismic view of the church. The members belong together, as in a body, and when one suffers all suffer and when one rejoices all rejoice. This kind of relationship is a New Testament view that is consistent with process philosophy, for every entity is connected with others. Howard Grimes suggests that there is a mixture of unity and community, so that the organic unity of the church consists of its members and more.[38] As Whitehead put it, "The many become one and are increased by one."[39] Thus,

37. See my *The Theory of Christian Education Practice* (Birmingham, Alabama: Religious Education Press, 1980), especially the first two chapters.

38. Howard Grimes, *The Church Redemptive* (Nashville: Abingdon Press, 1958), pp. 28–34.

39. Alfred North Whitehead, *Process and Reality* (New York: Macmillan Co., 1929, 1957) p.32.

there is a metaphysical base for the existence of the church as an organic unity without diminishing the individuality of its members. One is engrafted onto the body of Christ through baptism. The analogy here is that the child is born into a human family, an act over which the infant has no control, and also is figuratively born into that community which is the body of Christ. In time, the baby grows into a mature person and can make a decision for the family and for the church. The church becomes the redemptive community, a living and growing organism centered in Christ who is the head of the body.

Grimes summarizes it as follows: "Unless the life of the Church is carried on with a keen sense of its divine nature, that life may easily become secularized and the Church may become only a society for human betterment. Further, this view seems to be that which is most likely to bridge the gap between churches holding to congregational policy and those believing in the episcopacy in any form."[40]

This organic view of the church points to the value of the learner, who is seen as one of supreme value, as an end and not as a means for others. This valuing of a human being, which emerges from the whole Christian and Jewish traditions, fits into a process view of reality. Martin Buber has stressed the place of the I-thou relation in human community. At one level, it is a description of human relations that recognizes the value of each individual; at another level, which Buber would include in the total picture, is the relationship with God, who is also conceived of as personal. Thus, the interpersonal relationships between human beings are seen organically as well as interpersonally, and at the higher level God is experienced in an I-thou relationship.

When this is translated into educational terms, it places a tremendous demand on the teacher, the church as community, and the family of the learner. Martin Buber describes this process at some length. When the teacher is seen by the pupils as an object, as an authority figure, as someone to be scorned, the chances of a good

40. Grimes, *The Church Redemptive,* p. 33.

interpersonal relationship being achieved are slight. But the wise teacher knows this and takes steps to establish the fact that the teacher accepts each student as he or she is. The teacher's imagination or empathy makes it possible to feel the other's feelings, to become empathetic, in Whitehead's terms to prehend the other. The teacher gains humility and increased self-awareness which can lead to confidence. The student discovers that this teacher is a person who can be trusted, and so the pupil accepts the teacher as one who is participating in one's life. The pupil learns to ask new questions that probe new depths. The I-thou relationship has been achieved, at least for the moment. Thus the class becomes a unity, a group, without the loss of individuality.[41]

This view of the nature of the church places a great responsibility on the community to achieve a standard of living in relationship that is extremely difficult. This was the primary difficulty of the *Seabury Series,* which was built on the assumption that the local parish could be a redemptive community. Howard Grimes faced this problem in 1958 in *The Church Redemptive* and after establishing a view of the church as a redemptive community he worked out the programs and the administrative responsibilities for the reforming of the local congregation along these lines. He listed types of experiences provided by selected congregations where some of these goals were achieved, and there was a note of hope that others might follow along, but even the few illustrations that Grimes provided did not last. Likewise, the *Seabury Series* influenced a few parishes for a period of time, but enthusiasm died because there was no supporting structure in the parishes.

Process theology takes a look at the learner and sees a capacity for growth of the total person in relation to other persons. The potential is found in every human being for development. In the right kind of community, the creative mind will be stimulated and the affections stirred. The learner, however, is free to respond or to reject such

---

41. See Martin Buber, *Between Man and Man* (London: Routledge & Kegan Paul, 1947), pp. 83–117; see also my *Living with Anxiety* (Philadelphia: United Church Press, 1971), pp. 56–58.

stimuli. Many young people are turned off when they face a schooling situation that fails to meet them where they are, where there is no feeling for their own sense of worth, where there is an adversary relationship between pupil and teacher, and where they are not incorporated into the fellowship of the classroom, school, or church. But when they feel that their needs and desires are taken seriously, their own sense of worth is recognized, an atmosphere of mutual trust and acceptance exists, and a strong feeling of belonging to a community is experienced, learning will take place and it will become an exciting adventure for both pupil and teacher.

GOD AND EDUCATION

The freedom of the learner is guaranteed theologically by our view of God as one who has limited power but is unsurpassable except by self.[42] Charles Hartshorne says that "instead of saying that God's power is limited, . . . we should rather say: his power is absolutely maximal, the greatest possible, but even the greatest possible power is still one power among others, is not the only power. God can do everything that a God can do, everything that could be done by 'a being with no possible superior.' "[43] Whitehead believes that we have chosen the wrong model for God, and that this mistake occurred early in the development of Christianity. We have chosen the model of Caesar rather than that of Christ, stressing the brute power of an absolute monarch against the persuasive love of a tender companion. There is, says Whitehead, "the limitation for which no reason can be given: for all reason flows from it. God is the ultimate limitation, and His existence is the ultimate irrationality. For no reason can be given for just that limitation which it stands in his nature to impose. God is not concrete, but He is the ground for

42. See my "Process, Evil, and God," *American Journal of Theology and Philosophy* (May, 1980), pp. 60-70.

43. Charles Hartshorne, *The Divine Relativity* (New Haven: Yale University Press, 1948), p. 138.

concrete actuality. No reason can be given for the nature of God, because that nature is the ground for rationality."[44] "God is . . . the foundation of order, and . . . the goad towards novelty. 'Order' and 'novelty' are but the instruments of his subjective aim which is the intensification of 'formal intimacy.' "[45] The intervention of God in the world makes possible the order of the world and the creation of novelty.

According to process theology, God is affected by the world and affects the world. Because God is love at work and love is persuasive, human beings are affected by God and God feels our human feelings; there is "mutual prehension" between God and humanity. Love, however, has sharp edges and may be the source of judgment. In spite of all the talk about God as a tender companion, there is a coercive aspect as we come up against structures that can destroy us. Powerlessness as such cannot survive. The consequences of human action are not eliminated by forgiveness, although they are shared by God's love at work in our midst. Human freedom is restricted by the principle of limitation or concretion. There is, says Whitehead, "the remorseless working of things, . . . the ruthlessness of God can be personified by *Até,* the goddess of mischief. The chaff is burnt. What is inexorable in God is valuation as an aim towards 'order'; and 'order' means 'society' permissive of actualities with patterned intensities of feeling arising from adjusted contrasts. In this sense, God is the principle of concretion."[46]

With belief in this kind of deity, there is room for human freedom, chance, and evil. If God were only brute power, we would not want to worship him, but if God is persuasive and suffering love who shares our joys and sorrows, who is the source of our vision, "the immediate reaction of human nature to the religious vision is worship." "The power of God is the worship he inspires."[47] This leads us into the risk of adventure, into spontaneous and free deci-

---

44. Whitehead, *Science and the Modern World* (New York: Macmillan, 1925), Mentor edition, p. 179.

45. *Process and Reality,* p. 135.

46. *Process and Reality,* pp. 373–374.

47. *Science and the Modern World,* Mentor edition, pp. 192,191.

sions to align our wills with God's will, to seek the increase of value in the world. "The kingdom of heaven," says Whitehead, "is not the isolation of good from evil. It is the overcoming of evil by good. This transmutation of evil into good enters into the actual world by reason of the inclusion of the nature of God, which includes the ideal vision of each actual evil so met with a novel consequent as to issue in the restoration of goodness."[48] This is what we mean by grace in action, and our confidence in the working of God's grace leads to the infusion of new values into the world.

The educational challenge that emerges from such a theological base is considerable. If we believe that God works to bring about the growth of meaning and value in the world, then there is a basis for the hope that God's persuasive love will lure human beings into the orbit of love as a basis for their lives. The basis for hope is written into the nature of reality, so that no matter how dark with foreboding our view of the future may be, we believe that God is able to take what perishes and make it the basis for a new becoming, and thus God makes all things new.

We start with the present. It is all we have. The past can only be seen from the perspective of the present, although revisionist principles for reading history may be brought to bear on the data. We may reinterpret history, but we cannot remake it. This is so not only as we read the biblical story but as we tell our own stories. But we can learn to read history to discover what God has done. There is in the Bible a record of the mighty acts of God, based on the empirical facts of historical events, but given a theological explanation. This reading of history is not different for the process theologian from that of others. We can concentrate as Christians on the focal point, which is the coming of Jesus Christ into the processes of history. The Christologies that emerge will differ, and even the facts of historical occurrences will be read differently, but this may be due to a nontheological paradigm.

When one looks to the future, however, the process theologian is likely to be much less certain about any predictions in the light of

48. *Religion in the Making* (New York: Macmillan, 1926), p. 155.

current evidence. The key question is, Does God know the future? It is evident that human foresight has frequently failed. We still have differences among some groups about the timing of the end of the world. We do not read the signs of the times. The elements of chance and novelty come into the picture, and this makes all predictions tentative. But the process theologian is likely to go one step further. Because God works in the temporal sequence of creativity, the "not yet" is "not yet" even in the mind of God. God may be working his purpose out, but events may occur that will surprise God. If freedom and power can exist outside of God's control, which is the only way we can describe genuine freedom or power, the future remains open.

This places the locale of education within the present moment. It matters greatly what happens educationally in the time available, for the lost moment is permanently lost. From the perspective of the present, the learner looks at the past and the future as well as the present. There is no other perspective possible.

Knowledge, whether it be of the past, future, or present, does not have value. "That knowledge which adds greatness to character is knowledge so handled as to transform every phase of immediate experience."[49] This is why Whitehead claimed that all education is religious. He saw it as the inculcation of duty and the appreciation of beauty that led to newness of life. He would agree with Paul: "Do not be conformed to this world, but be transformed by the renewal of your mind, that you may prove what is the will of God, what is good and acceptable and perfect" (Rom. 12:2, RSV). This emphasis on the transformation of experience, when based on the making of all things new in Whitehead's thought, becomes an important factor in Christian educational theory and practice.

Such education, as we have asserted, is centered in worship. The organic nature of human community is strongly reinforced by genuine worship, the need to belong is satisfied to some extent by being in a community at worship, and the awareness of God at work in our lives comes alive in the experience of liturgy, hymn singing,

---

49. Whitehead, *Aims of Education* (New York: Macmillan, 1929), p. 32.

listening to scripture, proclamation and prayer. The corporateness of congregational worship can be understood in terms of God's prehension of the feelings and thoughts of the congregation and of each individual, and of the mutual prehension of the members of the congregation of each other in the act of worship, so that the interrelationships are manifold in their complexity. Martin Buber, with a different philosophy, described the human I-thou relationship as being inclusive of a divine I-Thou relationship, based on the idea of what it means to treat someone and to be treated as a person. Whitehead would say that what comes through strongly in such a relationship is the sense of worth, of oneself as a person valued by other persons and by God. It is within this context that Whitehead speaks of God as one who shares our pains and our joys, who "saves the world as it passes through the immediacy of his own life. It is the judgment of a tenderness which loses nothing that can be saved. It is also the judgment of a wisdom which uses what in the temporal world is mere wreckage."[50] The divine persuasion is "the power of love presenting the one purpose whose fulfillment is eternal harmony."[51] God "is the lure for feeling, the eternal urge of desire."[52] God saves the world; "He is the poet of the world, with tender patience leading it by his vision of truth, beauty, and goodness."[53]

The religious education that emerges from this theological position combines skill and imagination. As Whitehead reminds us, the acquisition of skills is a dull and repetitive process which is essential, but it may kill the imaginative zest which is what drives a person into the unknown future. Too much time spent on skills leads to degeneration, for the crux of education is that level of scholarship which unfolds the mystery and opens the channels for emerging novelty controlled by the order of things. We can receive from the past but we must live in the present. The perpetual perishing that is essential to Whitehead's understanding of process entails

50. *Process and Reality,* p. 525.
51. *Science and the Modern World,* Mentor edition, p. 192.
52. *Process and Reality,* p. 522.
53. Ibid., p. 526.

loss and finally death, which is the basis for a new becoming. Thus, we end with the biblical promise: "Behold, I make all things new" (Rev. 21:5, RSV).

Jan Struther concludes a hymn of thanksgiving with these words:

> We thank you, Lord of heaven, ...
> For zeal and zest of living,
>   For faith and understanding,
> For words to tell our loving.
>   For hope of peace unending—
> We thank you, Lord, for these.[54]

Two conclusions should be clear: (1) Theology of some kind stands in the background of any religious educational theory, and sometimes it may take over the content and give the learner a false evaluation of what it means to have a sense of worth. (2) When the right theology, which again must be open-ended, and not dogmatic, stands in the background and when grace and faith are in the foreground, the learner's sense of worth will be underscored and the teacher-pupil relationship will operate on an I-thou level within the broader community of the church, and the transforming power of the gospel will work to bring about a decision of faith in Jesus Christ.

It is not clear that process theology will be in the background for many educators. Both Sara Little and Norma Thompson see a variety of theologies as possibilities for the future of the theory of Christian education practice. The conservative theologies of the evangelicals have made strong gains in the past decades. The liberal theologies of the 1930s have a way of being resurrected without being identified. Much that Coe and Elliott and Bower wrote still has value for today's church. The relationship theology of H. H. Farmer, Reuel Howe, and Martin Buber maintains a validity in any theory that is concerned with how people relate to each other. It is

54. *The Hymnal 1940* (New York: Church Hymnal Corporation, 1943), No. 313, stanza 4.

likely that there will be a myriad of theologies at work, some more clearly articulated than others, and the conclusion of this essay is that all educators should be aware of their own theological assumptions and be capable of expressing these beliefs as they relate to educational practice.

Chapter 3

From Obstacle to Modest Contributor: Theology in Religious Education

GABRIEL MORAN

I

The relation that I wish to assert between theology and religious education is a fairly simple one, but it can be reached only by a circuitous route. I think that theology—a word used mainly but not exclusively by Christian writers—can supply part of the content of religious education. Theology cannot provide all of the content and theology has nothing directly to offer concerning the method, structure, and institutional form of religious education.

The reason why I must go a roundabout way is that theology has not functioned in the way I am proposing. Christian theology has usually been the guardian of the content of church education programs. Also, the premises of Christian theology have exercised a great influence on the methods of church education. This influence is illustrated by the strong tendency to equate teaching and preaching in church circles. If the content of a program is guaranteed by divine backing, then activites such as preaching, witnessing, or announcing are appropriate methods of presentation.

In the above paragraph, I referred to church educational programs rather than to religious education. If Christian theology determines the content and implies the method of education, then one has to ask whether the result is accurately named religious education. If a program is a branch of theology it is difficult to see how it can encompass all kinds of religious phenomena and how it can incorporate practices associated with the modern meaning of education. Some of that modern meaning of education may need challenging by religious people, but first there has to be a religious education if the challenging is to be very effective.

My claim is that the hegemony of theology over education programs in Christian circles is one of the obstacles to the emergence of religious education. My main interest in this article is removing or breaking through this obstacle. I will try to achieve my purpose by 1) examining the struggle to exist of religious education 2) looking at the word theology in relation to religious education 3) illustrating a religious approach through faith and revelation that disavows the assumptions of Christian theology while placing faith and revelation in a context of religious education.

Religious education as a distinct area of study and practice has been struggling to come into existence throughout the twentieth century. Its full emergence more likely belongs to the twenty-first century when the world will be forced to deal with religiously educating people or else be torn apart by warring sects. Despite some naive pronouncements in the 1960s about the end of religion, the religious element shows no signs of abating. Even when one acknowledges the lack of agreement on what to include under the words religious and religion there is still no denying that religion and religiousness by almost anyone's definitions are central elements in most of the world's trouble spots.

While religion and religiousness are alive and volatile, the case of religious education is not so clear. At the turn of the twentieth century a group of people in this country set out to invent an academic field and a new profession that would deserve the title religious education. Their intention and effort were admirable, but they were hampered by some of the cultural biases of the time. The bias is reflected in who they were—generally white, male, Protestant, and liberal. That composition of a group does not invalidate their work, but it did build some restrictions into their meaning of religious. From reading books like Adolph von Harnack's *What is*

Christianity (1900) or Walter Rauschenbusch's *Christianity and the Social Crisis* (1907) one can get an idea of the religion assumed by many writers of the period in which "the religious education movement" began.

This movement has not been a swelling tide of success during the last eight decades. In fact, the discernible movement has often been one of each religious group pulling back into its own narrow concerns of survival and self-protection. The 1970s on the whole seemed to be such a time for many Christian groups. However, the pressure on the churches to engage the modern world in its good aspects as well as bad, to use the tools of modern scholarship for reinterpreting traditional Christian positions, and to make intelligent understanding accessible to larger numbers of church people has not ceased. The Christian churches may in the coming decades recognize religious education not as a minor enterprise within churches but as a movement to which the church as a whole might contribute in partnership with Jews, Muslims, and other interested parties.

*   *   *

The contemporary picture can be very confusing both because what is contributing to the emergence of religious education is not so named and because the term religious education is tossed about in strange fashion. For example, in a recent article on John Dewey, Joe Burnett recalls attention to Dewey's interest in the religious: "This aspect of Dewey's thought could be most suggestive to us today, when religious education is swelling to vast proportions as an alternative to public education—no doubt for antidemocratic reasons in part, but perhaps in part because public education never has found a way to legitimately and adequately deal with religious experience as a phenomenon of ordinary experience."[1]

Several points in the above passage call for comment. On the positive side the reminder is helpful that John Dewey saw the work

---

1. "Whatever Happened to John Dewey," *Teachers College Record* 81 (1979), p. 205.

of the public school as religious. Indeed, one problem with Dewey is that he overemphasized the religious role that the public school could take. Nevertheless, his exaggeration in that direction does not excuse the continuing neglect of religion in the public school. Burnett also makes the helpful point that churches may be responding to the legitimate need for understanding religious experience even if their chief motivation is defensive and sometimes racist.

On the negative side it is not clear exactly what it is that Burnett sees "swelling to vast proportions." It would seem that what he refers to as "religious education" are the schools under church auspices (and perhaps some Jewish day schools). If so, the growth would seem much more modest than his phrase suggests. The growth of "Christian schools" in parts of the South and a slight resurgence of Roman Catholic schools after more than a decade of decline do not constitute a powerful movement nationwide. More problematic is a usage of the phrase "religious education" as "an alternative to public education." That comes dangerously close to asserting that *religious* and *public* are mutually exclusive terms or that public education is by definition not a place for religious education. If I grasp his intention correctly, I think Burnett wishes to go in the opposite direction and encourage public schools to assume responsibility for part of the religious education of children.

To conclude this comment on Burnett's statement: The continuance and expansion of Catholic, Jewish, and Protestant (often called Christian) schools is one piece of evidence for the need of religious education. On the other hand, the growth of such schools springs from a variety of motives. In any case, to equate a religious education movement with such schools is to obscure the possible emergence of religious education in many other places, including the public school and nonschool settings such as the family.

* * *

I have suggested that religious education was not actual—perhaps was not possible—before the twentieth century. We forget how recent is our meaning of religion—largely a development of the nineteenth century. We think today of religion as a set of n

elements, the elements having the names Jewish, Muslim, Hindu, Orthodox, etc. Indeed, in much of the world the query "Of what religion are you a member?" is still an unintelligible or unaskable question. Whether or not we think the existence of the question represents progress we should not forget that the question could not be asked much before the twentieth century.

I am not claiming that before this century nothing educational was done by Christian, Jewish, Muslim, or Hindu peoples. A young Jew or Catholic in the Middle Ages was immersed into the ways of one's ancestors and studied the prescribed texts. The child was participating in what today might get called religious education. But not only would they not have used that term, our application of it to them can be a misleading jump across the centuries. Using religious education in reference to the Middle Ages can obscure the fundamental change of context and means that ineluctably confronts us in the twentieth century. It would be like describing the United Nations in the thirteenth century when in fact the notion of nation state came later, not to mention an organization called United Nations much later still.

The activities by which boys and girls were initiated into Jewish, Muslim, or Christian life may have been appropriate and praiseworthy. We may and probably do have a lot to learn from that history. Nonetheless, all such practices have to be reconsidered in the twentieth century context. Now the question is one of religiously educating people in a world of Jews, Muslims, Christians, etc., instead of a world divided into "my people" (God's people) and "all the others" (infidels). The very existence of the term "religious education" implicitly acknowledges that there are people in the world who cannot be securely located on either side of the divide between the people who are God's and the people who aren't.

Religious groups still use a "binary" language when they speak intramurally. I will defend the legitimacy and what is very likely the necessity of such language for many intramural purposes (e.g. the celebration of traditional feasts). As H. Richard Niebuhr showed in a pertinent analogy, the U.S. celebration of the Fourth of July relies on the Declaration of Independence rather than the Cambridge history text.[2] A classroom, however, is a place not mainly for the singing of praise but for the critical examination of conflicting texts and competing interpretations. The very existence of religious education would call into question the adequacy of a binary language (God's people/infidels) for living in the modern world.

Many religious groups that are distrustful of everything modern, including modern education, act consistently when they oppose religious education. Even to say "Catholic education," "Christian education" or "Muslim education" is to let in some compromise with a modern way of speaking. Therefore, the defenders of the traditional way would immediately have to add that Christian education is simply another name for the true education. Islam is perhaps the clearest case in point. For several decades (though only recently recognized in most of the West) Islam has been making efforts to reestablish not "Muslim education" but simple and true education. That is, Islam is not the name of "a religion" which is somehow to qualify education but Islam is the truth, the way, and the life to which all education is subject. As Khurshid Ahmad puts it: "The primary purpose of education should be to imbue the students with their religion and ideology. . . . Education should produce men with deeply held convictions about the Islamic ideals of individual and collective life. It should develop in them the Islamic approach so that they may carve out their own way in the light of Islamic guidance."[3]

Those of us interested in religious education would do well to ponder statements like that of Ahmad's. What is not helpful is to call it a statement of religious education or even of Muslim education. Rather, it is a statement about education that describes education in such a way as to preclude the emergence of many religious questions and religious problems. One does not inquire about the religious in life; one submits to Islam.

It is difficult to find Catholic, Protestant, or Jewish writers who

2. See *The Meaning of Revelation* (New York: Macmillan, 1962).
3. Quoted in Edward Hulmes, *Commitment and Neutrality in Religious Education* (New York: Macmillan, 1979), p. 9.

advocate such a rigorously consistent meaning of education. That is, a meaning of "Christian education" that in effect renders the adjective Christian redundant would require a rejection of most of what the modern West calls education. Some Muslims say that they are willing to do just that. Catholics, Jews, and Protestants have been touched to varying degrees by modernization so that only the most extreme wing of each group can even consider being thoroughly consistent in their educational claim, that is, that their education is equivalent to acquiring the truth, the way, and the life.

Many right-wing fundamentalist groups profess to reject the modern world and to be fighting for the traditional way of life in all of its purity. What one often discovers is that their cantankerous arguments with the modern world are a rejection of what they see as profanations, but they are not entirely consistent in their rejection of possible benefits. Some prominent fundamentalists preachers are not averse to enjoying luxurious homes and first-class accommodations. The issue transcends the compromises of Christian preachers. When Shiite Muslims, beginning in 1979, attempted to reestablish true Islam in Iran, modern dress, music, and manners were designated enemies. However, much of the fervor for revolution came from students educated in U.S. universities. In addition, Ayatollah Khomeini lived in exile under protection of a Western democracy, sent his messages to Iran on audio cassettes, and when he returned to Iran he skillfully exploited ABC television. That is not to accuse Khomeini or other Islamic leaders of dishonesty, but it is to point out that a completely consistent rejection of the modern world is nearly impossible.

The Old Order Amish have tried to be consistent in their view of education and modernity.[4] As well as what other people agree are the profanations of technology (e.g., industrial pollution), the Amish have been consistent in rejecting what other people call the benefits of technology. They went to the highest court to protect their children against what the modern world calls the advantages of

4. See John Hostetler and Gertrude Huntington, *Children in Amish Society* (New York: Holt, Rinehart, 1971).

education. Whether they can maintain their protest against modern ideas or whether they are merely slowing down the march of modernity remains an open question. In either case, my choice of the Amish as example—a gentle, peaceful people—is to suggest that the struggle between the traditional way and the modern way is not necessarily a contest between sick or ignorant crackpots on one side and the obviously better specimens of humanity on the other side. A fear of things modern has a legitimate basis. The experiment called modernity is still at a precarious stage. For the traditional way, one needs induction into a consistent form of life. For the modern way, we need a complex pattern of religious education whose lines of development are not yet clear.

The difficulty of trying to live religiously within the modern context of pluralism and (supposed) progress was well formulated by J. H. Randall at the 1930 meeting of the Religious Education Association: "Can a man entertain all ideas as provisional hypotheses . . . and at the same time cherish in feeling and action the conviction of the prophet and the saint of old? Can he vigorously crusade for a right he knows is relative and tentative? Can he pour out his soul in worship of a force or an ideal he knows may be superseded tomorrow?"[5] One could possibly make changes in the wording of Randall's threefold question that would allow a positive response. As it stands, the question invites a negative reply by people serious about religion. Many people who fight against the emergence of religious education sense the doubtful outcome of living with the tensions that Randall lists. They are being consistent in trying to keep out the diversity, criticism, and openendedness that religious education entails.

Where I find inconsistency is in Christian or Jewish writers interchanging religious education with an enterprise that is defined by its Catholic, Protestant, or Jewish setting. For example, if a Catholic church gives instruction to present or prospective members it has every right to call that structure "catechetics." What it

5. Quoted in H. Shelton Smith, *Faith and Nurture* (New York: Charles Scribner's Sons, 1941), p. 113.

does not have a right to do is imply by interchanging the terms that catechetics is religious education (or even more peculiarly that religious education is a part of catechetics). What the Catholic church does in catechetical programs is undoubtedly significant for the development of religious education, but catechetics cannot pretend to be the whole thing nor is it a simple subset (along with Jewish, Muslim, etc.). What each group does internally undergoes challenge and some transformation when the setting is religious education.

II

For the development of religious education we need some penetrating and systematic thinking about religion and the religious. We have to consider the peculiar characteristics of a religious life that lead to a near contradiction between the words religious and education. The paradox can be stated this way:

1) The evidence is that to be Christian or Jewish or Muslim one should be committed to it as the truth, the life, the path. Each demands not an academic curiosity but a wholehearted commitment of oneself, not a general interest but an intense devotion.

2) The existence of a diversity of these "one ways" seems to undercut the possibility that Christian, Jewish, Muslim, or any other group can maintain its traditional position while accepting the "many ways" that modern education readily acknowledges.

This paradox—the existence of religions eliminates the possibility of being religious—has been with us throughout the twentieth century. The rationalists in the early part of the century thought that the problem was soluble by a further application of modern science which would finally turn religion into something completely rational or else would enlighten the masses so that they would no longer be religious. We still have this scientific approach to religion, with its roots in the nineteenth century. Such science has produced some valuable information and understanding, but its hoped for result—the transformation of either religion or the masses—has not occurred.

On the other side we still have Christian, Jewish, or Muslim leaders speaking the peculiar inner language of their respective traditions. They confidently assert what God thinks on the basis of what God has said in one text or another. They know what God wishes because they draw conclusions and make applications from the statements of his will in their possession. One group may look bemusedly on the superstitions of another, and some people claim to have extricated themselves from all such groups. Nonetheless, these inner languages, with their intense emotional drives, show no signs of disappearing.

What we have had for most of the twentieth century and what is liable to get much worse is a standoff between these two languages. Neither language alone can satisfy a human being. The defenders of "one God, one way" cannot allow any real diversity, nor will they submit to "mere human reason." The defenders of reason have no place for the irrationalities of religion except as an aberration to be explained. In its perfectly reasonable fashion, modern rationalism will gladly accept religion on the one condition that it cease to be religious.

I do not think I am exaggerating the severity of the conflict. There is an enormous difference between an ancient approach of praying over sacred texts and a modern approach which looks upon everything without exception as material for human analysis. The conflict is not always obvious because it is blurred from both sides. The modern scholar is taught a form of tolerance which avoids any open ridicule or disparagement of texts that are claimed to be from or about God. "Of course, that is the way religious people speak, and because we are open and tolerant we understand them." Those who speak for or about God have often learned the skills of modern scholarship. History, languages, and social sciences can be put at the service of a claim to speak with an authority that is above the uncertainties of human existence.

Neither of these two approaches to the religious life ("What did God say to my people?" "How do I understand this phenomenon of religion?") provides an adequate basis for a religious education. The demand of religious education is to think through the way of being religious in a context of education. That entails thinking through the meaning of one's own religious life in relation to both those who share that life and those who do not. Of those who do not, some profess no religion at all (not a puzzling fact in any era of history). However, others profess to be religious but in a way different from my people. It is this latter case that is the cause of confusion in the twentieth century and the reason why there is a need for religious education.

Can one allow the claims inherent to Catholicism or Islam and still carry on the relativizing (placing in relation) that is part of modern education? Note that the question is not mainly one of comparing Catholicism and Judaism, Catholicism and Islam; relious education does not mean one lone course in "comparative religion." The simpler but more shaking question is: Can one make sense of being a Catholic in a world where one acknowledges the existence of intelligent and holy Jews? An immediate and confident yes to this question may obscure the difficult issue of relating tolerance and religious commitment.

I think the most that anyone can claim today is to be reducing blatant intolerance while working to create categories that would allow for beginning conversation. Claiming to have done more than that is liable to stop a conversation. As an example of an excessive claim, consider this statement of Radhakrishnan: "When the Hindu found that different people aimed at and achieved God-realization in different ways, he generously recognized them all and justified their place in the course of history."[6] If this author had wished to claim that Hinduism is more tolerant (or less intolerant) than Catholicism and Islam he would have had a good case. But claiming to have "justified their place in the course of history" is indefensible for the simple reason that these other groups do not in the least accept that place. Christianity has often made analogous claims to generous recognition of others. With reference to Jews, for example, Christian teaching has always "justified their place in the course of history." Not only do Jews not applaud this justification, but they consider it a particularly objectionable form of intolerance.

6. *The Hindu View of Life* (New York: Macmillan, 1941), p. 16.

I think it is admirable if Hinduism in its inner language does not speak negatively of the Christ figure. Likewise, the removal of "perfidious Jews" from the Catholic liturgy is undoubtedly progress. But such accomplishments have to be seen as the first baby steps in a journey that will be decades long. No one yet has a position that can be easily reconciled with the demands of both religion and education.

Real progress comes with the recognition that the other people really are other. Instead of being a piece of our puzzle whose location we contemplate, they speak for themselves. They thereby threaten our complacent assumptions about our own identity. Only if we can acknowledge the threat posed by the other can the other eventually become a partner in a process mutually beneficial. "Once the assumption that the stranger is inferior is shattered, then he is experienced as a stranger. And once you admit that you do not understand *him* (or her), you are gradually forced to admit that you do not understand yourself."[7]

The religious language of religious education would have to be a language sensitive to the two different kinds of splits I have noted: 1) the inner language of one religious group and the inner language of other religious groups 2) the inner language of religious groups and the language which lies beyond devotion to any religious group. We need from the common fund of language at least some terms that can mediate these two divisions. In the latter part of this essay I will discuss two terms, faith and revelation, that have a good chance to be currency in intrareligious discussion (e.g., Christian-Muslim) and religious/nonreligious conversation. One would have to be consistent in distinguishing such terms from the meanings they assume in exclusively Christian, Muslim, or Jewish settings.

*   *   *

I have been claiming that for the development of an adequate field of religious education we need a comprehensive and systematic

7. Nicholas Lash, *Theology on Dover Beach* (New York: Paulist, 1979), p. 71.

study of the religious. Many people within the Christian churches would presume that I am referring to theology. It is possible that the study I refer to may some day be called theology, but on the basis of etymology, history, and present usage I think that is unlikely. Theology is too closely associated with the inner language, one of the conflicting parties not the mediator. If there has been an operative meaning of theology for seven hundred and perhaps up to fifteen hundred years, it does not change with a few writers saying: "The real meaning of theology is . . .". Christian theologians may claim that other people's religious discourse is "theological" but that is no more persuasive than Hindus "justifying the place" of Christians or Jews in world history.

Christian theology supplies some of the content for religious education. No Christian would take part in a field of religious education if it excluded the New Testament, various church doctrines, and some of the writings of people called theologians. The content taken from Christian theology would be subject to criticism when placed in the educational context of religious education. The first criticism would be directed at the *word* theology itself.

The word theology expresses the claim that a group deals with God. "Our way is guaranteed not by mere human wisdom but by the "word(s) of God." A religious education that is dealing with the double division described above must a) respect the group's claim and its symbolic ways of speaking b) not accept the claim at face value for the simple reason that there are competing claims. Can Catholics be "the people of God" and Jews be "the chosen people?" Possibly. But to begin exploring the issue requires a logic and language beyond the inner languages of either Catholicism or Judaism.

An instructive example of the operative meaning of theology is the case of Hans Küng in the Catholic church. In 1979 the Vatican declared that Küng no longer had an official mandate to teach Catholic theology. He was neither forbidden to teach or excommunicated from the Roman Catholic Church. Instead, the Vatican said that he had stepped beyond a line that made his writings no longer theology. Whatever liberal theologians have recently tried to make of the word theology, the Vatican had the centuries on its side. One could surely protest that the Vatican drew the line at the wrong place or even that their method of deciding where to draw the line needs reform, but a line between orthodox theology and heterodoxy has never been doubted in Catholic history nor in most of Protestantism.

Can the word theology be cut loose from its historical association with the question of orthodoxy? I doubt that it can, and I also doubt that most theologians would make that choice were it available. The limitation of orthodoxy is also the guarantee that one is dealing with more than passing fads. Theology avoids being merely academic because it lays claim to divine truth. If one takes this rich but narrow path one must abide by the consequences.

In a rather shrill commentary on the Küng affair, Jurgen Moltmann writes: "Within the church, theology is responsible for itself. To make it into a mere explicator and defender of a doctrine laid down by the church is to reduce it to impotence. Are theologians nothing more than apologists for church doctrine?"[8] If one gives a full enough meaning to the word apologist, I think that would be a good description of theologians. I would wager that most people within the Christian churches see theology that way and nearly everyone outside the churches. What is wrong with explicating the "doctrine laid down by the church" if one means by church not a Vatican official but two thousand years of Christian history. Occasionally a genius may arise who explicates the texts in a way no one previously has; he or she is liable to be in temporary trouble. A longer view of history may show that such a person was on the side of sound doctrine. In the middle of personal battles for one's reputation it is not easy to keep such a long-range vision of church history.

The work of biblical exegetes, church historians, and apologists for Christian doctrine is an invaluable contribution to the work of religious educators. Creative minds within any religious tradition

8. Jurgen Moltmann, "The Hans Küng Case," in *Christian Century* (February 20, 1980).

always experience some frustration when they encounter the current limits of orthodoxy. If they are willing to be patient and to be careful in recovering other strands of the tradition, they may succeed in expanding the limits of what is orthodox. If Küng, Moltmann, and others are unhappy in the role of theologian, perhaps they should consider becoming religious educators.

*   *   *

There are numerous proposals to change the "model" or "paradigm" of Christian theology. But such changes have gone on regularly for centuries. The choice of conceptual frameworks for explicating Christian doctrine has changed from one era to the next. There has been theology called monastic, scholastic, federal, dialectical, existential, etc. What Christian theologians seem unwilling to grasp or to admit is that today the question is not models of theology but theology as one model. That is, whatever variations exist within Christian theology, it is itself only one model (or better, one language) for religious speaking. Theology came into the Christian church from Greek ancestry when the church was trying to defend and explain itself. Some of the elaborate systems of theology have a beautiful consistency when taken on their own terms. They remain important to one part of church life, and they can provide some of the content for religious education. What they cannot claim to do is to own the field of religious language (and thereby the control of religious education).

An example of what strikes me as hopelessly misguided radicalism is Charles McCoy's *When Gods Change*.[9] The big enemy in this book is the "Constantinian paradigm of theology," a phrase that appears well over a hundred times. The writer wishes to transform theology so that it will no longer be the "function of a particular ecclesiastical conclave." His criticism of what the word theology has meant ever since the word entered Christian history provides strong evidence that what he is criticizing is not a paradigm but the thing itself. He could conceivably argue that the future is

9. *When Gods Change* (New York: Abingdon, 1979).

going to be different despite all the evidence of the past. Instead, he drifts into reference to a world that has never existed: "The transformation of theology points the way toward the return of theology into the university and societal context from which Constantinian theology in its more ecclesiastical manifestations withdrew."[10] I cannot imagine what era he is referring to before the advent of Constantinian theology when theology was in the university and had less of an ecclesiastical manifestation.

As a final note in this section I would like to comment on the extent to which my position is continuous or discontinuous with what I have written during the past two decades. In the mid-1960s, I was urging the need for sound theology in the catechetical movement of the Catholic church, claiming that it was theology which would make or break the movement. I would not today repudiate that position, but my context is fundamentally different. During the past decade, my interest has been a field of religious education within which Christian theology can play only a small role. In contrast, theology is almost by definition the guiding hand of catechetical instruction. There was a short period in the Catholic church when theology seemed to be on one side and the Bible/ liturgy on the other side. What I wrote against in the 1960s was the illusion that one could strip away theology to reveal a kind of naked narrative and simple piety.[11]

My emphasis on theology was not in opposition, for example, to the social sciences. I was advocating a reflected-upon theology as opposed to a biblical-liturgical approach that unreflectingly assumed a theology. Neither in the past nor the present would I disagree with James Michael Lee's premise that we need a "social science approach to religious instruction." I do not use that phrase, but I certainly think that a social psychologist would be more helpful than a theologian in the approach to religious instruction. The difference between Lee and myself has never been over a theological versus social scientific approach. Rather, we have dif-

10. Ibid., pp. 236f.
11. See my *Catechesis of Revelation* (New York: Herder and Herder, 1966).

fered over *what we are approaching.* His interest is "religious instruction," and though I have some interest in that topic it is almost
never my main concern. Furthermore, when I do refer to religious
instruction it is from a different angle of approach than does James
Michael Lee. We differ radically, I think, on the relation between
religious instruction and religious education. I am interested in the
institutional forms and political implications of education. I would
call my approach to religious education political/aesthetic. Theology and social sciences have definite contributions to make to Christian religious instruction. In my view, neither theology nor social
science should have the right to define what constitutes the overall
meaning of religious education.

*   *   *

I could end my essay here, having tried to state the important but
modest role that Christian theology has within the developing field
of religious education. However, I don't think I would have demonstrated why the question remains a sticky issue and how some
progress might be made. At one level my proposal simply seems to
mean: Let theology be a part of the content not the whole. But I
have also said that the word theology itself becomes problematic in
the context of religious education. As only one of the players in
the game theology becomes subject to outside criticism, starting
with criticism of the face value of the word theology.

Asking theology to submit to religious education may sound
equivalent to asking a college professor to be judged by a kindergar-
ten. Religious education as a context in which people are interested
in understanding and living religiously would be an uncompromising but kind judge. Material from Christian theology will be
judged not on whether it carries official approbation but whether
it humanly, religiously, experientially makes sense. Of course,
material from Christian (Jewish, Muslim, etc.) history can be
prematurely rejected as "irrelevant" or unintelligible when the
real problem is with the hearer. But the word theology itself,
because it lays claim to a status that the person engaged in reli-

gious inquiry may not be ready to accord the material, can be an obstacle to religious education.

If theologians wish to claim that the word theology can indeed cover the entire ground for the systematic study of religious life, their case would have to include these three claims: 1) that theology can be as much a non-Christian word as a Christian word 2) that theology can describe ways of speaking and writing that are presentational as well as discursive, which means that poetry or biography are not just lesser forms of a properly doctrinal theology 3) that theology is not under the direct or subtle control of guardians of orthodoxy. Because in practice Christian writers have assumed that theology extends to all religious speech, then it is difficult to ask questions in religious education that are clearly not theological questions (i.e., questions which assume premises of Christian theology). The problem extends to the Jew or Muslim. In the United States, a country which is 97 percent non-Jewish/non-Muslim, it is difficult to identify an available religious language once the Jews or Muslims step beyond the inner language of their own traditions.

III

What I wish to do in the remainder of this essay is to illustrate with two key terms, faith and revelation, the building of a two-pronged bridge between religions and between religious and non-religious speech. The question of faith and revelation is posed from within religious education; if Christian theology has any help to offer it will be welcome. As it is, Christian theology often functions as a block to asking this question. Theology was to such a large extent built upon the categories of "the Christian revelation" and "the Christian faith" that it may seem blasphemous to attempt radical surgery on these two terms. But the religious need of the day and an educational approach to religion require us to ask the meanings of faith and revelation as something other than theological questions.

At the base of Judaism, Christianity, and Islam there is an inter-connection of the words faith and revelation. I don't think one can easily include Eastern religion in what follows, although the word faith might be found there. In the Western religions the ultimate metaphor was revelation, a term that allowed Greek and Hebrew traditions to meet (in Jewish as well as Christian history). In the East the ultimate metaphor has been enlightenment; interestingly, this image has also dominated modern secularism in the West. Before the Western religions try to understand both modern sec-ularism and Eastern religions they ought to spend time understand-ing their own foundations in the terms faith/revelation. In current Christian writing the word revelation has almost disappeared, leav-ing the word faith to cover the whole territory. Faith is hopelessly outmatched in its attempt to be all things to all people.

*   *   *

My thesis here is a simple one: Jewish, Christian, and Muslim people can be described by saying that they each wished to believe in the only God there is. The word "monotheism" is a deadening modern distortion that turns these histories into abstract discussion about the number of Gods. It was not that they calculated that there is one deity but rather (in what sounds like a backwards formulation to modern ears) there is no other God except "the unnameable" who has appeared in our daily existence. One either believed in that more than nameable reality or one didn't; one lived faithfully or one was an infidel.

If Jewish, Christian, and Muslim worlds could have been segre-gated they might have worked through their "one and only faith in the one and only God" in three different ways. However, when the three are visible to one another then the illogic of three "one and only faiths in the one and only God" is literally intolerable. The intolerance of Christianity for Judaism took on a bloody form for centuries, a scandal that pressures Christian theology to search its foundations for the cause of that persecution. As for why Chris-tianity and Islam have not been able to coexist peacefully, a Muslim writer says: "Even to consider such a pacific possibility is to ignore the essential nature of living faiths—that they claim—they must claim—to have a monopoly of 'truth.' A 'living God' is a 'jealous God' and cannot tolerate competitors. . . . The relationship of the two religions could not but be wholly antagonistic in the Age of Faith. Interfaith tolerance and ecumenical movements are sure indications of a slackening of belief."[12]

I think that this statement is thoroughly and dangerously in error, but I also think most Christian writing has no response to the challenge because it manifests the same confusion, namely, an equating of faith and religion, and an equating of faith and belief. I will argue that the set of doctrines, practices, and institutions that carry the names Christianity and Islam should be called religions, not faiths. As a first step in clarifying the issue of faith, this point must be insisted upon without compromise: there is no Muslim faith, there is no Jewish faith, there is no Christian faith. There can be no clash between faiths if there is only one faith, and thus the problem of "interfaith tolerance" is dissolved.

Far from doing violence to Judaism, Islam, and Christianity, I am trying to locate the driving impluse in the originating documents of these three great historical movements. Each of the three groups was certain that there is only one God, one revelation of God, one will of God, one faith in God. I do not think that any one of the three religions can or should stray from this foundation. What each religion has to do is find the way to say explicitly (and not implicitly deny it a moment later) that faith is not exclusively in the domain of their own religious history. The basis for such a distinction resides within the history of each group. The Christian (Jewish, Muslim) community developed a multiplicity of signs to indicate who was and who was not of God; nonetheless, that judgement finally belongs to God. In Christianity, the church is important to the Christian, but no object nor the entire set of objects that make up this historical and social institution is equivalent to faith. There is no "Christian faith"; there is faith in God, and there are pointers to and expressions from the act of believing in God.

12. G. H. Jansen, *Militant Islam* (New York: Harper and Row, 1980), p. 49.

Catholic, Protestant, and Orthodox Christianity do not differ on this point.

While I have distinguished faith and religion in the preceding paragraph I have not separated them. The recognition that faith is not religion has often led to an opposition between the two. This position has been more typically Protestant than Roman Catholic, but it has flooded liberal Catholic writing in recent decades. For example, Gerard Noel in *The Anatomy of the Catholic Church* writes: "The 'religious' man does not find it difficult to talk to God, even if he often has to devise a special and rather stilted language. . . . To accompany the language, other paraphernalia is introduced: music, candles, incense, incantations, relics, rubrics, and rituals. The man of faith however, barely talks to God at all. God talks to him; and man listens."[13] The sexist language of this description is not accidental. The choice is between promethean man inventing his religious gods and the lonely man of faith to whom God talks. What such language precludes is considering the fact that "believing in" is what children do with their parents and what women and men do with each other. The religious "paraphernalia" can be an integral display of men, women, children, and nonhumans accepting life together.

The rich meaning of faith that came out of the religious traditions is still embedded in contemporary English. A misused or reduced meaning of faith is also part of the language so that one must fight for the richest meaning of faith, but it is not a quixotic endeavor. The trouble with much Christian writing is that it is not content to fight for the word faith, allowing and inviting other religious people to join the effort. Christian writers wish not to recover faith but to establish "Christian faith," a term which confuses and undercuts the securing of faith.

The most positive meaning of faith is as a verb and refers to a personal attitude. The clearest, even if somewhat clumsy, way to indicate the meaning is to substitute "to believe in." The preposi-

---

13. *The Anatomy of the Catholic Church* (Garden City: Doubleday, 1979), p. 256.

tion "in" indicates that not only is there someone doing the believing but that there is someone (or something of a personal nature) that is believed. The English word faith carries two other meanings: "to believe that" (followed by an object, often in the form of a statement) and "beliefs," meaning that which one believes. Thus, there are two verbs and one noun in this complex term; more confusing still, it is one of the verb meanings that Christian, Jewish, and Muslim writers are trying to recapture from a word that in English is grammatically a noun.

One or several of the following images can render this meaning of faith (to believe in): 1) to be open, 2) to say yes, 3) to trust, 4) to give one's heart to, 5) to listen, 6) to respond. The meaning of faith has reemerged in the twentieth century within philosophy, psychology, economics, and dozens of other places. Underneath all of a person's knowledge and choices there is an attitude toward life and death. A person "believes in" in order to know but even more basically to be. Much of eighteenth and nineteenth century philosophy would be amazed if it could awake to discover that faith is not only alive but flourishing in every area of human life. Some of those hard-headed empiricists would call this development a failure of nerve or a lack of brains. However, it may also be that the humans having got near the limits of their promethean posturing are now more sanely aware of their tininess, vulnerability, and interdependence in a world not of their own making.

Christian writers are attracted to and encouraged by the resurgence of faith (to believe in), but that meaning is available only if one accepts the limitations of the word. The price of the richest meaning of faith (to believe in) is that one not try to extend its meaning beyond the simple human act of trust toward God and thereby everything (or toward everything, thereby God). The word takes no qualifiers except terms like greater/lesser to indicate the direction of a life.

In the other two senses of faith ("to believe that," "beliefs") one could say Christian faith, but it would be clearer to say "Christian belief." Like religion, of which beliefs are a part, I would not at all disparage believing that and beliefs. Beliefs are indispensable as one of the expressions of and helps toward faith as believing in. Two points must be stressed with reference to beliefs: 1) beliefs are not a peculiarity of religion; to refer to a religious group as believers seems to imply that Southern democrats, Soviet bureaucrats, or Midwestern farmers are not believers; 2) beliefs are only a small part of the complex structure of religious objects. Dance, architecture, or immersion into water may be more important than anything formulated into a belief.

The above two points are connected. As the religious life of a people is reduced to statements of belief then the distinguishing mark appears to be that they only *believe* things, while in the rest of the world people really *know* things. W. Cantwell Smith makes a good point, though I think he overstates it, in writing "that religious people are expected to believe something is a modern aberration."[14] I think more accurately it could be said "that religious people are the only ones expected to believe something and that religious people are only expected to believe something is a double modern aberration."

Beliefs do play a part in religion, and it is dangerous to speak of religious beliefs as dispensable or negative. When belief is the first question it is usually the wrong one. What can be identified as beliefs are usually residues of the past or an outer fence for the present group. In the television series *The Long Search,* the commentator persistently asks each group: What are your beliefs? To which each group with a somewhat puzzled look responds in effect: Why ask that question? If you wish to understand our way of life, come watch the way we live.

I described the beliefs of a religious group as an outer fence. Much of Christian difficulty comes from talking of official creeds and Christian doctrine as "expressions of faith." No doubt they were once the expressions of someone's faith. Today these doctrines could be stimulating enough to lead a person into inquiry about the Christian church. Instead of an expression from faith, they could be taken as an impression into faith. For church members, doctrine

---

14. *Faith and Belief* (Princeton: Princeton University, 1979), p. 38.

should have a mainly negative meaning, that is, one should not fly directly against these doctrines or one is liable to be outside the church. A lot of grief could be avoided by people who are not sure whether they can assent to all the doctrines of the church.

Jewish practice is clearer than Christian here. For the Jew only the explicit denial of a few key doctrines central to the tradition would be a sign of "loss of faith."[15] What may appear to the Christian as a burdensome legal structure can for the Jew be an outer fence that lets life proceed within. The Christian tendency to encompass the Bible and doctrine under "Christian faith" leads almost inevitably to making the profession of faith (i.e. beliefs) the test of being Christian and of being faithful. Better signs of faith, such as struggling against injustice, are thereby neglected. Ironically, the Christian doctrines that could make up some fascinating content for religious education (whether in church institutions or not) are seldom investigated that way.

In summary, we cannot understand what other people see, experience, and know while we keep asking: What do they believe? We cannot even ask what we see, experience, and know so long as we talk about Christian faith. Religious education is an exploration of those religious structures by which we might understand ourselves and others. One must begin by presuming that we are all joined in faith, or at least that none of us is totally lacking in faith. Lack of faith or "bad faith" is a condition that needs proving by multiple signs. When we wish to refer to the objects of the Christian religion we would do well to say Christian scripture, Christian sacraments, Christian doctrine, Christian beliefs, etc. So long as "Christian faith" floats about then Christian writers confusedly mix the exalted but subjective meaning of faith with the concreteness of reference to objects designated as Christian.

*　*　*

It is time to turn to the missing piece of the puzzle in contemporary Christian writing: revelation. In the past, the terms faith and

15. See Martin Buber, *Two Types of Faith* (New York: Harper Torch, 1961), p. 43.

revelation had to go together: faith was in response to a revelation of God, or the revelation of God called forth a response of faith. While the word faith has regained a positive meaning in contemporary thought, the word revelation has suffered a decline. Yet the matter cannot be left there. Faith cannot stand alone, because the positive, modern meaning is one that is inner, subjective, and individual. There is nothing wrong with a word's meaning being inner, subjective, and individual if it is embedded in a language that has words denoting the outer, objective, and collective. Even better would be words that refer to the relational, interpersonal, social, political, and ecological.

Revelation has been a difficult, almost embarrassing word for modern students of Christianity. Having slowly withdrawn the meaning of the word revelation into an isolated part of Christian theology, theologians made the term indefensible. It is assumed to mean information not accessible to human reason, a notion which most of Christian theology would rather not try to explain or to defend. Somewhere and somehow God gave us "the Christian revelation" which is what theology presupposes. A recent article opens with the sentence: "With a fair degree of unanimity, theologians would be willing to describe revelation as the action of God whereby he communicates to intelligent creatures knowledge or awareness of what normally lies beyond their ken."[16] That is a fair statement of eighteenth-century theology and, to the extent that contemporary writers seldom investigate the intelligibility of the claim, the statement is probably accurate. Christian theology still assumes that Christians (or some Christians) have a knowledge from God that lies outside normal human knowing.

To great numbers of people, including some church people, this assumption of theology is peculiarly arrogant and stops conversation with anyone who does not make that assumption. The problem here is similar to that of faith. As soon as one says "Christian faith" one is no longer referring to the inner attitude of believing in but to some

16. Avery Dulles, "The Symbolic Structure of Revelation," in *Theological Studies* 41 (March, 1980), p. 81.

object within church definition. As soon as one says "Christian revelation" one is referring not to the whole pattern of the universe where God acts but to an object (knowledge that is discussed by theologians).

The proposal I make here is the same as with faith: there is no Christian (Jewish, Muslim) revelation. There is the revelation of everything and thereby God; there is the revelation of God and thereby everything. Is the word necessary at all if it refers to everyone and everything? The answer is yes for reasons which must be stated negatively, the peculiar form that religious language takes. Revelation is a word that reminds us that reality is not reducible to a set of facts and objects but is the unveiling of mystery. Revelation is a reminder that what is attained by human beings is not theirs by conquest but theirs by gift; all truth is an unveiling. Both reminders if pushed far enough lead to a recognition of the universe as a personalizing place where something greater than our private egos is being born. Revelation as ultimate metaphor is neither attitude nor object but a way of being in relation.

The Jewish, Christian, and Muslim religions all attempt to be (not have) that revelation. All three religions, when they are self-critical, admit that they are not and never will be that revelation. What they can strive to be is a re-presentation of the revelation of God/creation. All three religions in less self-critical moments speak as though each respectively is (or has) the revelation. While in previous ages it may have seemed a minor distortion to say "Christian revelation" when one meant the revelation of God more or less accessible to the Christian through the Christian church, the use of the phrase Christian revelation is inexcusable today.

We need ways of speaking that allow for convergence toward a unity of religions. Jewish, Christian, or Muslim are not parts of the unity (no religion accepts that position); they are serious, though flawed, attempts to represent the whole. What was probably unthinkable in the fourteenth century may be commonplace today, namely, that the only revelation of the only God might be clearer in some ways to a Christian through Jewish history than through the church. The solution is not necessarily that this Christian should become a Jew. The answer lies in recognizing that no object of religion or all of one's religion or the totality of religions is the object of faith. The "object" (i.e. the transubjective referent) for faith is the whole of creation revelatory of God.

Religious education becomes possible only under two conditions: 1) the rites, doctrines, symbols, and institutional forms of religion are taken with utmost seriousness and reverence as capable of revealing God; and 2) no ritual, book, doctrine, or office is identified with the word revelation. If anything is called "the revelation," presumably in contrast to other things which are not, then religious education is stymied. I hardly need add that action for social improvement is all but excluded.

As an example of the relation of social change and revelation, Jane Smith has an interesting article on women in Islam that concludes: "To a people for whom God's word has been absolutely revealed and whose law had developed under God's guidance, change is a slow and problematic process. When it does come, Muslim men and women agree, it must be within the framework of that revelation. Equality will carry an Islamic, not a Western definition, and in the Muslim mind the role of women must evolve in a pattern consistent with God's ordered plan for humankind."[17]

Smith's attempt to understand Islam from its own perspective is admirable. I still think one must ask whether much change is possible so long as the notion of revelation apparent throughout the article is not challenged. To demand "equality" for Muslim women could be a form of Western imperialism. To criticize the Muslim notion of revelation is not imperialistic provided that Christians are willing to admit the unintelligibility of "Christian revelation." Smith refers in her opening sentence to the Qur'an as "God's verbatim revelation for humankind." One can respect Muslims while still arguing with them—partly through appeal to other strands of their own tradition—that they commonly use revelation in a way

17. "Women in Islam: Equity, Equality, and the Search for a Natural Order," in *Journal of the American Academy of Religion* 47 (December, 1979), p. 530.

that is logically incoherent and ecumenically unacceptable. For this delicate task we need the setting of religious education (and other settings such as communities of prayer) rather than polemical essays or political arguments.

Islam is the least hesitant of the Western religions today to use the word revelation. It has the most obvious problem, but it may also be a clearer, more manageable problem than in the church where "the Christian revelation" is somewhere vaguely in back of it all. Islam insists upon the text of a book as mediating God's revelation of God's self. That text itself, however, warns the reader (as the Hebrew Bible and the New Testament do) not to collapse the difference between the meaning of revelation and the text of the book. "I believe in whatever book God may have revealed" (XLII, 15) is a startling reminder of the Qur'an not to assume that God's revelation is held in your hands. And the very meaning of book opens beyond itself: "One of the characteristics of the Qur'an as the last Revelation is that at times it becomes, as it were, transparent in order that the first Revelation may shine through its verses; and this first Revelation, namely, the Book of Nature, belongs to everyone."[18]

Islam will have to find its own way in making some distinctions. It may find it possible to put together nature, people, book, and piety in a way superior to the inadequate job of Christian thought in recent centuries. We have a right and perhaps a duty to warn Islam when the direction seems wrong. For example, a Muslim reformer writes: "Any real reconstruction of religious thought in Islam needs to be based on the principle that the area of unquestioned revealed truth needs to be narrowed, but not diluted."[19] That statement seems to me advocacy in the wrong direction. The writer should try a few other metaphors: dilute and narrow are not a logical pair. What he really needs to examine is the phrase "unquestioned revealed truth."

18. Martin Lings, *What is Sufism?* (Berkeley: University of California, 1975), p. 23.
19. Jansen, *Militant Islam,* pp. 201f.

That point brings me to my conclusion concerning the word revelation. We need a religious education context in which to try out images and languages that would be compatible to diverse traditions and make sense in contemporary English. In Christian history the distinctions of public/private, general/special, natural/supernatural are part of an intramural language not at all adequate to today's task.

Reconstructing the category of revelation will include using aesthetic, ecological, and political languages that convey a sense of form together with a drive toward what is beautiful, good, and true. Of course, religious people do not have to start from zero here. Much of what already exists in the religious institution is revelatory of God/creation. In addition, one can find images and experiences beyond the religious institutions that help to support a religious life. If some people wish to call the explication of this material "theology" that is their choice, but I would prefer to call it the religious part of religious education.

Chapter 4

Black Theology: A Challenge to Religious Education

OLIVIA PEARL STOKES

Introduction

In this chapter we shall be concerned with the definitions and scope of black theology, its major central themes and some educational implications of these for religious education. Since most black theologians have written within the context of the Christian religion, the main emphasis will be on black theology and Christian education.

The black church, the major free agent of black people, and the central, most historically valid organization in the black experience and black community, is the locale for this educational process. "The black preacher is still the natural leader and the black church continues to be the richest source of ethically innovative leadership, lay and clergy, in our community."[1]

The value of understanding black theology for all religious education is that it may provide some new theological insight, from the black perspective, into the contemporary search for the truth found in the gospel. John Bennett, a distinguished theologian, states, "It

1. Gayraud S. Wilmore and James Cone, eds. *Black Theology—A Documentary History, 1966–1979* (Maryknoll, N.Y.: Orbis Books, 1979), p. 347.

has deepened my awareness of the fluid spots of white theologians, beginning with myself."[2]

Black Theology Defined

"Black theology is a systematic interpretation of the meaning and significance of the Christian faith for the worshiping, witnessing, and proclaiming black Christian community," says Joseph A. Johnson of the Christian Methodist Church. *Black*—because our enslaved fore-parents appropriated the Christian gospel and articulated its relevance to our freedom struggle with incisive accents that black women and men have sounded since. *Theology*—because our people's perception of human life and history begins with God, who works in the person of Jesus Christ for liberation from every bondage.

Therefore, black theology is "God talk" that reflects the black perspective of the Christian experience of God's action and our grateful response. Black theology understands the "Good News" as freedom and Jesus Christ as liberator.

Black, an ethnic and psychological concept, first appeared in the late 1960s. It is formulated from our reading the Bible as we experience our suffering as a people. Black theology moves between our church and our community: the church proclaims the message, and the message reverberates back upon the church, enhanced by the religious consciousness of black people, including those who stand outside of the institutional church but are not beyond God's grace and his revelation.

Black theologians aim to present a new understanding of the worth and dignity of black people as children of God. "Black theology is Christian theology precisely because it utilizes God's revelation in Jesus Christ, as its point of departure."

Major Themes in Contemporary Black Theology—1976

On June 13, 1969, the first statement on black theology was issued from Atlanta by a group of black religious scholars, church-

2. Ibid., John Bennett, "Critique of Black Theology of Liberation," pp. 174.

men, and theologians. It heralded a new beginning for a movement in Afro-American Christianity that was at least as old as the first murmur of protest against slavery and oppression among Christian slaves in the United States. Its restatement at the end of the turbulent 1960s served notice to the world that the faith of the posterity of the slaves was expressed by a qualitatively different interpretation of Christianity than that of the posterity of the slavemasters.

From the beginning, our ancestors reflected theologically upon the meaning of their condition in relation to the revelation of God in Jesus Christ and the scriptures. Jesus was for them the liberator. They interpreted his person and work in spiritual songs, sermons, and prayers as the promise and the assurance of liberation in both this life and in the life to come.

In concise theological language, the 1969 statement of black theology reiterated the persistent theme of liberation in black Christianity and declared that the function of theological reflection in the black church is to show that the gospel of Jesus Christ, the liberator, is consonant with the aggressive effort to achieve and preserve the humanity of black people. Further, the 1969 statement called for significant programs of social change on the part of white Christians to abolish oppression of blacks. It affirmed that nothing less than white repentance and reparation could consitute a new beginning for shared power and responsibility.

The following statement is another explication of major themes in contemporary black theology by the Theological Commission of the National Conference of Black Churchmen. It reaffirms the historic statement of 1969 and seeks to illumine issues of urgent theological import that face the black church in 1976: Black theology's independence from both white Christian liberalism and the new conservatism, black theology as the theology of the black ecumenism, black theology as the theology of the black Messiah, and black theology as a political theology.[3]

3. Ibid., National Conference of the Black Theology Project, 1977, "Message to the Black Church and Community," pp. 345–348.

BLACK THEOLOGY AFFIRMS BLACK SPIRITUALITY

Black theological reflection takes place in the context of the authentic experience of God in the black worshiping community. That worship is, and has always been, about freedom under the reign of God—the freedom to suffer without self-pity, to struggle without despair, to win victories without vindictiveness and to celebrate worldly pleasures and happiness without anxiety and guilt. It is the freedom and blessedness, promised to the poor and oppressed, in the promise that theirs is the kingdom of heaven.

But the worship of the black church cannot be separated from its life and ethical praxis. It is in the struggle against racism and oppression that the black church creates and recreates its theological understanding of the faith and expresses it in shouts of praise and sounds of struggle, for the liberation of the oppressed.

Black theology is open to critical examination and dialogue with all who come to it in sincerity. But black theology does not belong to white theologians. It will not be dictated to by those who want to enlighten the outmoded spirituality of the black church with the utilitarian reasonableness of the liberal democratic civil religion or the abstractions of the modern scientific world view. Nor will black theology be authenticated as legitimate Christian theology only when it agrees with those white theologians who presume to define heresy by carefully balanced declarations that avoid taking sides in the struggle for justice.

Black theology is ultimately corrected and authenticated by the inseparable life and worship of the black church. It is rooted in neither American liberalism nor conservatism, but in black spirituality and black struggle. Its appropriation of the Christian faith and the ethical imperatives of the gospel is grounded in the revelation of God contained in the inspired preaching, prayer, and praise of black worship informed by the Holy Scriptures. It is controlled by the revelation of God in the history of black people that gives purpose, meaning and transforming power to the black struggle for humanity and liberation.

BLACK THEOLOGY AFFIRMS BLACK ECUMENISM

Black theology is the theology of the black church. It seeks the reunion of all black Christians, Protestant and Roman Catholic, in one church encompassing the totality of the black religious experience and the history and destiny of all black people. All efforts to reunite and renew the black church serve the ultimate purpose of confirming the catholicity, apostolicity, and holiness of the whole church of Jesus Christ, in which every race and nation joined together, each contributing properly and equally, upbuilds the one church of Christ, in love and justice. Black theology does not deny the importance of interdenominational and ecumenical efforts toward church unity with white and other Christians. Rather it asserts the operational unity of all black Christians as the first step toward a wider unit in which the restructuring of power relations in church and society and the liberation of the poor and oppressed will be recognized as the first propriety of mission.

Jesus Christ reveals himself to black people as the liberator of the black people of Africa, the Caribbean, and Latin America, as well as those of North America. The gospel was known among African people by the end of the second century, long before it finally extended north and east beyond the Mediterranean basin. But even if the earliest religious traditions of black Africa cannot be shown to have been penetrated by elements of Christian belief, black theology affirms that God did not leave himself without a witness in Africa before the arrival of Christian missionaries.

God shows no partiality. His eternal power and deity was shown to all mankind from the creation of the world and his wrath and mercy have fallen upon every race and nation because of universal sin and disobedience, in the face of his revealed truth in Jesus Christ.

This truth of God was hidden in the traditional religions of Africa which awaited their fulfillment in the revelation of Jesus, the liberator. It is within the ancient substructure of black religion, and in the struggle for freedom and independence experienced by black churches everywhere, that black theology seeks evidence of divine revelation, suppressed on both sides of the Atlantic, and retained in the earliest expressions of slave religion in North America and the Caribbean.

The rediscovery of truth revealed to Africa by the indigenization of Christian theology in African culture, and the unity of black and African Christianity, with its common experience of white racism and oppression, are basic goals of a black ecumenism shaped by black theologians in America working with colleagues of the African continent. Black theology is an ecumenical theology which seeks to justify and enhance the search for unity among black denominations in the United States, and among black Christians everywhere, as one aspect of obedience to the will of God that all may be unified and liberated in Jesus Christ.

BLACK THEOLOGY AFFIRMS THE BLACK MESSIAH

Black theology symbolizes Jesus Christ as the black messiah to remind black people in the most forceful manner that God, through Christ, takes upon himself the badge of their suffering, humiliation, and struggle, transforming it by the triumph of his resurrection.

Blackness is a symbol of the being, the humanity of black people. In the context of the experience African and Afro-American people have had with Europe and America, blackness has meant inferiority and oppression. Insofar as Jesus Christ was subjugated and humiliated without cause to save the world, he is recognized by black theology as the oppressed man of God who took upon himself the undeserved suffering of all oppressed people. Insofar as he is the conqueror of death and all the principalities and powers, he is the black messiah who was raised from the dead to liberate the oppressed by the power of the God who delivered Israel from the hand of Pharoah and revealed himself as a strong deliverer and liberator from every oppression of human existence.

Blackness in these terms is more than skin color. Even though it is a symbol that rises from the historic meaning attached to black skin color in Western civilization, it points beyond mere color to the solidarity, in suffering and struggle, of the descendents of all colonized people. The identification and affirmation of blackness by black theology is the affirmation of a mystery about a particular people and history that have an affinity to the mystery of the Cross. As the oppression and crucifixion of Jesus Christ is the mystery of blackness that proleptically encompasses the whole history of black people, so the dethronement of powers of evil and the victory of the resurrection is the eschatological destiny of blackness that gives meaning and provisional foretaste of victory in the historic struggle of the oppressed.

Black theology affirms this double meaning of blackness and seeks to interpret it theologically, homiletically, and liturgically in the life of the black church. By so doing it unveils and gives a symbolic reference to a mysterious reality in which sin and suffering, grace and liberation are inexplicably conjoined in the experience of the oppressed and in all existence that is truly human.

BLACK THEOLOGY AFFIRMS A POLITICAL PROGRAM

Black theology is a political theology. The encounter of black people with God takes in the area of history and involves ethical judgments and decisions having to do with liberation from racism, poverty, cultural and political domination, and economic exploitation. Black people see the hand of God, not only in personal salvation, but in social and political deliverance.

Even if black people were to obtain complete freedom and justice throughout the world, new forms of injustice and oppression would demand their identification with those who suffer from man's perennial inhumanity to man. Black theology seeks to interpret the world-wide revolution against inhumanity, exploitation, and oppression in which black people have played a major role and which is the work of Jesus Christ and the mission of his church. Black theology affirms that the faiths and ideologies of the oppressed masses, can be used by God as instrumentalities of their liberation.

It teaches black people to be radically critical of both American status quo and also of their own political strategies for change.

Because some forms of socialism, which stress humanism and cooperation, are more Christian and more contributive to justice and morality than American capitalism, black theology does not shrink from the exploration of socialistic alternatives to the idolatrous worship of the dollar, the chaotic individualism and corroding materialism of the American economic and political system. Black theology affirms that "the earth is the Lord's" and opposes any politics which are based on a theory of adherence to absolute self-interest, the precedence of private to public ownership, and the ascendancy of the profit motive and property rights over the public good.

Black theology, seeking to follow Jesus in his concern for the whole person in the whole community, presents a vision of the world in which all persons can find fulfillment, in families and natural communities linked by bonds of love and affection. Such a vision includes the institution of governments of the people committed to peaceful coexistence and self-determination for all races and cultural groups, universal human rights—including the right of revolution for just cause, equal justice, the fair and equitable distribution of wealth, the protection of the weak and helpless, and the fostering of human fulfillment by the enhancement of culture and religion.

Black theology as a political theology seeks to inculcate this vision in America, and then equip the black church to be an agent of its realization. The specific content of political strategy for its actualization will evolve in the wrestling of the black church with the meaning of the gospel of liberation, the realities of each historical situation, and the collective judgment of those who bear the greatest burden of suffering and deprivation.

Black theology is a theology for political reconstruction under the Lordship of Jesus Christ. Within its prayerful reflection and praxis reverberates God's call to black Christians to join the people of the Third World in the social revolutions of this century—to overthrow every structure of domination and injustice as a faithful response to the prophetic ministry of Jesus Christ who said, "The spirit of the Lord is upon me to set at liberty those who are oppressed."[4]

Some Current Black Theologians

Many great black preachers have been unpublished theologians throughout the history of the black church from slavery to the present.

Today theological seminaries have black theologians as scholars on their faculties, James Cone at Union Theological Seminary in New York being among the first. These faculty are popularly known as the new black theologians.

Let's look at short background statements of some of these leaders in both groups.

Martin Luther King, Jr. in *Where Do We Go From There: Chaos or Community* (1967), predated the black theology development, but his faith and teachings have made him the most revered of black theologians. His central teaching was "love your enemies, effect societal change through nonviolence, peace and goodwill, and human rights."

J. Deotis Roberts, in *Liberation and Reconciliation: A Black Theology* (1971), expressed belief in a global Christian vision and saw black theology as compatible to God's gift of reconciliation among all peoples. His proposition is that of being pro-black without being "antiwhite." Rather, he aims at presenting the Christian faith so as to make man's life more human for all God's people.

Roberts, while endorsing black power, places emphasis on Christian ethics in his effort to stimulate men of good will—black and white—to join in the struggle for racial justice as followers of Christ, and just as decent human beings.

"Liberation is revolutionary—for blacks it points to what they ought to do. Black Christians desire radical and rapid social change;

4. Ibid.

we believe that Christian faith is avowedly revolutionary and, there-fore, it may speak to this need with great force."[5]

Howard Thurman, *Jesus and the Disinherited* and *The Luminous Darkness: A Personal Interpretation of the Anatomy of Segregation and the Ground of Hope.* In these two studies, Dr. Thurman, grandson of slaves, relates the long and heart-breaking struggle of the Negro to pierce the veil of separation in the American society and the tragic price which white people have paid to maintain it. He establishes a genuine basis for hope that this troublesome problem is on the way to resolution. In *The Growing Edge,* his sermons deal with truths that are eternal.

James H. Cone, is the first and most prolific exponent of black theology. His thesis in *God of the Oppressed* (1975) is that Chris-tianity is a religion of liberation, that God is God of the oppressed, and his son, Jesus Christ, is the liberator who enables the black oppressed community to struggle for its freedom. Cone asks white theologians the piercing question: "What has God to do with the weak, the oppressed, the powerless—struggling for justice, equality, and freedom?" Cone challenges white theologians to exam-ine the oppressive society of which they are members, societies that hold minorities in oppression.

The basic foundation for Cone's thesis of liberation in black theology is found in the dialogue between black religious experi-ence, the tradition and practice of the black church, oral stories, spirituals, sermons, and the Bible. The black religious experience in the black church has values, theological insights, and God's revela-tion for humanity as a source of theology. *God of the Oppressed* (1975) embodies his black theology of liberation in its totality.

Cecil W. Cone, in *The Identity Crisis in Black Theology* (1975), takes issue with the thesis of his brother, James Cone, in that he be-lieves that black theologians fail to recognize the irreconcilability of black power and the accepted white theology. His belief is that black theology should build solidly on the black religious experience and

5. Ibid., "Black Theology in 1976," Statement by the Theological Commis-sion of the National Conference of Black Churchmen, pp. 340–344.

tradition. This, he believes, would decrease the identity crisis in theology. For him, the experience of an Almighty Sovereign God is the take-off point for black theology.

William R. Jones, in *Is God a White Racist?* (1973), poses the question of evil in the disturbing question, "Is God a White Racist?" Jones, in this controversial study, challenges the existing presuppositions of Western theology as adequate for meaningful dialogue with the world's oppressed peoples. This book is a call for radical theological reconstruction in order to credit the black experience in the U.S.A. with value in the Christian context.

Major J. Jones, in *Christian Ethics for Black Theology* (1974), takes a serious look at the ethical implications of strategies for the liberation struggle. He supports Martin Luther King's method of nonviolence as both a theology and action method for social change. Jones writes of King's nonviolence: "For him, nonviolence was not a capitulation to weakness and fear; rather, nonviolence demanded that difficult kind of steadfastness which can endure indignation with dignity. For King, nonviolence always attempted to reconcile and establish a relationship rather than humilate the opponent. For King, nonviolence was always directed against the evil rather than against the person responsible for the evil."[6]

Gayraud S. Wilmore, in *Black Religion and Black Radicalism* (1973), has provided an examination of the black experience in religion. In this historical and theological study, black pride, black power and pan-Africanism find their past in the black church and the black religious experience. This study develops and contributes to one's understanding of paradoxes of the black church in that it is the most reactionary and the most radical of black institutions, and yet often evidences its deep acceptance of white American values. The pride, independence, and power of the black church are clearly evident as the race's most significant force.

Wilmore has been at the heart of most of the black theological consultations and conferences in the U.S.A., the Caribbean Islands,

---

6. Major J. Jones, *Christian Ethics for Black Theology* (Nashville, Tennessee: Abingdon Press, 1974), p. 142.

Asia, and Africa. These documents reflect his dynamic theological insights and understanding of the Almighty God, Christ as liberator, and the black church.

William A. Jones, *God in the Ghetto* (1979). Jones, in this book, raises challenging and burning questions. How does one change a social system that is deeply demonic? What method does one employ to overcome a system whose holy trinity is capitalism, racism, and militarism?

He believes the white church has capitulated to culture and serves as the soothing conscience rather than the critical conscience of the state. He considers the black church to be the most viable instrument in the nation to give leadership to the black people's struggle for justice, equality, and freedom. He believes that liberation "is the black church." He says this because the black church is numerically strong; it has historical continuity; and it has the most clear and most discernible affinity with the religion of Jesus Christ of any church in the American culture.

As the struggle continues, he believes, the black church, when properly performing its prophetic functions, will seek reconciliation between the oppressors and the oppressed, but only through equity and justice. Thus, the black church's mission is to "deal with the victimizers in terms of judgment and demands for justice, and that of healing the victims torn and riveted by the evils of the system."[7]

Albert Cleage, *The Black Messiah* (1968). Cleage believes Jesus is, indeed, the black messiah. He believes black Christianity is the exclusive and only true expression of the religion of the Old Testament Israel and the New Testament Jesus, both originating in Africa. Cleage limits his concept to a black nationalistic interpretation of biblical religion and the black church. His purpose was to urge acceptance of the black church as the most important power in the black struggle for justice and freedom. This work has had relatively little impact on the black church. It evidenced no ecu-

---

7. William A. Jones, *God in the Ghetto* (Elgin, Illinois: Progressive Baptist Publishing House, 1979), p. 116.

menical vision and black religionists could not associate with his ideas of "black messiah" and "black nation."

Joseph Washington, *Black Religion: The Negro and Christianity in the United States* (1964). This study is an assult on the authenticity of the black church as a viable Christian community with a theology. Black theologians rejected the thesis and responded with studies in black theology.

It is interesting to observe that all of these spiritual leaders have a common assessment of Christianity as it is practiced in Western culture.

Black Theologians' Assessment: Poverty of Soul of Traditional Christianity

A basic critique of traditional Christian theology by black theologians has been the failure of American Christianity to understand Jesus Christ's concern for the theological, as well as the spiritual nature, of human beings. The churches have, with few exceptions, addressed the spiritual needs of people, assuming that understanding of these would lead to Christian behavior and actions to change the physical and material needs of persons.

Black theologians have pointed out that traditional theology has failed to understand that salvation and historical liberation form an inseparable synthesis of the indivisible gospel of Jesus. Therefore, in the black church, in the black community as Christians, preachers and laity must deal with the issues of their lives as they perceive them and understand and speak the truth of God.

Traditional theologians have, by and large, been insensitive to the pain and conflict of the earthly life of most of the world's oppressed peoples throughout history. Christ died not on an altar nor in a temple, but out on a hillside in the pain of life. Martin Luther King, Jr., was shot dead on the balcony of a Memphis, Tennessee, motel as he led the campaign for better jobs and working conditions of the garbage workers of that city. The contemporary church must take the inspiration and the spiritual insights gained within its stained glass meeting houses of worship out among the urban, suburban, and rural centers of life, where there is unemployment, labor-management conflicts, mothers crying, uneducated children and youth searching for meaning in the new lifestyles, amid the search for new values, in the climate of drugs, alcohol, and sexual excursions.

The issue in black America is survival. The few social and legal gains that have been made come not as much through attitudinal changes as through legislation and laws that are often inadequately implemented. Too often blackness has been defined as evil and inferior, or as degradation. This is forcefully pictured in every system of society in the film-strip, "From Racism to Pluralism," by the Foundation for Change, supported in part by the Ford Foundation.[8]

Black theologians proclaim against the disorders of the society and advocate the development of societal structures that enable power and self-determination among blacks. Black churchmen, in their analysis of the source of the crisis, state that the "root problem is human sinfulness which nurtures monopolistic capitalism, aided by racism and abetted by sexism. . . . Exploitative, profit-oriented capitalism is a way of ordering life fundamentally alien to human value in general and to black humanity in particular."[9]

The roots of the survival crisis are in the economic, social, educational, and political power systems that prevent blacks from managing the controls over their daily lives. Let us examine the uniqueness of the black church.

The Origins and Power of the Black Church

Historically, beginning with slavery and continuing into the 1980s, the black church has been the most powerful force of the

8. Filmstrip, *From Racism to Pluralism* (New York: Foundation for Change, 1840 Broadway).

9. Gayraud S. Wilmore and James Cone, eds., *Black Theology—A Documentary History, 1966–1979,* National Conference of the Black Theology Project, 1977, "Message to the Black Church and Community," (Maryknoll, New York: Orbis Books, 1979), pp. 345–349.

black people's struggle for justice, equality, liberation, and free-dom. The black church has been the communities' protest center, the spiritual powerhouse, and the fellowship community center for radical unity, talent launching, and fund raising for survival causes.

The worship of the black church, allowing emotionalism, has often served unconsciously as therapy for persons suffering from oppression and poverty. As its spiritual powerhouse, the sermons and songs of black preachers and choirs have refueled black people's hopes, faith, and courage.

Dr. Benjamin E. Mays, the president of Morehouse College for twenty nine years, and the inspiration and role model for Martin Luther King, Jr., reminds us "that the black church is always pointing black people to a better day, both in the present and in the future."[10]

The power of the black church is in "people power" and "presence" and provides the richest sources of ethically motivated leadership, lay and clergy, in the black community.

SOME EDUCATIONAL IMPLICATIONS OF LIBERATION THEOLOGY FOR RELIGIOUS EDUCATION

In the black church, in general, there have been two basic theories of religious education. First, the black churches in predominantly white denominations have followed their denominational middle-class curriculum based on liberal Christianity which often lacked depth of biblical study and was based on progressive education methodology. Second, the historical black churches, and many independent storefront churches, relied on a curriculum from the very conservative and often highly fundamentalist publishers. These appealed because the curriculum resources were literally Bible-centered. The Uniform Lesson series were the curriculum materials for almost all grade levels in many denominations.

10. Benjamin E. Mays, *The Negro's God as Reflected in his Literature* (Boston: Chapman and Grimes, 1938).

From the perspective of the theology of liberation, neither of these forms of religious education is contenporary, or relevant from the black theological point of view.

The failure of the ungraded and Bible-centered approach is best analyzed in the writings of Paulo Freire in his book, *The Pedagogy of The Oppressed:* "Education is suffering from narration sickness." Narration, with the teacher as narrator, leads the student to memorize mechanically the narrated content. Worse yet, it turns students into containers—into receptacles to be filled by the teacher. The more completely he fills the receptacles, the better teacher he is. The more meekly the receptacles permit themselves to be filled, the better students they are. Education thus becomes an act of "depositing" in which the students are the depositories and the teacher is the depositor.

Instead of communicating, the teacher issues memory work and makes deposits which the student patiently receives, memorizes, and repeats. This is the "banking" concept of education in which the scope of action allowed extends only as far as receiving, filling, and storing the deposits. Students do, it is true, "have the opportunity to become collectors or cataloguers of the things they store; but in the last analysis, it is men themselves who are filed away, the lack of creativity, transformation, and knowledge, and this, at best, is misguided education."

Among the mainline Protestant denominations, the United Methodist, The Lutheran Church, the JED group (Disciples, Episcopalians, United Church of Christ, and the United Presbyterian) and others have established educational commissions or task forces mandated to produce supplementary educational resources relevant to the black constituency within their denominations. The United Methodist Church in its Abingdon catalog lists these educational materials as "Special Groups—Black American Resources."

In black denominations, the black educators, some pastors, and higher education scholars who have been enlisted as part-time curriculum writers have created resources mainly with a focus on black history from the beginnings of slavery to the present: few theological materials have been produced. The United Methodist and the

JED group, however, have developed some materials based on the theology of liberation.

These innovative supplementary educational resources or units, and their founders, received their early grounding in the National Council of Churches' Black Christian Education Project (1966–1973) which represented the six historical black denominations constituent to the NCCC—the African Methodist Episcopal Church, the African Methodist Episcopal Zion Church, the Christian Methodist Church, the National Baptist Convention, Inc., the National Baptist Convention of America, the Progressive Baptist Convention, and representatives, as consultants, from the black caucuses of the predominantly white denominations.

The Black Christian Education Project began in 1966, in the Department of Education Development of NCCC, and had as its major purpose the development, interpretation, and promotion of black church educational cooperation. This coalition aimed at enabling program leadership development, research, and the creation of curriculum resources addressed to the needs of black churches.

In July-August of 1971, the NCCC Project produced a special issue of *Spectrum* (the old *International Journal of Religious Education*) on "Christian Education In the Black Church." This document became the springboard for inspiring relevant denominational resources from the black perspective.

One wonders if the Christian Education Movement among Protestants has not been more philosophical than theological. Philosophy has been defined as "the art of asking the right question," the critical exposition of key issues and problems, according to Whitehead in *The Aims of Education*. This approach could lead to poverty of the soul. Theology, however, goes beyond philosophy, and is concerned with the projection of appropriate answers to man's ultimate life question. This is the aim of black theology.

The NCCC Black Christian Education Project, in a September, 1969, conference on "The Educational Role of the Black Church," developed its unique perspective on the mission and education task of the black church: "Christian mission today requires radical change in our present structures, practices, and ideologies. This means revolt against many religious, social, educational, political, and economic structures."

Thus it is the educational task of the black church to join theological reflection with those processes which expose the structures which enslave, to develop techniques for freedom, and give structure to those values of the black experience for building community for God's people.

The late Bishop Joseph Johnson, in an address to the 27th General Conference of the Christian Methodist Episcopal Church in May, 1970, stated the problem of blacks in America in these words:

> The history of the black man in America has been one of endless struggle against the forces of racism, oppression, and exploitation. We are no longer held in physical bondage, but we are nonetheless bound by a history of social, economic, and cultural oppression which has been more damaging in its effects than physical enslavement. The black man in America has used a variety of strategies and programs. We have tried the vocational education program of Booker T. Washington, the legal persuasion of the NAACP, the emigrationism of Marcus Garvey, and the moral and ethical persuasionism of Martin Luther King, Jr. . . . However, we are still oppressed. Even though some progress has been made, yet we remain on the fringe of American society. We are politically, socially, economically, and culturally enslaved.
>
> The situation of the black man in America is desperate and baffling. Our situation is radical, unique, and complicated. It requires a new orientation of the black man's thinking about the society in which he lives and about himself. It demands a new understanding of the black man. It has forced the black man to draw on those resources, spiritual and moral, deeply imbedded in the black tradition and in the black religious experience. . . . The humanity of all those who have lived under the yoke of racism—whether black, white, or brown—has been distorted and all but destroyed. We must bear in mind that racism is an extreme form of departure from Christ's mandate that in the kingdom of heaven there is neither Jew nor Greek, male or female. . . .
>
> Christians, we believe, are called upon to play a vital role in

the midst of disunity, discontinuity, disorder, and violence. We are called upon to bring a gospel of hope, love, and promise of redemption. Above all, we are called upon to act in fulfillment of our Christian mission to find new creative ways of thinking about racism and to help build new structures out of which reconciliation can develop."[11]

Christian education in the black and white churches must answer the question posed by the black poet, Margaret G. T. Burroughs, in "What Shall I Tell My Children Who Are Black?"

WHAT SHALL I TELL MY CHILDREN WHO ARE BLACK

(Reflections of an African-American Mother)

1963

What shall I tell my children who are black
Of what it means to be a captive in this dark skin
What shall I tell my dear ones, fruit of my womb,
Of how beautiful they are when everywhere they turn
They are faced with abhorrence of everything that is black.
Villains are black with black hearts.
A black cow gives no milk. A black hen lays no eggs.
Bad news comes bordered in black, black is evil
And evil is black and devils' food is black. . .

What shall I tell my dear ones raised in a white world
A place where white has been made to represent
All that is good and pure and fine and decent.
Where clouds are white, and dolls, and heaven
Surely is a white, white place with angels
Robed in white, and cotton candy and ice cream
and milk and ruffled Sunday dresses
And dream houses and long sleek cadillacs
And angel's food is white. . . all, all . . . white.

11. Joseph Johnson, *The Black Preacher* (Nashville, Tennessee: Christian Methodist Episcopal Church, 1977).

What can I say therefore, when my child
Comes home in tears because a playmate
Has called him black, big lipped, flatnosed
and nappy headed? What will he think
When I dry his tears and whisper, "Yes, that's true.
But no less beautiful and dear."
How shall I lift up his head, get him to square
His shoulders, look his adversaries in the eye,
Confident of the knowledge of his worth,
Serene under his sable skin and proud of his own beauty?

What can I do to give him strength
That he may come through life's adversities
As a whole human being unwarped and human in a world
Of biased laws and inhuman practices, that he might
Survive. And survive he must! For who knows?
Perhaps this black child here bears the genius
To discover the cure for . . . Cancer
Or to chart the course for exploration of the universe.
So, he must survive for the good of all humanity.
He must and will survive.
I have drunk deeply of late from the fountain
Of my black culture, sat at the knee and learned
From Mother Africa, discovered the truth of my heritage,
The truth, so often obscured and omitted.
And I find I have much to say to my black children.[12]

INDICTMENT OF RELIGIOUS EDUCATION

Christian education is the great failure of contemporary Judeo-
Christian life. The Jewish, Roman Catholic, Protestant, and Or-

12. Margaret Burroughs, "What Shall I Tell My Children Who Are Black?" in
Education in the City Church, (New York: Board of Christian Education, United
Presbyterian Church in the U.S.A., 1967), p. 23. Used by permission of the
author. Dr. Margaret Burroughs is Director, Du Sable Museum of African-
American History, Washington Park, Chicago.

thodox churches have historically established elaborate religious education programs in beautiful modern buildings attended by many children and youth. But in 1981 neither attractive building nor impressive statistics can cover the ugly fact that Judeo-Christian education schools have failed to produce an American Judeo-Christian nation of equality and justice.

Religious education in America is unable, it seems, to establish a viable education for its constitutents, in its Judeo-Christian values and hopes and expectations.

It is painful to indict religious education after all the connected efforts of denominations and religious leaders through these 300 or more years of American history. But if we are to be honest, inequality, racism, injustice, oppression, and materialism are the ugly realities of America in 1981 notwithstanding the minority gains of the 1960s and early 1970s. The backlash has come and the scene reminds the blacks of life following slavery.

Christian education seems ineffectual to bring about Christian behavior. White Christian educators must honestly face the great failure of religious education. Children and youth trained or educated in the traditional Protestant and Roman Catholic educational program are not behaving as committed Judeo-Christian youth in schools or as adults, in management-employee relations, in human rights in USA or the Third World, in economic or political systems, or in the general educational systems of the society.

America was founded on a religious base and if it is unable to assure its young a solid grounding in its traditional spiritual values and culture its very existence as a democratic, Judeo-Christian nation is endangered.

"Love they neighbor as thyself" is not the prevailing philosophy in the U.S.A. in 1981. Daniel Yankelovich, in his article "New Rules in American Life: Searching for Self-Fulfillment In a World Turned Up-side Down," in the April, 1981, issue of *Psychology Today,* states that his social research findings reveal (1) that nearly 80 percent of the U.S. population is engaged in the search for self-fulfillment; (2) that in place of the traditional ethic of self-denial and sacrifice, we now find an ethic that denies people nothing; (3) that at the core of the cultural revolution is a contradiction between the goals of the self-fulfillment seekers and their means; (4) that our culture and our economy are on opposite courses: while the culture calls for freedom, the economy calls for constraint; (5) that the most ardent seekers of self-fulfillment fallaciously view self as an endless series of gratifiable needs and desires; (6) that surveys reveal the virtual abandonment of some of our most deeply held Judeo-Christian beliefs about marriage and the family; (7) that for the first time in American society, only minorities, as adults, report discomfort at having a friend who is homosexual; (8) that most Americans now believe it is OK to be single and have a child; (9) that norms about whether a wife should work outside the home have reversed themselves in a single generation.

Whether one agrees with the analysis of Daniel Yankelovich in his book, *New Rules,* the moral change is being shaped by a cultural revolution that is transforming the norms of American life and moving persons in this society into a totally uncharted life, unlike the Judeo-Christian lifestyles of the past. The critical question is how can Christian educators deal effectively with the tragic news of the world, the almost total disappearance of political liberalism, the new economic constraints, the emergence of fundamentalist groups—all opposed to ERA, abortion, and sex education in the public shcools?

A second major question for Christian educators is one Reinhold Niebuhr dealt with in *Christ and Culture:* Is Christianity to be in alliance with or tension with the culture? The distinguished religious educator Randolph Crump Miller in his preface to *Christian Nurture and the Church,* says that "the educational aim of the church is primarily to educate people to be the church."

Given today's un-Christian society, one wonders if from a methodological point of view religious education hasn't been the giving or transmission of factual information and its meaning rather than the church having provided its members with a nurturing environment which provided an atmosphere and involved relationships that gave expression in words and action to the acquired biblical information? Has Christian education within the church looked too much within its own community of baptized believers and not led these to address the real life issues within the society—or, in other words, the church educating believers to build a strong faith to serve in society as individuals, and as the church? This black theology aims to do. Have religious educators relied too heavily on secular educational philosophies and theories and their significance for religious education rather than developed a unique theological discipline and methodology for Christian education? Have religious educators failed to recognize that the parents are the prime religious educators of their offspring? How can Christian education compete with general education when it instructs, indoctrinates, or teaches for only one to three hours per week versus twenty-five hours of public education? The parents have their children and youth in a family community for many more hours. Historically Christian education has focused on the child for too few hours per week and not on Christian education of their children supplemented by the formal church school and through the week church educational programs. Have modern Christian educators been more concerned about the newest scientific social science research findings than with deep biblical study and the meanings of Christianity in today's complex rapidly changing world? Has the pride in and search for knowledge of the latest in educational theory blinded Christian educators to the need for theological study and reflection as an essential discipline in Christian education?

Have our denominational educational teacher training workshops been methodological skill shops turning out techniques and technicians more excited about how to teach than what was being taught? Have religious educators too often failed in Christian education because the emphasis has been on "saving" the individual, rather than enabling the church to be the body of Christ in life and society?

Randolph Crump Miller's question of 1952–3, "What is the religious readiness of the child?" is as relevant today as then. I'd go further to ask: What is the religious readiness of the church to deal with the issues of the society?

BLACK THEOLOGY AND EDUCATIONAL THEORY

Black theology affirms that it is relevant to the problems of a people oppressed in the American and African societies. Christian education has too often been theologically deprived and church schools have done little to help. As Randolph Crump Miller states in *The Theory of Christian Education Practice,* "The purpose of Christian education is to place God at the center and to bring the individual into right relationship with God and one's fellows within the perspective of the fundamental truths about all of life. The major task of Christian education is to discover and impart the relevance of Christian truth."[13] Christian education within white churches has deprived their students (children, youth, and adults) of the right relationship with black people—black Christians as one's fellow human beings. It has failed to grapple with the relevance of the oppressive and racist situation and the condition of the poor and minorities in light of the relevance of Christian truth. If in Dr. Miller's definition, theology is "the truth-about-God-in-relation-to-humanity," Jewish and Christian educators have to a great extent failed to be theologically oriented in their education. Black theology is the black theologian's perceived truth about God in relation to all humanity, not just blacks. Black theology is experiential or situational and not abstract or irrelevant to black people or poor people's condition, and God's relationship to them through Jesus Christ.

Black theology asserts Jesus Christ as liberator, concerned that provides knowledge of black people and their historical and present situation in this society and the world, knowledge of the data of the Holy Scriptures, development of Christ-like character, and life within the black Christian church and universal Christian community through the fellowship of the church and involvement in the larger community as Christian change agents.

Black theology assets Jesus Christ as liberator, concerned that persons emulate him as the model of God's will for all men. Jesus

13. Randolph Crump Miller, *The Theory of Christian Education Practice* (Birmingham, Alabama: Religious Education Press, 1980), p. 156.

taught most often out among the common people in their work places or homes, through the situational method of parables. Have Christian educators taught historical biblical truths as fact without enabling students to discern their implications for today's life situations? Somehow, biblical truth must be relevant to today's economic, political, sociological, and educational factors within the situations of this present life.

In theological education, there needs to be a marriage between the theologians and the educator. Such a relationship within a department of theology would require problem identification and analysis of man and society, the state of the church historically and contemporarily, the nature of being human and the way believing persons are related to God in a committed community.

Curriculum in such a relationship would include the basic concepts of black theology, from Howard Thurman's *Jesus and the Disinherited* to Martin Luther King, Jr.'s theology of redemptive love found in *I Have A Dream.*

IMPLICATIONS FOR TEACHING BLACK THEOLOGY IN CHRISTIAN EDUCATION

How to teach black theology in Christian education needs to be discussed in an ecumenical, interracial, intercultural arena of Christian educators. Presently there exists the idea that black theology is exclusively for black persons in the black church. This is no more true than is the notion that only blacks should support the NAACP. It's an association for the advancement of black people, thus any persons committed to its purposes are eligible to become involved. Black theology is Christian theology from the perspective of revelations and insights given by God to black theologians. These may be richer, truer, and more relevant than general Christian theology being taught in American churches and theological seminaries. Assuming that "theology is the truth about God in relation to humanity," black theology contributes to truth about God as it relates to blacks and others in our nation and world. The problem is compounded by the fact that neither black or white theoreticians in Christian education have in-depth knowledge of the data of black theology. The resources are new and the various theologians have written only since the 1960s. Within the national black denominations, there have been limited experiences with writing curriculum materials. In the predominately white denominations the Christian educators lack the intimate knowledge of the black experience which would limit their Christian insights and answers. Thus an integrated ecumenical task force of Christian educators could make a real contribution to their field by their collaborative work.

Black theoreticians can help the practitioner understand the "how to" question—showing the practitioner how to clarify major or key issues and cite examples of possible responses. The "how to" is relevant when specifics are addressed educationally in terms of black life problems.

TOWARD A THEORY OF BLACK THEOLOGY IN CHRISTIAN EDUCATION

In trying to suggest a way of approaching the teaching of black theology, I am suggesting a normative theory and not offering it as a fully developed educational strategy or philosophy.

The basic underlying principle of the proposed conception is that black theology is Christian theology from the perspective of a deeply religious ethnic group, a historically oppressed and contemporary people who have shared a common past, present, and future, as well as common mores, moral values, religious experience and values, and a common oppressive past. The religious dimension of these people has been central in their life of survival throughout their history in America and one of its unique elements. Religion in the Black Experience in U.S.A. has been one of the defining elements of black people; therefore, the strong ties with the Christian community, though racially isolated, are not so by choice.

The educational implications of these assumptions are that (1) Christian education should be concerned with the transmission of the truths of black theology and (2) since black people are a part of U.S.A. and the human race, Christian education must include teaching about blackness as a gift of God and as valuable as whiteness. Blackness is God-given personal identity, and black Americans constitute a visible group and a social phenomenon. The ultimate meaning of blackness is in terms of its value in the character formation of the individual. Teaching the worth and beauty of blackness relates to the development of self and character of black persons.

Black theology should be taught as a basic dimension of Christiantiy, which holds a world view, a Christian-value system, a social force that proposes and aims to help persons develop a Christ-like self.

In the development of the black child, the character education process should include cognitive, affective, and behavioral dimensions of growth. Black theology implies educationally that black children in character development should be prepared to deal with a lifestyle that struggles for equality, justice, freedom, and liberation. Christian educators in white churches should educate their children and youth and adults to understand how Christian truths are perceived in the black religious experience because of inequalities in the church and society. They will want to educate for justice and equality of all persons. Black theology is understood very differently by different groups of persons within the black church. The goals are the same for all, but the methods for achieving liberation are as different as the many leaders. Thus, Christian education of black persons encompasses the ideal Christian life, and the reality of life in America, as blacks struggle with racial injustices and inequality in all America's social systems and institutional structures.

The gigantic task before black and white Christian educators is the translation of black theology and its underlying concepts and implied theoretical assumptions into goals, objectives, curricula designs, educational materials, and teaching methodologies.

While some noble attempts have been made to achieve this task, the proposed plan is larger in scope, and needs an ecumenical interracial task force. The field testing of curricula resources after implementation should be evaluated in both black and white churches and then discussed together, for the goal is a just and equitable Christian society.

For blacks, teaching black theology in both black and white churches is corrective of Christian theology and presents the distinctive revelations of God to black theologians in their struggle to be like Christ in U.S.A. and the Third World. The concept of blackness as a gift of God. is important for black Christians—for persons are created in the image of God. The concept goes beyond color to psychological and philosophical dimensions in American Western society. Teaching black theology might be best presented in terms of interactions with an ideal theory of Christianity with a theory of teaching, with the realities of educational situations.

Teaching black theology should deal with such issues as: the meaning of blackness from the perspectives of blacks and whites, the meaning of Christianity, the meaning of learning and teaching and practical education situations.

IN CONCLUSION

This chapter has tried to point out that comtemporary Christian education has not integrated the Christian insights and theological revelations of black theologians into present Christian educational theory or curriculum resources to a significant extent for either black or white churches. In some black churches black history is being taught because of its omission from the general education texts of public schools. The Christian theological insights from black theology—redemptive love and suffering, the meaning of liberation—have yet to be developed for the educational resources of most black and white churches.

Christian educators may want to be students of black theology for the purpose of understanding God's revelations of truth from the black perspective. Since education may take place in a nurturing community, interpersonal relationships between minority and majority Christians at every age and in a variety of settings—family, school, local community, and church—can give relevance to the development of the Christian goal of justice and equality.

Black theology does not lead to indoctrination as an educational methodology, because there are no commonly-agreed-upon doctrines, beliefs, or values that are prescribed without examination. Learners are free to examine the autonomy of the black theological writers.

Black theology provides the opportunity to question biblical data, sociological data of the black experience, and the ability to make inferences, and to choose live and not forced options.

Black theology defines what the black church will determine to be the content of Christian education. Black theology includes the writers' beliefs of God, and his relationship to oppressed black humanity. Black theology helps persons understand how God relates to his world and his creatures. Education enables reflection on life experiences in the light of theology.

The challenge to Christian education is to find the new insights brought by black theology and using these with insights gained from social and educational psychology, the sociology of learning and cultural anthropology, enrich our teaching-learning process to end in the development of Christ-like persons.

The chapter raises as many questions as it may answer, and the author invites the reader to dialogue, for space does not permit what a book could further explore. The exploration has just begun.

Chapter 5

The Authentic Source of Religious Instruction

JAMES MICHAEL LEE

The title of this article indicates that my discussion will revolve around two major topics, namely the reality of religious instruction and the theoretical approach which adequately explains this reality. Before beginning the main lines of my exposition, I think it would be helpful to clarify what is meant by religion and instruction on the one hand, and by theory on the other hand.

RELIGION

Religion is that form of lifestyle which expresses and enfleshes the lived relationship a person enjoys with a transpersonal being as a consequence of the actualized fusion in his self-system of that knowledge, belief, feeling, experience, and practice that are in one way or another connected with that which the individual perceives to be divine. This definition suggests that religion is an activity of the whole person. This definition also suggests that religion is different both from faith and from theology.

Religion differs from faith as the whole differs from one of its parts. Faith is an encounter between God and a human being in which the individual enters into that kind of compact with God by giving his total and free personal assent to God as the Lord reveals himself in

100

written and ongoing form.[1] Faith, then, is one aspect of religion—other aspects of religion include hope and love, among others (1 Cor. 13:13).[2] Faith is necessary but not sufficient for religion. Faith is necessary for religion because a person cannot be religious without faith. But faith is not sufficient for religion because religion also

1. This definition is severely limited in that it simply reflects a certain strand of post-World War II Christian theology. Throughout the history of the church, there have been and still are legitimate definitions of faith which differ sharply and are even contrary to the one I am advancing. The confusion—and one could almost say conceptual anarchy—which has reigned in Christian theology with respect to the meaning, parameters, and potency of faith stems from the fact that faith has typically been defined almost exclusively from a speculative or from a stipulative base rather than making heavy use of a nonhistorical empirical foundation. Biblical theologians derive a definition of faith from their scholarly, speculative study of the Bible, regardless of whether or not their study is tethered to or tied in with a *theologia orativa*. But because of the nature of the sociopsychological functioning of each interpreter, these definitions have had a wide variety of different and even contrary formulations over the centuries. Ecclesiastical bodies and their theologians have sometimes defined faith stipulatively, namely, the definition of faith has been formulated on the basis of what that ecclesiastical body and/or its theologians say it is. But because stipulations *eis ipsis* reflect the views and interpretations of the church body and its theologians, these definitions of faith exhibit a great variety and sometimes go counter to one another. If faith is indeed a denotation of a set of human behaviors, then its adequate and genuine definition must rely heavily on, and in an important sense be grounded in, a genuine and robust empirical study of faithing. *Ascertaining empirically how faith behaviors actually do operate will go a long way in telling us what faith really is, and will contribute in no small measure to ending the centuries-old conceptual confusion about the meaning and scope of this term.* The careful empirical study of faith in no way eliminates the role or minimizes the importance of the biblical hermeneuticist; rather such rigorous empirical investigation constitutes an invaluable and indispensable major source for the biblical hermeneuticist in his efforts at arriving at a true understanding of what and how the Bible means by faith. Surely there is no double truth: faith cannot be described and prescribed in the Bible in a manner fundamentally different from the way in which faith is lived in the lives of religious persons today.

2. Obviously I am here considering faith in the sense in which it is used in theology and in religious instruction, namely faith in God and in divinely revealed reality. Faith as a trusting, fiduciary orientation which is more global, such as faith in one's political leaders, is not the focus of my discussion here.

The disagreement over the meaning and extension of the construct "religion" is analogous to the point I make in footnote 1 about the confusion in Christianity over the meaning and extension of the construct "faith." Wilfred Cantwell

requires the exercise of other virtues such as hope and love if it is to be made operative.[3] Some religious educationists[4] have made the gratuitous, unhistorical, dualistic, and illogical claim that religion consists simply of so-called externals like institutions or creeds or buildings or outward human conduct, while faith comprises the

---

Smith's historical research concludes that the term "religion" has been used in a wide variety of combined and discrete ways throughout the history of Christianity (pp. 15–50). Merton Strommen and the editorial committee of the monumental *Research on Religious Development* decided against providing the contributors with any definition of religion because the construct "religion" seems to be one on which it is exceedingly difficult to obtain consensus (p. xvi). In contemporary Christianity, the theories of Karl Barth and Dietrich Bonhoeffer have endeavored to discard the construct and referent "religion" as destructive of deep and authentic Christian living. The influence in this regard of Barth and Bonhoeffer on James Fowler is not clear, if indeed such an influence does exist at all. Still, Fowler seems to conceptualize the construct "religion" (pp. 9–11) along the lines of what he construes to be the interpretation offered by his old professor Wilfred Cantwell Smith, namely a particular cumulative tradition of the past which includes scripture, law, creeds, rites, myths, and so on. (I am uncertain whether Fowler correctly interprets his old professor in this regard. As I read the Smith book which Fowler uses as his source, I do not see this comparative religionist claiming that the construct "religion" as used in Western Christianity consists only in a cumulative tradition of the past; Smith clearly asserts that religion as this term is used in Western Christianity also consists in personal piety. Indeed, Smith wishes to abolish the construct "religion" precisely because it is a term typically used to denote an amalgam of the cumulative tradition of the past with personal faith, and hence is conceptually unmanageable (pp. 193–195). Smith also proposes that the terms "Christianity" and "Buddhism" be dropped—a proposal with which Gabriel Moran would probably agree). Though the construct "religion" is peripheral to his admirable research, nevertheless I think that Fowler would have been better served if he rigorously surveyed the various scholarly interpretations of the construct "religion" rather than relying on the work and conclusions of only one researcher, however skilled this researcher may be.

My own conceptualization of religion as offered in the definition given in the body of the text preserves the very dynamic amalgam which Smith would like to eliminate. Religion is first and foremost a human activity and as such must necessarily be a living amalgam of self and situation, of one's personality and tradition-dimension of one's interactive environment. My position resonates with Talcott Parsons' view that religion is involved in at least three of the four systems constituting human life (pp. 30–79). These four systems are the physiological system of the organism, the personality system of the individual, the social system of the group, and the overall system of the culture. My position also resonates with Gordon Allport's contention that religion is a multifaceted texture and thrust of one's entire personality structure. My position is highly sympa-

so-called internals like interior commitment. This claim is gratuitous because its proponents have freely asserted it without adducing
any supporting evidence; what is gratuitously asserted can just as
gratuitously be denied. This claim is unhistorical since Christianity
throughout its existence has generally conceptualized religion as

---

thetic, also, to Carl Jung's view that religion is intensely personal because its
rites, symbols, and dogmas (yes, dogmas) ultimately reside in the deepest recesses
of a person's unconscious. Jung radicates his conceptualization of religion in a personal experience of the numinosum (p. 6). My definition of religion as presented
in the body of the text is heavily influenced by sources such as those mentioned
above, the sources mentioned in the relevant section of *The Shape of Religious
Instruction,* and particularly by what I regard as the seminal composite picture
painted by Charles Glock (pp. s-98–s-100).

It should be underscored that James Fowler's vitally important theorizing and
research are directed not toward religion or even toward religious faith, but
toward faith in any and all of its forms whether religious or not. In Fowler's
research and theorizing, faith is thus a broader (Fowler would say a more fundamental) construct than religion. There is a sense in which I concur with Fowler on
this point. I do not concur with Fowler's contention, however, that faith constitutes "the most fundamental category in the human quest for relation to transcendence" (p. 14). My view is, and always has been, that the most fundamental
category of all human living, including the quest for transcendence, is love. In
my view, faith is born out of love, is animated by love, works through love, and
in the very end is absorbed into and consumed by love. See Wilfred Cantwell
Smith, *The Meaning and End of Religion* (New York: Macmillan, 1963); Merton P.
Strommen, "Introduction," in Merton P. Strommen, ed., *Research on Religious
Development* (New York: Hawthorn, 1971); James W. Fowler, *Stages of Faith*
(New York: Harper & Row, 1981); Talcott Parsons, "An Outline of the Social
System," in Talcott Parsons et al., eds., *Theories of Society,* volume 1 (New York:
Free Press, 1961)—see also Talcott Parsons, *Societies* (Englewood Cliffs, N.J.:
Prentice-Hall, 1966); Gordon W. Allport, *The Individual and His Religion* (New
York: Macmillan, 1950); Carl Jung, *Psychology and Religion* (New Haven, Con-
necticut: Yale University Press, 1938); Charles Y. Glock, "On the Study of
Religious Commitment," in *Religious Education,* research supplement LVII
(July–August, 1962).

3. Historically, faith has sometimes divided family from family, person from
person, Christian from Christian. Persons of faith have been known to revile,
ostracize, persecute, and even kill other persons of faith primarily because of a
perceived or real difference in faith. Not a few world religions, including some
prominent Christian confessions, taught officially by many centuries that the
faith of their adherents required or at least strongly suggested that heretics and
infidels be reviled, ostracized, persecuted, and even killed. If faith has sometimes
divided people from one another, love has always tended to join people together
and heal human wounds.

involving the totality of a person's lived relationship to God and not merely the so-called behavioral or artifactual externals.[5] This claim is dualistic in that it posits a fundamental and unwarranted dichotomy between inner faith and outer religion. The available empirical research strongly suggests that the person is in all likeli-

---

It is logically fallacious, empirically fallacious, and possibly even theologically fallacious to claim that faith includes love. This claim is logically fallacious because at bottom it is a reductionist one—it ultimately reduces two distinct though intertwined sets of human behaviors (faith and love) to only one behavioral set (faith). Such a reductionism is in some way analogous to asserting that the cognitive, affective, and psychomotor domains are all really cognitive because each of these domains is operative in some degree when a person is thinking. The claim that faith includes love is empirically fallacious because there is an abundance of past and present evidence which indicates that persons appearing to exhibit a high degree of faith have been notoriously unloving in certain respects. For example, there have been officially canonized Catholic saints who, in the Middle Ages, publicly reviled and even incited mobs against the Jews. The claim that faith includes love might possibly be theologically fallacious since there is a substantial and continuing theological tradition within Christianity which holds that faith is born, shaped, and perfected by love.

The point I am making in this footnote is twofold. First, the confusion and disagreement over the essence of faith brought about by speculatively and stipulatively grounded definitions make it necessary for religious educationists to embrace due caution and to eschew grandiloquent sureties when delineating the nature and parameters of faith. Second, since faith is distinct from hope and love, the global outcome for which the Christian *ecclesia* should be teaching ought not to be faith, but rather a reality which includes hope and love as well as faith. This reality is called religion by many persons, including myself.

My views as expressed in this footnote are rather traditional (I write "traditional" and not "conservative") throughout Christianity. Thus Bernard James Diggs observes that love is being as perfective. Consequently love is a force which binds and reconciles. Love is the fruit of unity in goodness. In this same vein, Henry Bars states that faith is the entry, while charity is the goal and source. In Bars' analysis "faith holds diplomatic relations with reason; but it strictly distinguishes the teachings of revelation from all the rest." Charity, on the other hand, "always approaches, for it is made to approach all things." Indeed, "charity reconciles man, and the world which supports him, to their God." Thomas Aquinas' well-known statement runs as follows: "Charity is the form of faith in that the act of faith is perfected and formed by charity." Paul Tillich remarks that "faith is the state of being ultimately concerned." Love, on the other hand "is the power in the ground of everything that is, driving it beyond itself toward reunion with the other one and ultimately with the ground itself from which it is separated." Rosemary Haughton puts the relationship between faith and love in arresting terms. "It remains in this chapter to wonder if an act of faith whose goal

hood *homo integer,* so that virtually all human behaviors (including those classified as faith or religion) have simultanelously an "inner" and an "outer" face. If faith exists as a human act, then by any kind of definition it is a functional dimension of the whole person. If faithing is indeed a human act, then it follows that faithing is an

---

is explicitly God has any advantage as a human act over those that have not: . . . and why acts of faith so often end up by denying themselves—that is, by failing to be acts of love issuing in love." From the biblical perspective, the scholarly conclusions of Donatien Mollat and Viktor Warnach are highly illuminative. From his careful analysis of the First Epistle of John, Mollat concludes: "L'effet de la foi est la victoire de la charité de Dieu qui nous donne la vie éternelle. . . . Dans ce sens se réalise la plus intime connexion de la charité qui révèle, de la charité absolue, réalité ultime. Si l'objet de la foi est la charité, si la réponse de foi est l'acceptation de la révèlation divine, la charité doit contenir, étroitement liées, toutes les conditions de la perception de l'amour divin par l'homme." Viktor Warnach's scholarly study of charity in the New Testament puts it pithily: "Mit überzeugender Eindringlichkeit wird im NT der Vorrang der Agape von allen Motiven ausgesprochen." Bernard James Diggs, *Love and Being* (New York: Vanni, 1947), pp. 143–157; Henry Bars, *Faith, Hope, and Charity,* translated by P. J. Hepburne Scott (New York: Hawthorn, 1961), pp. 18–65, 143; Thomas Aquinas, *Summa Theologica,* II-II, q.4, a.3, translation mine; Paul Tillich, *Dynamics of Faith* (New York: Harper and Row, 1957), p. 114; Rosemary Haughton, *Act of Love* (Philadelphia: Lippincott, 1968), p. 157; Donatien Mollat, *Lumière et Charité d'après la Première Epître de Saint Jean* (Rome: Institut Pontifical des Recherches Ecclesiastiques, 1971), p. 161; Viktor Warnach, *Agape: Die Liebe als Grundmotiv der neutestamentlichen Theologie* (Düsseldorf, Deutschland: Patmos, 1951), p. 472.

4. See, for example, John H. Westerhoff III, *Will Our Children Have Faith?* (New York: Seabury, 1976), pp. 21–23.

5. Thus, for example, Thomas Aquinas writes that religion properly denotes a person's total relationship with God, his orientation to God. Aquinas' view is supported by a wealth of scholarship. For example, Ninian Smart's cross-cultural study of religion suggests that religion is a broad term which in various eras and cultures includes such personal "inner" activities as one's experiences, feelings, beliefs, and myths, as well as such visible "outer" forms as rituals, symbols, institutions, and creedal statements. These "inner" and "outer" dimensions of religion are in continual existential dialogue since they are simply dimensions of the same unified total entity called religion.

Karl Hermann Schelkle's scholarly treatment of the historical theology of the Bible reveals that in the non-Greek texts, faith was something as fully "outer" as "inner." Thus in the Old Testament, faith was Abraham's "inner" and "outer" submission to God's will. Faith was also Israel's visible living within her own geographical boundaries, the visible subjection of a whole nation to God's command, and the "outer" expression by the whole godly man of his own personal

activity of the whole person, and not simply of his allegedly inner self. Finally, the claim that faith is inner and religion is outer is illogical because it reifies faith. *Faith is a construct. Consequently faith is a logical being and not a real being. Faith is simply a label given to a certain set of behaviors which enjoy a certain similarity to one another.* The purpose of a construct is heuristic, namely to help us analyze particular behaviors more clearly and more carefully. Faith, therefore, does not exist in the soul or anywhere else. What exists is that

---

experience with God. It is only with the Greek Bible that the words "faith" and "to have faith" acquired the intensive significance of primarily but by no means exclusively "inner" activity. In the New Testament, especially in Mark and Luke and Paul, faith is both an "inner" commitment and an "outer" set of visible decisions and actions.

Erich Heck's careful review of the concept of religion in the works of Peter Abelard, Thomas Aquinas, Raymond Lull, Nicholas of Cusa, Martin Luther, Ulrich Zwingli, John Calvin, Hugo Grotius, John Locke, Immanuel Kant, Friedrich Schleiermacher, Friedrich Nietzsche, Sigmund Freud, and Carl Jung found that while the concept of religion comprises the unified "inner" and "outer," it always includes the lived "inner" relationship which man has with God, a relationship made inextricably observable by the "outer."

Scholarly studies such as those made by Günter Lanczkowski, Winston King, and William Tremmel in the history of world religions find no basis for claiming that religion is "outer" and faith "inner." To be sure, the history of religions clearly shows that religion is an act of the whole person involving both "outer" and "inner," with the so-called "inner" being the core.

Johann Baptist Metz nicely summarizes the view of contemporary Christian theology that the act of religion encompasses not only an act which totally and radically involves the whole person "inner" and "outer," but is also an act in which the whole person "inner" and "outer" is caught up in both the self-transcending act of involvement with God and in the *descensus* of God's love for all creation, especially other persons. Thomas Aquinas, *Summa Theologica,* II-II q.81, a.1; Ninian Smart, *The Phenomenon of Religion* (New York: Macmillan, 1973), pp. 1–120; Karl Hermann Schelkle, *Theology of the New Testament,* volume III, translated by William A. Jurgens (Collegeville, MN: Liturgical Press, 1970), pp. 82–97; Erich Heck, *Der Begriff religion bei Thomas von Aquin* (München: Schöningh, 1971), pp. 8–17; Günter Lanczkowski, "Religion: II: Science of Religion: B: History of Religion," in Karl Rahner et al., editors, *Sacramentum Mundi,* volume V (New York: Herder and Herder, 1970), pp. 262–276; Winston L. King, *Introduction to Religion* (New York: Harper and Row, 1954); William C. Tremmel, *Religion: What is It?* (New York: Holt, Rinehart, and Winston, 1976); Johann Baptist Metz, "Religious Act," in Karl Rahner et al., editors, *Sacramentum Mundi,* volume V, pp. 287–290.

particular set of behaviors which certain human beings classify as faith. In other words, faith is a word used to designate a functional set of human behaviors. Faith is a description of one way in which persons organize and implement their lives as persons. Thus it is nonsensical to state that faith is "in there."

If the claim that faith is inner and religion is outer is fallacious, so also is the claim made by some religious educationists[6] that faith cannot be taught because it is a lifestyle gift of God's grace. This latter claim is fallacious logically, theologically, and pedagogically. The claim that faith cannot be taught is logically fallacious because it gratuitously makes an empirical assertion about a matter for which no empirical evidence is adduced. It is a rule of logic that any valid assertion about an empirical matter must be supported by empirical evidence. The claim that faith cannot be taught is theologically fallacious because in theological theory all reality and not just faith is regarded as a gift of God's grace. If it were true that faith could not be taught because it is a gift of God's grace, then nothing in this world could be taught by any human being since all reality is a gift of God's grace. *The issue, then, is not whether gifts of God's grace can be taught, but rather how these gifts are given and received. To be sure, this is the central issue in religious instruction,* and it will not be satisfactorily addressed by begging the question as has been done by those persons who claim that faith cannot be taught because it is a gift of God's grace. Understanding how the gifts of God's grace are given and received is central to religious instruction because teaching deals with the way God's grace is given and learning deals with the way God's grace is received. The claim that faith cannot be taught is pedagogically fallacious because all manner of lifestyle behaviors can and indeed have been successfully taught by human beings.[7]

6. See, for example, Berard L. Marthaler, "Socialization as a Model for Catechetics," in Padraic O'Hare, editor, *Foundations of Religious Education* (New York: Paulist, 1978), p. 75.

7. To claim, as Berard Marthaler explicitly does, that only a cognitive meaning (theology) of faith can be taught, and that faith as lifestyle cannot be taught, is rationalist reductionism. If such a preposterous claim were true, then all Christian religious instruction would be constitutionally permissible in American

Religion differs from theology as two realities with substantially distinct natures differ from one another. A definition of religion was given at the outset of this section. Theology may be defined as that form of cognitive investigation which uses both reason and divine revelation to systematically discover and elaborate the truths concerning God and his activities.[8] Religion and theology, consequently, differ on-

---

public schools since it is legal to teach theologically about faith on public property. To adhere to Marthaler's unsupported claim is to ultimately allege that faith can never be learned at all because learning takes place in unintentional or nonintentional education. But if faith cannot be learned, then how does a person acquire faith and grow in faith?

8. Definitions of theology offered by some standard reference works and by a few prominent theologians might be instructive in this connection. The *Encyclopedia of Religion and Ethics* states that "theology may be broadly defined as the science which deals, according to the scientific method, with the facts and phenomena of religion and culminates in a comprehensive synthesis or philosophy of religion, which seeks to set forth in a systematic way all that can be known regarding the objective grounds of religious belief." In *Sacramentum Mundi* the following definition is given: "Theology is the science of the faith inasmuch as the Christian faith is the basis, norm, and goal of this science. . . . Theology is the critical and methodological reflection on faith." *Theological Dictionary* defines theology as "essentially the conscious effort of the Christian to hearken to the actual verbal revelation which God has promulgated in history, to acquire a knowledge of it by the methods of scholarship, and to reflect upon its implications. . . . This methodological effort to acquire knowledge of a complete, internally unified subject must be called a science. . . ." The *New Catholic Encyclopedia* states that theology "is a branch of learning which a Christian, using his reason enlightened by divine faith, seeks to understand the mysteries of God revealed in and through history." Paul Tillich writes as follows: "Theology is the methodological explanation of the contents of the Christian faith. This definition is valid for all theological disciplines." John Macquarrie has this to say: "Theology may be defined as the study which, through participation in and reflection upon a religious faith, seeks to express the content of this faith in the clearest, most coherent language available." In a thought-provoking statement of especial relevance to those religious educationists and educators who regard religious instruction as nothing more than theology, Helmut Thielicke writes: *"In view of its structure, theological thinking is in some way an 'alien' medium into which statements of faith must be transposed."* D. S. Adam, "Theology: Definition," in James Hastings, editor, *Encyclopedia of Religion and Ethics,* volume XII (New York: Scribner's, 1925), p. 293; Karl Rahner, "Theology," in Karl Rahner et al., editors, *Sacramentum Mundi,* volume VI (New York: Herder and Herder, 1970), p. 235; Karl Rahner and Herbert Vorgrimler, editors, *Theological Dictionary,* edited by Cornelius

tically in several substantial respects. Religion is a lifestyle activity involving the personally-lived fusion of knowledge, belief, feeling, experience, and practice; theology is primarily a cognitive affair. *Religion is basically a way of living; theology is principally a scientific way of knowing.* Religion is the personal way in which an individual lives a God-like existence; theology is one of the most important cognitive vehicles for helping the individual come to a valid knowledge of God as he reveals himself to us. *Religion is a way of life; theology is a theory about this way of life.* [9] The test of religion is the degree to which it leads and indeed embodies a life lived in unity with God in his revelation; the test of theology is the degree to which it cohesively inserts all the relevant concepts, facts, and laws into an adequate theory of God and of religious living. Religion as experiential has an absolute character to it in that religious experience *is* always valid as such; theology as theory has a tentative character in that a theological theory only *may be* valid as such. Religion exists primarily and directly to enable individuals to live enriched God-filled lives; theology exists primarily and directly to provide cognitive information on God and his revelatory activities, information which is also required or helpful for living an enriched religious life. Religion is a way of life, and hence makes lifestyle and often confessional demands upon the learner when it is facilitated;

Ernst and translated by Richard Strachan (New York: Herder and Herder, 1965), p. 456; G. F. van Ackeren, "Theology," in *New Catholic Encyclopedia,* volume XIV (New York: McGraw-Hill, 1967), p. 39; Paul Tillich, *Systematic Theology,* volume I (Chicago: University of Chicago Press, 1951), p. 28; John Macquarrie, *Principles of Christian Theology* (New York: Scribner's, 1966), p. 1; Helmut Thielicke, *The Evangelical Faith,* volume II, translated and edited by Geoffrey W. Bromiley (Grand Rapids, Michigan: Eerdmans, 1977), p. 3, italics added.

9. *There is, of course, a discrete ontic difference between a reality and a theory of that reality. Thus a person can be a superb theologian and not be very religious.* No empirical evidence has been adduced to support the empirical claim made by some theologians that personal Christian faith acts must necessarily accompany the theologian's theologizing. To be sure, recent biographies and histories of some major Christian theologians suggest that by the accepted standards of their own Christian denominations, the quality of much of their religious life appears to have been somewhat weak. *In short, religion will necessarily get a person into heaven, while theology will not necessarily eventuate in salvation.*

theology is a cognitive science, and hence makes no lifestyle or confessional demands upon the learner when it is facilitated.[10] Religion and theology, then, are distinct entities: Christian living and thought concerning God are not the same thing. Though religion and theology may intersect each other under certain circumstances, nonetheless they are basically different modes of human activity. Theology is dependent upon religion but is not identical to religion.[11]

INSTRUCTION

Instruction is to education as a part is to the whole. Thus to properly understand instruction, it is helpful to briefly define and discuss education.

Education

Education may be defined as the broad process whereby a person learns something. Whenever a person's behavior is changed, he is *eo ipso* learning something, that is to say he is acquiring education. There are two major types of education, namely, nonintentional and intentional. Nonintentional education consists in all those learnings acquired from sources or in milieux in which learning outcomes are not purposely sought. Intentional education consists in all those learnings acquired from sources or in milieux in which learning outcomes are purposely sought. The purpose of intentional educa-

10. This characteristic of theology constitutes the ultimate foundation of academic freedom for theological programs (and for theologians) in church-related universities. *Theology is an autonomous intellectual science and hence is not directly part of the pastoral mission of the bishop, clergy, or church elders.* Also this characteristic of theology constitutes the constitutional basis for the inclusion of theology courses and degree-programs in government-operated universities situated in countries like the United States which sponsor religiously-neutral schools.

11. Thus Bernard Lonergan can write that theology "makes thematic what is already part of Christian living." Bernard J. F. Lonergan, *Method in Theology*, p. 144.

tion is to make learning more efficient, more rapid, and easier than would be the case if the same learning were acquired from nonintentional sources and in nonintentional milieux. The claim made by some religious educationists[12] that all education is intentional is both empirically false and logically false. This claim is empirically false because it is an empirically demonstrated fact that nonintentional education, including nonintentional education in religion, sometimes and in certain cases often yields more significant learning outcomes than intentional education. This claim is logically false as is illustrated in the following dilemma: "If all education is intentional, then it is correct to assert that those learnings acquired from nonintentional sources or in nonintentional milieux are noneducational. But if these learnings are noneducational, what are they?" Scholars and practitioners in the field of education typically identify three basic types of intentional education, namely instruction, guidance, and administration.

Instruction

Instruction may be defined as that kind of intentional educational process by and through which desired learning outcomes are actually facilitated in some way. According to both time-honored dictionary usage and long-standing professional pedagogical parlance, *instruction is a term which is synonymous with teaching. The instructional process is enacted in the interplay of four major variables: teacher, learner, subject matter, and environment. These four variables are always present in one way or another in every teaching-learning act.* Because these major variables are variables, they can and do admit of both primary change and secondary change. A major instructional variable undergoes primary change when its particular make-up is altered in some basic way. Thus, for example, the teacher variable might consist of a person or a person-designed teaching machine, a priest or a layper-

---

12. See, for example, John H. Westerhoff III, "Risking an Answer: A Conclusion," in John H. Westerhoff III, *Who Are We?: The Quest for a Religious Education* (Birmingham, Alabama: Religious Education Press, 1978), p. 264.

son, a parent or a schoolteacher. A major instructional variable undergoes secondary change when one of its particular subordinate features is altered. Thus, for example, the priest (teacher) giving his Sunday sermon might change his voice tone and adjust his subject matter as a consequence of his observation that some of the congregation are seemingly going to sleep. The instructional process, therefore, is not necessarily tied in with any particular kind of teacher, any particular kind of learner, any particular kind of subject matter, any particular kind of environment. Subject matter is still subject matter, regardless of whether it is cognitive or affective or lifestyle, or whether it is biblical or nonbiblical. Similarly an instructional environment may be formal (school, church) or informal (home, playground). The fact that an instructional environment is not setting-bound (that is, not restricted simply to one or another particular setting) clearly points up the fallaciousness of the claim made by some religious educationists[13] that instruction is synonymous with schooling. *By virtue of both its definition (teaching) and its composition (varying environments), instruction is perforce setting-free.*[14] (Parenthetically, I should note that since setting constitutes only one of four major variables within the entire structure of the teaching-learning process, it is erroneous to allege that schooling itself is a global mode of teaching/learning, as has been claimed by

13. Thus, for example, John Westerhoff typically uses the expression "schooling-instructional paradigm" to syntactically as well as denotatively link schooling inextricably with instruction. Prescinding from the grammatical inaccuracy of his terminology, Westerhoff has no valid theoretical, logical, historical, or lexical basis for any linkage which necessarily ties schooling with instruction. See John H. Westerhoff III, *Will Our Children Have Faith?* pp. 6–9.

14. At the outset of *The Flow of Religious Instruction* (Birmingham, Alabama: Religious Education Press, 1973) I specifically stated that religious instruction is of its very essence setting-free. Furthermore, the detailed analyses of the religious instruction process which I have given in my various writings from 1959 to the present unambiguously indicate that instruction (teaching) must by its very nature and function be setting-free. Persons who claim that the social-science approach is restricted solely or even primarily to the school setting neither have read my writings with requisite care nor have grasped the basis of my theory. See Jack L. Seymour, "Contemporary Approaches to Christian Education," in *Chicago Theological Seminary Register* LXIX (Spring, 1979), pp. 1–10.

at least one religious educationist.[15]) Instruction refers to the teaching process in its entirety. Instruction, then, is not procedure-bound (that is, not restricted to one or another particular pedagogical procedure). The fact that instruction is not procedure-bound reveals the fallaciousness of the claim made or implied by some

15. Gabriel Moran gratuitously defines schooling as a molar mode or form of learning which may occur in both school and nonschool settings. Moran appears to predicate schooling as coextensive with intentional education regardless of the setting in which it is enacted. To the term "schooling" he juxtaposes "laboratory," a term which he seems to conceptualize as nonintentional education and hence the contrary of schooling. Moran's gratuitous definitions and distinctions not only introduce conceptual confusion, but also could result in a decided retrogression in religious education if they were taken seriously. Moran's gratuitous definition of schooling as simultaneously a major mode of education (intentionality) and setting-free (not coextensive with a school setting) is at once lexically inaccurate, historically blind, and logically bizarre—lexically inaccurate since the dictionary defines schooling as typically setting-bound, historically blind since educationists and educators down the centuries have typically regarded schooling as setting-bound, and logically bizarre because it senselessly introduces an unwarranted chasm between a noun and its directly derivative gerund. Moran's gratuitous and strange definition of "laboratory" is also without lexical, historical, and logical foundation. Two examples should suffice to illustrate my point that Moran's gratuitous definitions and conceptualizations of "schooling" and "laboratory," if taken seriously, could cause serious retrogression in religious education. First, Moran places the family in his laboratory (nonintentional) mode of teaching/learning. Yet one of the major empirically-based insights of this century has been that the family (and indeed the entire community) can and surely does play a powerful role as intentional (as well as nonintentional) educators not only of children but also of other family (and community) members. Second, one of the major theoretical and practical advances made in education has been in transforming schooling from a wholly didactic, teacher-talk enterprise into an authentic organized laboratory, a laboratory in which learners can optimally fuse [intentional] instruction into their whole here-and-now lives. To be sure, the Swiss educationist Johann Pestalozzi (1746–1827), the German educationist Friedrich Froebel (1782–1852), the Italian educationist Maria Montessori (1870–1952), and the American educationist John Dewey (1859–1952) all rejected the distinction between schooling and laboratory on both theoretical and practical grounds. All these educationists—who incidentally operated laboratory-schools at one time or another in their careers—repeatedly emphasized that schooling should be of such a cast that it is a laboratory for enriched intentional learning. Moran's positing, from out of the blue, of laboratory as comprising nonintentional education could arrest the possible development and expansion of the laboratory emphasis in a religious school setting. My

religious educationists that instruction is restricted to a teacher-centered lecture-type technique.

Religious Instruction

Religious instruction is that kind of intentional educational process by and through which desired religious learning outcomes are actually facilitated in some way. *My essay in this book deals principally with the religious instruction sector of intentional religious education. Any global treatment of intentional religious education should, by definition and comprehension, deal with religious instruction, religious guidance, and the administration of religious education activities.* However, I will confine my analysis to religious instruction, for three basic reasons. First, the space allotted to this essay is too short to permit even a minimally adequate treatment of the relation of theology to religious instruction, religious guidance, and the administration of religious education activities. Second, my primary though by no means exclusive scholarly interest resides in the area of religious instruction. The third, and in some ways the most important reason lies in the fact that when writers, professors, and speakers in religious education discuss the field, they almost always deal with religious instruction rather than with religious guidance or administration. Rarely do persons publicly identified as religious educationists or educators deal with the theories and procedures of religious counseling or religious administration when these individuals discuss reli-

---

own empirically-based contention, as stated in books and speeches dating back to the early 1960's, is that *as far as possible, all religion teaching, regardless of the setting in which it takes place, should be a laboratory for Christian living.* See Gabriel Moran, *Education for Adulthood* (New York: Paulist, 1979), pp. 33–35, 105–129. See also Johann Heinrich Pestalozzi, *How Gertrude Teaches Her Children,* translated by Lucy E. Holland and Francis C. Turner, edited by Ebenezer Cook (London: Sonnenschein, 1894); Friedrich Wilhelm August Froebel, *Gesammelte pädagogische Schriften,* Herausgeber Richard Lange (Berlin: Enslin, 1861 & 1862); Maria Montessori, *The Montessori Method,* translated by Anne B. George (Cambridge, Massachusetts: Bentley, 1965); John Dewey, *The School and Society* (Chicago: University of Chicago Press, 1900).

gious education *per se et nominatim.*[16] One of the major reasons why Christian religious educationists and educators continue to erroneously identify the part (religious instruction) with the whole (religious education) is that the instructional sector of religious education, unlike the guidance and administration sectors, has not yet become a profession and therefore has not yet developed its own special identity, definitions, conceptualizations, and language.

The term "religious instruction" clearly indicates the two primary components of religious instruction, namely religion and instruction. Religious instruction is only religious instruction when that which is occurring is the teaching of religion. *Theological instruction is not religious instruction.* Language instruction is not religious instruction. Religious architecture is not religious instruction. Religious music is not religious instruction. Theology, language, architecture, and music may be used in the work of religious instruction, but of themselves they are not religious instruction *per se.*

Viewed formally, religious instruction is composed of two primary and fundamental contents, namely structural content and substantive content. In terms only of religious instruction itself, neither of these two contents can be said to enjoy independent or autonomous existence. Each of these two becomes a content of religious instruction only at such a time as it is compounded with the other to form the religious instruction act.

The structural content of religious instruction is the teaching process. This content assumes many and varied shapes, depending upon the dynamic interaction in the religious instruction act of the four major variables involved in all teaching. These four major variables are the learner, the teacher, the subject matter, and the environment. In terms of both the practice and the formal theory of teaching, these four basic variables are always interactively present in one way or another.

16. When religious educationists or educators, for example, discuss the administration of religious education programs, they are usually careful to specify that they are discussing the administration of religious education activities rather than treating the whole of religious education.

The substantive content of religious instruction is religion. This content assumes many and varied shapes, depending upon the emphasis and arrangement of the subcontents contained in substantive content. On the basis of empirical investigation, I have been able to identify eight discrete subcontents of substantive content as these subcontents exist in the religious instruction act: (1) product content; (2) process content; (3) cognitive content; (4) affective content; (5) verbal content; (6) nonverbal content; (7) unconscious content; (8) lifestyle content. In terms of both the practice and the formal theory of religion teaching, these eight basic substantive contents are always interactively present in one way or another.

Religious instruction consists in the religious instruction act, nothing more and nothing less. When a person speculates on religious instruction, theorizes on religious instruction, or does empirical research on religious instruction, his speculations or theories or research are not religious instruction but rather are about or on religious instruction. Consequently any adequate speculation or theory or research about/on religious instruction cannot start from any a priori position, but rather must necessarily start from the religious instruction act itself. It is impossible to develop an adequate view of play unless one's views are carefully drawn from and are constantly tethered to the act of playing. It is impossible to develop an adequate view of prayer unless one's views are carefully drawn from and are constantly tethered to the act of praying. It is likewise impossible to develop an adequate view of religious instruction unless one's views are carefully drawn from and are constantly tethered to the act of teaching religion. A great deal of the contemporary writing on religious instruction is so vacuous and downright ridiculous because a great deal of contemporary writing is drawn simply from the authors' armchair musings rather than drawn from and tethered to the religious instruction act. When authors of books and articles purporting to treat of religious instruction do not draw their views from a rigorous analysis of the religious instruction act itself, then their views are only their own opinions and hypotheses, opinions and hypotheses which only coincidentally may bear an intrinsic relationship to religious instruction.

THEORY

A theory is a statement or group of statements organically integrating interrelated concepts, facts, and laws in such a fashion as to offer a comprehensive and systematic view of reality by specifying relations among variables.[17] A theory, then, is a tentative statement which attempts to make molar sense out of the facts from which it is necessarily constructed. Facts simply are: they have no meaning and significance in and of themselves. *Without theory, reality would be personally meaningless and without past or present or future significance.*

A theory intrinsically has at least two fundamental properties, namely comprehensiveness and systematicness. A theory is comprehensive in that it includes the entire range of concepts, facts, and laws which in some way are organically or operationally related to the phenomena or class with which theory purports to deal. A theory is systematic in that it assembles the entire range of relevant concepts, facts, and laws in such a fashion that they form an organized whole. The adequacy, fruitfulness, and power of a theory is determined in part by the degree to which it is comprehensive and systematic.

17. In my treatment of theory, I have utilized the contributions of a great number of authors. A few of these include David E. Apter and Charles F. Andrain, editors, *Contemporary Analytical Theory* (Englewood Cliffs, New Jersey: Prentice-Hall, 1972); Hubert M. Blalock, Jr., *Theory Construction* (Englewood Cliffs, New Jersey: Prentice-Hall, 1969); Robert G. Colodny, *The Nature and Function of Scientific Theories* (Pittsburgh: University of Pittsburgh Press, 1970); Jürgen Habermas, *Theory and Practice*, translated by John Viertel (Boston: Beacon, 1973); Abraham Kaplan, *The Conduct of Inquiry* (San Francisco: Chandler, 1964); Nicholas Lobkowicz, *Theory and Practice: History of a Concept from Aristotle to Marx* (Notre Dame, Indiana: University of Notre Dame Press, 1967); Bernard J. F. Lonergan, *Method in Theology,* 2d edition (New York: Seabury, 1972); Melvin H. Marx and Felix E. Goodson, editors, *Theories in Contemporary Psychology,* 2d edition (New York: Macmillan, 1976); F. S. C. Northrop, *The Logic of the Sciences and the Humanities* (Cleveland: World, 1947); Robert M. Pirsig, *Zen and the Art of Motorcycle Maintenance* (New York: Bantam, 1974); Karl Popper, *The Logic of Scientific Discovery* (New York: Harper and Row, 1965); David Tracy, *Blessed Rage for Order* (New York: Seabury, 1975); Walter L. Wallace, *The Logic of Science in Sociology* (Chicago: Aldine, 1971).

A theory intrinsically performs three fundamental functions, namely explanation, prediction, and verification. A theory explains a delineated class of reality by providing the basic meaning and significance about why the concepts, facts, and laws within that delineated class of reality are the way they are and interact the way they do. A theory predicts new interactions among the concepts, facts, and laws with which it deals, and also points to gaps in knowledge as well as to dimensions or areas not previously or adequately explained or explored. A theory verifies the existence and operation of the concepts, facts, and laws within a delineated class of reality. A major goal of every science, including social science and theological science, is to so broaden the explanatory, predictive, and verificational power of a theory that in the end there will remain the smallest number of possible theories, each possessing the strongest and widest power of explanation, prediction, and verification.

An adequate and fruitful theory is absolutely necessary for religious instruction. Without theory, for example, there could be no explanation of how and why a particular teaching procedure works at one time but not at another, how and why a given curriculum flops, and so on. Without theory, for example, the religious educator would be utterly unable to make any reasonable prediction about whether x pedagogical procedure will be more effective than y procedure in a certain instructional situation, or whether z curriculum will be a success with his learners. Without theory, for example, there is no way to ascertain whether that which is acquired really has been learned, whether that which the teacher is doing is really teaching, whether that which is taught does or does not constitute an integral aspect of the curriculum, and so forth. Theory, therefore, is indispensable both to the satisfactory understanding of religious instruction activity and to the effective enactment of religious instruction practice. Indeed there is a sense in which the adequacy and fruitfulness of a particular religious educator's pedagogical practice is contingent upon the adequacy and fruitfulness of his theory of religious instruction.

It is a truism that the most practical thing in the world is a good theory. This is so because theory explains how and why practice works the way it does, and also predicts which practices will tend to work in a given situation and which ones will tend to fail. If a religious educator does not know why a particular practice works, it is highly unlikely that he will know how to make that practice work in the way he wants it to work. Theory helps save the religious educator from the very failures which theory would have been able to predict.[18] *Religious educators of the practicalist variety who imagine themselves to be exempt from the influence of theory are often the unwitting slaves of some defunct or inoperative theory.*

Theories vary in their efficacy and "goodness." Some theories are better than others because some theories are more helpful for practice than others. The nature and work of theory suggests nine key litmus criteria by which the adequacy, validity, and goodness of a theory can be judged: form, consistency, procedural correspondence, comprehensiveness, systematicness, fruitfulness, explainability, predictability, and verifiability.

Theory is fundamentally different in structure and intent both from a tract and from speculation. A tract is a popular short book or pamphlet written in a zealous and titupping manner for the purpose of rousing persons to action. The adequacy and validity of a tract stem from the degree to which it echoes its author's personal passionate persuasion; hence a tract may be adequate and valid even though it contains empty slogans, fallacious reasoning, gross imprecisions, factual errors, and internal contradictions. Speculation is the exclusive use of conceptual, judgmental, and inferential processes in order to ascertain the truth about any matter of concern or interest. Speculation, then, consists in the contemplation of and reflection on all or part of the nature and/or workings of some reality. Speculation is primarily a particular form of thinking, and as such is directly opposite to empiric. Theory, as I observed at the outset of this section, is a statement or group of statements organically integrating interre-

18. Kenneth Gergen comments that knowledge of a theory enables one to avoid being ensnared by its predictions. Kenneth J. Gergen, "Social Psychology as History," in *Journal of Personality and Social Psychology* XXVI (May, 1973), p. 316.

lated concepts, facts, and laws in such a fashion as to offer a comprehensive and systematic view of reality by specifying relations
among variables. *A theory is constructed by carefully establishing concepts
and facts, and then systematically inserting these concepts and facts into
those kinds of laws and theory which comprehensively explain the interactive
variable relations among the concepts and facts.* In theoretical work, the
theorist constantly and consciously endeavors to directly relate his
premises, statements, descriptions, and conclusions to some overall
theory. In theorizing, the power, adequacy, and validity of any
premise, statement, description, and conclusion comes primarily
from the degree to which it finds its organic place within one or
another theory. Theory, then, is constructed and elaborated in a
manner which is basically different from the ways in which a tract
and speculation are conceptually constructed and elaborated. As a
consequence, theory performs a fundamentally different function
than does either a tract or speculation.

I am underscoring the fundamental difference among theory,
speculation, and tract because many religious educationists and
educators do not seem to be aware of this crucial distinction.[19]
*Almost all the writing in the field of Christian religious instruction in this
century has taken the form of speculation or tracts. Very little has been
theoretical.*[20] Speculative writings and tracts have their usefulness, of

19. See, for example, Gabriel Moran, *Education Toward Adulthood*, pp. 1–2.
20. *Quite possibly a major reason why there has been so little theorizing in religious
instruction in this century is the seemingly built-in aversion to theory and its properties on
the part of the advocates of the theological approach to religious instruction. The fact that
theory by its nature is comprehensive and systematic is at basic variance with one of the most
cherished (but unproven) claims made by most advocates of the theological approach,
namely that the facilitation of religious instruction outcomes is the proximate result of the
wholly mysterious and totally unfathomable action of the Holy Spirit. Thus Françoise
Darcy-Bérubé, a representative of this position, is able to state that even the most sophisticated religious instruction theory cannot explain or predict how or whether religious
outcomes are facilitated through teaching. The consequence of such a position is the
fundamental disvaluation of theory and the enthronement of all sorts of wild and near-wild
speculations and tracts. Because theory is remanded to the rubbish heap by most advocates of
the theological approach, the explanation and prediction and verification of religious
facilitation becomes totally relativized, with the opinions of any one speculationist or
tractarian being just as good as another. Paradoxically, Darcy-Bérubé's disvaluation of*

course. However, they can never substitute for theory since they
severely lack the power of a theory to comprehensively and systematically explain, predict, and verify religious instruction phenomena.
To be sure, the scarcity of genuine theory in the field of Christian
religious instruction during this century constitutes a major cause
for the undeniable fact that the field has been enfeebled by conceptual trinketry and riddled with procedural gimmickry.

THE BASIC ISSUES

The purpose of this article is to examine the relationship between
religious instruction and theology. There are two major issues
which must be considered when exploring this relationship. The
first of these basic issues deals with the appropriateness and adequacy of theology as a macrotheoretical approach to religious instruction. The second of these basic issues deals with the shape,
role, and function of theological content in religious instruction.
These two basic issues can only be first understood and then resolved
by continuously relating them to the three primary realities with
which these issues deal, namely religion, instruction, and theory.

THEOLOGY AS THE MACROTHEORETICAL APPROACH TO RELIGIOUS INSTRUCTION

Until the early 1970s, theology was generally regarded as comprising the macrotheoretical approach to Christian religious instruc-

---

*theory and its ability of making comprehensive explanations/predictions/verifications on
religious matters has the effect of destroying her cherished claim that theology has the
proximate primacy in properly interpreting all reality and its workings. Theology, after
all, is fundamentally a theory. If, as Darcy-Bérubé purports, a theory seriously lacks the
ability to comprehensively explain/predict/verify religious reality, then theology has little
utility for religious reality including religious instruction.* See Françoise Darcy-Bérubé,
"The Challenge Ahead of Us," in Padraic O'Hare, editor, *Foundations of Religious
Education*, p. 116.

tion.[21] As the macrotheory of religious instruction, theology was alleged to possess the power of explaining and predicting and verifying the entire range of religious instruction phenomena. Thus it was claimed that theology is capable of devising and testing effective teaching techniques, of explaining the conditions under which religious learning could or could not take place, of directly devising successful religion curricula, of predicting who would or would not be an effective religion teacher, and so forth. In 1971 a book was published which frontally challenged this centuries-old view of theology as the macrotheory of religious instruction. This book, *The Shape of Religious Instruction*[22], claimed that it is social science and not theology which constitutes the only adequate and valid macrotheory for religious instruction. Since 1971 the issue of whether theology or social science is the proper macrotheory has been one of the most recurrent and most hotly debated issues in the field. It would appear that the social-science approach is gaining the upper hand over the theological approach—so much so, in fact, that a prominent advocate of the theological approach could lament that all of religious education is now beginning to take its direction from the social sciences.[23] However, the adequacy and validity of either

21. A macrotheory is an overall and global form of theory into which are inserted theories and subtheories of a lesser scope. For example, the theory of grace is a major macrotheory in theological science. The atomic theory is a major macrotheory in chemical science. Macrotheory is of an essentially different order than metatheory. The term "metatheory" usually denotes the theory of theory, a critical theoretical examination of the nature and structure of theory in general.

22. James Michael Lee, *The Shape of Religious Instruction* (Birmingham, Alabama: Religious Education Press, 1971).

23. John H. Westerhoff III, "Value Catechesis," in *New Review of Books and Religion* IV (June, 1980), p. 3. The other two areas of religious education, namely religious guidance/counseling and the administration of religious education activities, long ago rejected the theological approach as their macrotheory, and instead adopted the social-science approach. Religious instruction for years was the lone holdout. But then again, this is not surprising since religious instruction always seems to lag behind. In 1976, Thomas Groome claimed, without adducing any supporting evidence, that the social-science approach was on the wane. Yet only four years later he published an important book espousing religious education as a political activity consisting of a pedagogical method which he terms "shared Christian praxis." The theory and explanation of political activity is generally

the theological approach or the social-science approach cannot be satisfactorily resolved by appeals either to venerableness or to recent ascendancy. *The adequacy and validity of any theory (and macrotheory) can only be gauged by ascertaining the degree to which it does what a theory or macrotheory is by its very nature supposed to do, namely explain and predict and verify the phenomena under its purview.* This section of my essay will be devoted to such an investigation. Restrictions of space permit only the sketchiest treatment of the many points I will advance.

In order to satisfactorily investigate whether theology or social science is the appropriate macrotheory for religious instruction, we must always keep as the center and as the touchstone that with which we are dealing, namely the nature and actual operation of religious instruction endeavor. The results of this kind of investigation will reveal the appropriate macrotheory for religious instruction. A theory or macrotheory is by its very essence a tentative overall explanation of the concepts, facts, and laws which it treats. Consequently, a valid and adequate macrotheory must be drawn or inferred from the actual operations of religious instruction activity itself. Thus neither the relationship between religious instruction and theology nor the role of theology in religious instruction can be determined a priori. It is invalid both logically and ontically to assert a priori that just because religious instruction deals with faith that it is therefore essentially theological. Conversely, it is invalid to assert a priori that just because religious instruction deals with the facilitation of learning that it is therefore essentially social scientific. The proper and valid determination of the appropriate nature and macrotheory for religious in-

---

conceded by contemporary scholars to fall directly within the range of social science. Furthermore, the way in which Groome defines and validates the instructional method of shared Christian praxis is fundamentally social-scientific in nature. Though Groome has consciously or unconsciously adopted a theory in which certain specific features are significantly different from the macrotheory I espouse, nonetheless his is also, in germ at least, a genuine social-scientific approach to religious instruction. Thomas Groome, "Review," in *Living Light* XIII (Winter, 1976), p. 630; Thomas H. Groome, *Christian Religious Education* (New York: Harper and Row, 1980).

struction can only come from keeping central in our investigation the way in which theology and social science do indeed function in the religious instruction act. By the term "religious instruction act" I do not mean exclusively or even primarily the classroom teaching act. A religious instruction act is that particular kind of endeavor in which religion teaching of any sort occurs. A Christian liturgy, for example, is fully as much a series of religious instruction acts as a classroom situation. Much of the recurring confusion and fuzzy thinking gripping religious educationists and educators concerning the relationship between religious instruction and theology occurs precisely because these individuals all too often conceptualize this relationship on an a priori basis rather than by grounding their investigation in the way in which religious instruction and theology actually work together in the real order, namely in the religious instruction act itself.

Before embarking on our all too brief investigation, two recurrent but patently erroneous claims can be quickly dispatched to the logical rubbish heap.

The first patently erroneous claim is that both the basic nature and overarching macrotheory of religious instruction must be fundamentally theological because the aims of religious instruction, the operations of religious instruction, and macrotheorizing on religious instruction all contain hidden or manifest theological presuppositions.[24] This claim is devoid of merit because it fails to recognize primary ontic and functional distinctions among realities. After all, in a world which God created and suffuses, every human activity contains certain theological presuppositions. There is a sense in which art, conversation, medicine—even football, farming, having a baby—have certain theological presuppositions. *To claim that religious instruction is fundamentally theological because it has theological presuppositions is as silly and as pretentious as claiming that art, conversa-*

24. See, for example, Randolph Crump Miller, "Continuity and Contrast in the Future of Religious Education," in James Michael Lee, *The Religious Education We Need* (Birmingham, Alabama: Religious Education Press, 1977), pp. 38–39; Randolph Crump Miller, *The Theory of Christian Education Practice* (Birmingham, Alabama: Religious Education Press, 1980), pp. 2, 153–164.

tion, medicine, football, farming, and having a baby are fundamentally theological because each of these human activities also have certain theological assumptions. If one were to take the presupposition-equals-essence position seriously, then one could make a strong case that the essence of theology is really philosophy because theological activity utilizes a great many prior and influential philosophical presuppositions. After all, much theological reflection is itself based on prior and more basic philosophical tenets such as the validity of knowledge (epistemology), the canons and criteria of reasoning (logic), the fundamental nature of existence (ontology), and so forth. Furthermore, the general and specific ways in which various Christian theologies developed was a direct and linear result of the philosophical and cultural ecology in which these theologies were formed, took root, and developed. The shape and thrust of Western Christian theology, for example, has been decisively conditioned by the Hellenistic philosophy and culture upon which Western theological categories and modes of investigation are directly built.

The second patently erroneous claim is that religious instruction is essentially a form of practical or pastoral theology because it is a type of the ecclesia's practical or pastoral work. This claim is devoid of merit because, like the first claim, it also fails to recognize primary ontic and functional distinctions among realities. *There is a vast ontic difference between the theology of ecclesial practice and the practice itself. Theology is one kind of cognitive reflection on ecclesial practice; theology is not coextensive with ecclesial practice.* Furthermore, there is a great deal of ecclesial practice which is not basically theological and for which an overriding theological macrotheory is therefore inadequate and invalid. For example, *a particular ecclesia, as part of its pastoral work, might sponsor a parish dance, a teen-club picnic, a fundraising event, an architectural renovation of the church building, a religious instruction program, and so on. It is flagrantly silly to assert that the nature and operations of these types of pastoral work are adequately or validly explained by theology. There may or may not be a theological dimension to, or even some theologizing taking place in a dance, in a picnic, in fund raising, in architectural renovation, in religious instruction. But to claim that these pastoral works are satisfactorily explained by theological macrotheory because they have a theological dimension and may involve some theologizing is essentially the same kind of fallacy as claiming that these pastoral works can satisfactorily be explained by linguistic theory because language is a dimension of and is used in all these pastoral works.* Dancing is properly explained by a theory of dance, and not by theology. Architectural renovation is properly explained by a theory of architecture, not by theology. Religious instruction is properly explained by a theory of religious instruction, and not by theology. There are, then, two basic points which should be kept in mind when assessing the claim that religious instruction is a form of practical or pastoral theology because it is a type of the ecclesia's practical or pastoral activity. First, a dimension is not at all the same as the whole, or even the same as the basic ontic or functional nature of the whole. Each of God's creations has a theological dimension, just as each has a philosophical dimension. But the nature and workings of each of God's creations such as dance or architecture or teaching cannot be satisfactorily explained in terms of any one of its dimensions; otherwise a competent theologian would automatically be a competent dancer, a competent fund raiser, a competent architect, a competent engineer, a competent teacher, and so on. Second, the use to which a reality is put does not change the basic nature of that reality. Few realities are pastoral by nature. A reality can be put to pastoral use, but this pastoral use neither fundamentally affects the basic nature of that reality nor replaces the theory which adequately explains the reality. For example, religious psychology is a branch of the discipline of psychology. When it is used in pastoral work such as in the religious counseling of terminally-ill patients or in retreats for youth, the subdiscipline of religious psychology still retains its fundamental psychological and social-scientific character.[25]

The key to an effective investigation of whether theology or social science constitutes the appropriate macrotheory for religious in-

---

25. On this point, see James Michael Lee, "Christian Religous Education and Moral Development," in Brenda Munsey, editor, *Moral Development, Moral Education, and Kohlberg* (Birmingham, Alabama: Religious Education Press, 1980), p. 354.

struction is to attend constantly to the basic nature and fundamental functions of religious instruction itself. A macrotheory of religious instruction is adequate and valid only to the extent that it comprehensively and systematically explains, predicts, and verifies the religious instruction process. But what is the religious instruction process? What does religious instruction do? Religious instruction facilitates religious learning. The validity of this assertion can be easily demonstrated by the answer to the question: "How can we know when teaching actually has taken place?" The answer to this question, obviously, is "When learning has occurred." *The basic nature of religious instruction is properly described in terms of the causation of desired learning outcomes. If learning outcomes have not occurred, then there has been no religious instruction, no matter how holy or how theologically erudite the religious educator is.* An appropriate macrotheory for religious instruction, therefore, has to be able to comprehensively and systematically explain, predict, and verify how teaching actually takes place, namely how the four major variables involved in religious instruction interact in such a way that desired learning outcomes are thereby facilitated. This is and must be the touchstone of any investigation of the appropriate macrotheory for religious instruction.

The major point made in the preceding paragraph can be further sharpened by posing two pointed questions. Does a religious educator's knowledge of and proficiency in theology directly bring about desired learning outcomes? Or, on the other hand, does a religious educator's knowledge of and proficiency in social science directly bring about desired learning outcomes? These questions can be further refined in the following comparative example. Religion teacher *A* understands that he and the learners are redeemed in God's grace. He is deeply aware that despite this redemption, he and the learners still suffer some of the deleterious after-effects of original sin. He knows full well that he and the learners are members of the mystical body and can cooperate with each other to further God's kingdom in religious instruction activity. This religion teacher is also proficient in theologizing about these and other theological concepts involving the teacher and the learner and the instructional process. Religion teacher *B,* in contrast, knows the dynamics of the teaching-learning process. He understands the substantive content (religion) and the structural content (pedagogical practice) of religious instruction as these contents are related to the here-and-now religion teaching situation. This religion teacher is also proficient in social-scientifically structuring the pedagogical variables in such a way that the desired learning outcomes take place. Which of these religion teachers is the more likely to be successful as a direct consequence of his knowledge and proficiency? The answer to this question provides an important clue to the solution of the basic issue under discussion, namely the issue of whether theology or social science is the adequate macrotheory for religious instruction.

The Six-Component Test

The correct identification of the appropriate macrotheory for religious instruction can only be satisfactorily made by rigorously analyzing the basic nature and operation of religious instruction in terms of the macrotheories which purport to explain, predict, and verify religious instruction phenomena. A particularly fruitful way of analyzing religious instruction in operation is the category system devised by Harold William Burgess.[26] Burgess' category system analyzes the workings of religious instruction in terms of six major variables which he has found to be present and indispensable in all religious instruction activity; aim, subject matter, teacher, learner, environment, and evaluation. Burgess rightly maintains that the relative merits and potency of a macrotheoretical approach to religious instruction can be ascertained by testing the adequacy to

26. Harold William Burgess, *An Invitation to Religious Education* (Birmingham, Alabama: Religious Education Press, 1975). As far as I am able to ascertain, this splendid volume is the most widely-used textbook for foundations courses in religious education in Protestant and Catholic graduate schools and seminaries in North America. Thus this book has exerted considerable influence in the field, and is well respected.

which competing macrotheoretical approaches can explain, predict, and verify the six variables separately and as a whole.

Aim. Advocates of the theological approach to religious instruction characteristically declare that the aim of religious instruction is to be found in theology.[27] The task of religious instruction is to act merely as a delivery system to faithfully transport theological content and processes intact from educator to learner. Every aim of religious instruction is theological: it is theological because it directly and explicitly enfleshes theological content and/or because it contains basic theological presuppositions which might be more hidden than manifest.

A social-science approach to religious instruction states that the aim of religious instruction is to be found in the learner as he interacts with his environment. The task of religious instruction is to facilitate the learner's religious development in such a way that he is optimally fulfilled as a person. Every pedagogical aim is basically social scientific because there can be no taught-learned aim which is in any way separate from the learner's here-and-now developing self-system.

In an earlier section I treated the issue of theological presuppositions in religious instruction. Consequently I will center my attention here on the locus (extrinsic or intrinsic) of the religious instruction aim.

By stating that the aim of religious instruction is theological, advocates of the theological approach thereby contend that the aim of religious instruction is extrinsic to the learner. But to assert that the aim of religious

27. John Westerhoff states that the aim of religious instruction is theology. Like virtually all members of the Catechetical Establishment, Berard Marthaler holds that the basic aims of religious instruction are only found in that kind of theological formulation specifically approved by the Roman Catholic magisterium and propounded in official ecclesiastical documents. John Westerhoff, "A Discipline in Crisis," *Religious Education* LIV (January-February, 1979), pp. 10–11. Marthaler has devoted most of his professional life to translating and commenting upon catechetical documents issued by the Vatican and by other Catholic ecclesiastical hierarchies. See, for example, Berard L. Marthaler, "Evangelization and Catechesis: Word, Memory, Witness," in *Living Light* XVI (Spring, 1979), pp. 33–45.

instruction is extrinsic to the learner is to assert that religious instruction is not first and foremost a human activity. By definition, every human activity has the person not only at the center but also existentially involved in every speck, movement, and perimeter of that process. Human learning means that the person interacts with environmental variables (including theological subject matter) in such a way that these variables, when learned, lose their autonomous ontic character and become incorporated into the individual's dynamic self-system. In order to learn, all extrinsic variables (e.g. theological subject matter) must become intrinsic (learner) on the learner's own dynamic existential terms according to where he is developmentally and how he is becoming a person. For example, when a person learns the Ten Commandments, the result is not the autonomous ontic structure of the Ten Commandments somehow existing independently in his mind. Rather, what is learned are the Ten Commandments as *he* has heard them spoken or seen them written, as *he* has perceived them, as *he* has conceptualized them, as *he* has interpreted them, as *he* has incorporated them into *his* self-system. What has been learned, then, is not the Ten Commandments in themselves, but *his personal* acquisition of the Ten Commandments. Hence there can be no such thing as extrinsic aims where human learning is concerned.

It is precisely because the aims of religious instruction are intrinsic rather than extrinsic to the learner that the theological approach is incapable of devising proper or adequate aims for religious instruction, and why, in turn, social science possesses this capability. Social science, after all, is that confluence of disciplines which, by definition and comprehension, explains, predicts, and verifies *human behavior.* Learning is a word used to signify a certain kind of human behavior.

No satisfactory aim of religious instruction can be erected primarily on presuppositions, hypotheses, forces, or institutions outside of or extrinsic to the developing learner. This statement does not mean that the aims of religious instruction are devoid of extrinsic theologies, philosophies, and ideologies of one sort or another. Rather, this statement asserts that the way in which extrinsically derived aims are incorporated into religious instruction activity in its processes or goals must be done in a manner consistent with and indeed based upon the learner's developmental self.

If religious instruction is to work, its aims must be framed in such a way that they can be taught and learned. If aims are such that they cannot be taught or learned, they are not religious instruction aims. My analysis in the preceding three paragraphs implies that theological principles and content cannot be stated as aims of religious instruction unless they are stated religiously and social-scientifically. *Theological content must be cast into religious form if religious instruction is to remain* religious *instruction. Theological content must also be cast into social-scientific form if it is to be rendered teachable and learnable.* The teaching-learning process is a behavioral activity governed primarily by social-scientific laws. A quick way to render religious instruction unteachable and unlearnable is to state an aim in terms of theological content.

To assert that theological aim must be fundamentally reconceptualized and restated into social-scientific aim is in no way to assert that religious instruction lacks a theological dimension. Rather, it is to assert that in the work of religious instruction, theology in one way or another takes on the processive shape and flow of the social-scientific activity of religious instruction. Perhaps an analogy will illustrate my point. Let us say that a theologian asks a sculptor to make a statue which conveys the theological aim of the evil of sin. Unless and until the sculptor radically reconceptualizes this theological aim into a sculptural aim, and then operationalizes this aim into specific sculpturing procedures, he will never be able to carve a statue. To carve the statue, the sculptor must always adhere to the aims and procedures of sculpting, not of theology. The statue which he finally produces is the fruit of sculptural aim, not theological aim. Further, the statue was made by the procedures of sculpture, not by the procedures of theology. The end result, the statue, was not the work of theology, but the work of sculpture. The statue possesses a theological dimension, but it itself is not theology, nor is it primarily theological in aim or execution.

Subject Matter. Advocates of the theological approach to religious instruction typically state that the substantive subject matter of religious instruction is theology in one form or another. The source and type of theological subject matter is determined on the basis of the particular brand of theology which the denominational religious education officials mandate, which the religion schoolteacher or parent prefers, and so on.

A social-science approach to religious instruction states that the substantive subject matter of religious instruction is religion—religion as it is actually taught-learned in the religious instruction act.

The theological approach maintains that the substantive subject matter of religious instruction is theology. But such an assertion is *prima facie* false. As its name and hence its definition unambiguously indicates, religious instruction is religious instruction and not theological instruction. As I indicated in the first section of this essay, religion and theology have essentially distinct natures.

Another consideration intrudes itself. Because the theological approach is perforce rooted in one or another specific theology, it is fundamentally defective as a macrotheory explaining, predicting, and verifying all of religious instruction. An adequate macrotheory for religious instruction must, by definition, explain, predict, and verify all kinds of subject matter which are present in all kinds of religious instruction acts. This is a task which the theological approach is incapable of accomplishing because of its very nature. For example, an Evangelical Protestant advocate of the theological approach would understandably deny that the theological approach taken by a conservative neo-Tridentine Roman Catholic would be adequate or acceptable as a macrotheory explaining, predicting, and verifying the selection and implementation of substantive subject matter in religious instruction. *The social-science approach, on the other hand, is value-free in that it not only accomodates all sorts of diverse theological views as a dimension of subject matter, but is admirably capable of explaining, predicting, and verifying the effective selection and implementation of the entire spectrum of complementary or conflicting religious subject matter.*[28]

28. Some religious educationists and theologians erroneously claim that I hold social science to be value-free in the sense that it neither presupposes nor embodies certain values. Such a claim is palpably false, as the persons who make it would readily know if they had bothered to read my books with even a minimum of attention. I specifically state in my books that value-freedom in social science

To equate substantive content with focused revelation and with the Bible, as is common with many leading Evangelical Protestant religious educationists like Herbert Byrne and Lawrence Richards, strengthens rather than weakens the position developed in the previous four paragraphs. To live in and with revelation is religion, or at least a major dimension of religion. Revelation is not primarily or even essentially theology. Theology is just one way of cognitively reflecting on the nature and meaning of revelation. To live in and with the Bible is religion, or at least a major dimension of religion. The Bible is not primarily or essentially a piece of theology. The Bible is simultaneously a religious instruction document and a history of God's religious instruction activities with human beings. Theology is just one way of cognitively reflecting on the nature and meaning of the bible.

Teacher. Advocates of the theological approach to religious instruction generally pay scant attention to the teacher. This statement holds true especially with regard to what the teacher actually does in the religious instruction act. Most proponents of the theological approach claim that effective religion teaching can be explained, predicted, and verified by any one or more of the following theories—the personality theory, the witness theory, the dedi-

---

means, among other things, that (1) social science is not normative with respect to religious and moral values; hence social science cannot state what ought to be religiously or morally; (2) social science of itself cannot assign moral or religious value to any reality; (3) social science can deal with a wide variety of morally and religiously value-laden areas without having to necessarily express a preference for one another value based on the intrinsic moral and religious merits of that value. I can only conclude that persons like Richard McBrien who grossly distort my position on this matter are guilty of sloppy scholarship. I would not like to think that their distortions are deliberate. To be sure, in making their claim the way they do, McBrien and others implicitly erode in a serious manner theology's self-styled privileged claim on moral and religious value judgment. It is indeed ironic that persons like McBrien who deny any value-neutrality in social science are typically the very ones who are most vocal in their assertion that social scientists, physical scientists, and the like, have no business proposing moral and religious value agendas for individuals or communities on the basis of their competence in social science or physical science. See James Michael Lee, *The Shape of Religious Instruction,* pp. 143–144, 207–208; Richard P. McBrien, "Toward an American Catechesis," in *Living Light* XIII (Summer, 1976), p. 174.

cation theory, the authenticity theory, or the blow theory. These theories hold, respectively, that religion teaching can be explained, predicted, and verified primarily or even exclusively by the educator's personality, the educator's Christian witness, the educator's dedication, the educator's authenticity, or by the mysterious unfathomable action of the Holy Spirit.[29]

The social-science approach pays a great deal of attention to the teacher. The social-science approach is always concerned with laying bare those pedagogical variables in the religious instruction dynamic which have been empirically demonstrated to correlate positively with effective religion teaching.

None of the various theories of religion *teaching* advanced by the proponents of the theological approach is an adequate theory of religion teaching precisely because none of them is capable of doing what a theory must perforce do if it is to be a genuine theory, namely to comprehensively and systematically explain, predict, and verify the laws and phenomena of religion *teaching* in a satisfactory manner. Each of these so-called "theories" highlights one and only one factor which *might* be responsible for the successful facilitation of learning in a *particular* situation. But there is no available empirical research to indicate that any one of these factors—or indeed all of them combined—are in themselves sufficient to adequately explain, predict, or verify how the religion teacher actually facilitates desired religious learnings.

It is not at all surprising that the advocates of the theological approach to religious instruction have proposed such fatally flawed pseudotheories of religion teaching. After all, *the construction of a workable and valid theory of teaching is a matter of social-scientific competence since the pedagogical process by definition and classification falls under the domain of social-scientific fact, law, and theory. Theological theory simply lacks the capability to explain, predict, and verify nontheological realms of being, such as teaching, dentistry, politics, economics, loving,*

29. For a brief discussion of these theories, see James Michael Lee, *The Flow of Religious Instruction* (Birmingham, Alabama: Religious Education Press, 1973), pp. 149–196.

and the like. When advocates of the theological approach to religious instruction propose one or another "theory" to explain, predict, and verify religion teaching, these persons do, in fact, unwittingly utilize the social-science approach rather than the theological approach. Since these individuals are usually untrained in and indeed are often antipathetic to social science, their incognizant attempts to devise social-scientifically based teaching laws and procedures on the basis of theological premises typically fall flat on their faces. Theology can no more validly or effectively generate social-scientific procedures such as teaching practice than social science can validly or effectively generate theological procedures such as Bible-based methods of inquiry into the existence of God.

While the theological approach looks to the nature and operation of theology as the basis for constructing a valid and workable theory of teaching, the social-science approach looks to the nature and operations of the actual here-and-now teaching/learning process as its basis for devising instructional theory. A social-science-based teaching theory, then, is derived from *descriptive* statements of the empirically demonstrated causal relationship between the religious educator's antecedent pedagogical behaviors and the learner's consequent performance behaviors. A social-science-based theory of religious instruction, then, holds that the significant variables which explain, predict, and verify the process of teaching religion are those involved in the effective modification of the learner's behavior along religious lines. A social-science-based theory of religious instruction shows how and why the four major variables present in every teaching act (teacher, learner, subject matter, and environment) dynamically and continuously interact in such a fashion as to yield desired religious outcomes. Thus, in the end, a general theory of instruction becomes essentially *prescriptive* in setting forth rules concerning the most effective pedagogical procedures for facilitating desired learning outcomes.[30]

30. See H. Edward Everding, Jr., Clarence H. Snelling, Jr., and Mary M. Wilcox, "Toward a Theory of Instruction for Religious Education," unpublished paper presented at the October, 1976 meeting of the Association of Professors and Researchers in Religious Education.

Learner. Proponents of the theological approach to religious instruction view the learner and the learning process primarily and often exclusively from the vantage point of one or another theological interpretation of the learner. Thus when advocates of the theological approach do discuss the learner, they typically deal with him *sub specie* a responsible person who can respond in faith to those initiatives made by the Holy Spirit in the context of fellowship and the Christian community.

The social-science approach, on the other hand, views the learner and the learning process from the perspective of how, in fact, the learner actually functions as a human being and how, in fact, the learner actually learns.

It would appear that the claim of the theological approach with regard to the learner and the learning process represents the logical fallacy of *ignoratio elenchi,* namely that of avoiding the central issues of learning in general and of learning as it occurs in the religious instruction act. The central issue around which all dimensions of the religious instruction act must proceed is how the learner does indeed function religiously and how the learner does indeed learn. All interpretations of the learner and learning, be these interpretations theological or philosophical or psychological or biological, must be continuously grounded in and tightly tethered to the actual reality of human functioning. In the final analysis, a theological interpretation of the learner and the learning process does not substantially affect the ongoing psychophysiological nature and functions of the learner or the learning process. Psychophysiological facts and laws of human functioning hold true regardless of whether one interprets the learner and his learning from a Calvinistic theological stance, from a Tillichian perspective, from a neo-Tridentine position, from a Mormon viewpoint, and so on. *To be sure, any valid and fruitful theological interpretation of the learner and the learning process must be based on or at least be in compliance with verified facts and established laws of psychophysiological reality.*[31]

---

31. In classical theological method, this is called the negative check on theology.

The basic set of empirically verified facts and laws relating to the learner and the learning process can be summarized in one short sentence: All learning takes place according to the mode of the learner. Advocates of the theological approach tend to ignore or uneasily bypass this basic and pivotal assertion. These individuals concentrate instead on high-sounding but vague statements such as "The person is God's masterpiece," or "Learning takes place mysteriously because it is the Holy Spirit who prompts the person and brings learning to pass." While sweet and pious, such statements are useless for religious instruction because they fail to address themselves to the all-important religious instruction issue of how and in what manner learning actually takes place. The fact of the matter is that the learner acquires, for example, a knowledge of the Ten Commandments (cognitive outcome), a love of the Ten Commandments (affective outcome), and an obedience to the Ten Commandments (lifestyle outcome) primarily according to the on-going laws of his own human development and not primarily to the logical structure or eternal import of the Ten Commandments themselves.

There is no empirical research evidence to suggest that a person learns religion (or even theology) in a way fundamentally different from the basic manner in which he learns any other area of reality. Consequently, the attempt by some advocates of the theological approach to exempt religious learning from the laws governing the learning process itself on the basis of appeals to the Holy Spirit's mysterious activity is an attempt utterly without foundation. Furthermore, those persons typically fail to explain why the Holy Spirit operates in religious (or even theological) learning but not in other types of human learning. (Parenthetically, one is tempted to inquire how so-called nonreligious learning takes place if the Holy Spirit is not present in these kinds of learning also. Can any reality exist or function without God's continuous and continual cooperation?)

Environment. Advocates of the theological approach to religious instruction largely ignore both the environment in which religious teaching takes place and the environmental variables outside the intentional teaching situation which dynamically interact with the learner. Most advocates of the theological approach seem to regard the learner's spiritual powers plus God's grace as constituting the key factors in religious learning, with environmental variables so negligible as to be hardly worth mentioning.

The social-science approach to religious instruction places great stress on the environment in the work of religious instruction. Based as it is on the empirical study of what actually occurs in the teaching-learning dynamic, the social-science approach contends that the environment is of tremendous importance precisely because it constitutes one of the four major interactive variables present and operative in every pedagogical situation.

There is a whole host of empirical research data which suggest that religious learning, and indeed all other kinds of human learning, are significantly affected by the structure and flow of one's interaction with the environment.[32] A valid macrotheory and usable approach to religious instruction, consequently, must utilize the all-important environmental variable as one of its central features. The social-science approach does indeed make extensive use of the environment in explaining, predicting, and verifying the work of religious instruction. The omission of the environment from axial consideration by proponents of the theological approach constitutes a major and indeed fatal deficiency in the validity of this approach as a macrotheory purporting to explain, to predict, and to verify the work of religious instruction.

Even a cursory look at the religious instruction act reveals how the learner is continuously and elementally interacting with environment variables such as the place in which the process is taking place, the socio-emotional climate, the other persons involved in the situation, the pedagogical materials—even with such frequently overlooked but often influential factors as temperature, light, and spatial arrangement. Usually the religious educator himself is the most potent aspect of the instructional environment because it is he

32. See, for example, James Michael Lee, *The Flow of Religious Instruction,* pp. 65–73; Merton P. Strommen, editor, *Research on Religious Development* (New York: Hawthorn, 1971).

who structures the features of the environment (including his own activity) in such a fashion that learning is thereby facilitated. *I suspect that one major reason accounting for the gross neglect of the environment by advocates of the theological approach is that they tend to concentrate their attention on theology rather than on the real-life situation in the here-and-now religious instruction act.* It is difficult to imagine any approach which focuses its attention on what is really happening in the here-and-now religious instruction act failing to take the environment into account as a central, major, and inextricable variable in the teaching-learning of religion.

The theological approach really does not come to grips with environmental variables by issuing vague and amorphous statements about the Holy Spirit or the faith community providing the environment for effective religious pedagogy. *Unless and until the advocates of the theological approach can factually demonstrate that the Holy Spirit and/or the faith community actually do exert one or another particular specifiable environmental influence on religious instruction, their statements to this effect must remain gratuitous.* Even if it were assumed or proven that the Holy Spirit and/or the faith community do indeed exert one or another particular specifiable environmental influence, little or nothing has been gained by such information which is useful for religious instruction. To be practical and useful for religious instruction, advocates of the theological approach must not simply state *that* the Holy Spirit and/or the faith community act as powerful environmental factors, but *how* these environmental forces specifically affect religion teaching and learning. *It makes much more sense to assert that the Holy Spirit works according to the laws of the nature he has made and keeps in continuous existence than to assert that the Holy Spirit somehow directly intervenes or withholds himself in each and every pedagogical act.* If this statement is true, then assertions about the Holy Spirit as the basic environmental factor mean nothing beyond what is known empirically about the specific effects which various environmental factors have on teaching and learning.

Evaluation. Supporters of the theological approach generally accord little or no integral attention to a careful or systematic evaluation of religious instruction. A great many advocates of the theological approach claim that the real effects of religious instruction are spiritual, unfathomable, and mysterious gifts of the Holy Spirit— hence these effects are not able to be evaluated. Other exponents of the theological approach claim that theology itself has the broad task of evaluating religious instruction insofar as it compares what is learned in religious instruction against theological standards.

The social-science approach considers evaluation to be an integral and vital dimension of religious instruction. The social-science approach contends that evaluation is a crucial and indispensable factor in the work of religious instruction for several reasons: evaluation helps discover whether the learner has indeed learned, it ascertains what he has learned and the degree to which he had learned it, it finds out how he has learned it, and it provides valuable information to both educator and learner about their respective progress in the teaching-learning dynamic.

The advocates of the theological approach end up in intellectual nihilism when they claim that religious instruction cannot be evaluated because its processes and effects are spiritual, unfathomable, and mysterious gifts of the Holy Spirit. If this claim of the theological approach were true, then it would be impossible to judge anything (including even chemical or physical reactions) since all reality is a once and continuing gift of God. If the processes and effects of religious instruction cannot be known or evaluated because they are mysterious and unfathomable, then it is manifestly impossible for anyone, including advocates of the theological approach, to make any meaningful or valid statement about the actuality of the religious instruction dynamic. [33] If the processes and effects of religious instruction are mysterious and unfathomable, then there is no way for the educator

33. William Jacobs urges religious educators not to be "particularly conscious of results. God alone knows them and this is quite sufficient." Despite such a sweeping laudation for the human unknowability of and unconcern for results, Jacobs devotes his entire article in attempting to persuasively demonstrate that the religious educator's living Christian witness will surely bring about the results which the religious educator consciously desires. William J. Jacobs, "The Catechist as Witness," in J. T. Dillon, editor, *Catechetics Reconsidered* (Winona, Minnesota: St. Mary's College Press, 1968), pp. 85–89, quote on p. 88.

to know the success or failure of any of his pedagogical procedures, or for the learner to know if he has gained anything from his participation in the religious instruction endeavor.

I find it a source of amusement that virtually all those advocates of the theological approach who claim that the processes and effects of religious instruction are mysterious and hence cannot be evaluated are the very people who most unambiguously claim that their own pet proposal for improving religious instruction is more effective than an alternate proposal or that their own favorite pedagogical procedure in religious instruction has proved effective time after time. Obviously there is a basic contradiction between claims of the mysteriousness and unfathomability of the processes and effects of religious instruction on the one hand, and claims of the superior workability and effectiveness of their own proposals and procedures on the other hand.

To claim that theology itself has the broad task of evaluating religious instruction insofar as theology compares what is learned against theological standards is to seriously beg the question on at least two counts. First of all, religious instruction is religious instruction and not theological instruction. Hence to evaluate the religious instruction act on the basis of theological standards is irrelevant in terms of religious instruction. Second, because of its nature and structure, theology simply does not possess either the means or the procedures to evaluate how and to what extent the four major variables in the religious instruction dynamic interact in such a way as to bring about learning outcomes. *In the final analysis, all theology can do is to state whether some of the effects of religious instruction square with this or that theological proposition. Thus theological activity does not evaluate either the processes or the religious outcomes of the religious instruction act, but rather evaluates only the theological dimension of some of the effects of religious instruction.* Perhaps an analogy will further clarify this point. Theology may legitimately evaluate the theological dimension of some of the effects of a certain dentistry procedure; however, this kind of evaluation is of a far different genre than that of theology attempting to evaluate the interactive dynamics of the dental process itself or of attempting to evaluate the dental effects of this process.

By Your Fruits You Shall Know Them

One of the most important and significant tests of the adequacy and validity of a theory is its fruitfulness, namely the degree to which it gives rise to new practice. It is an astounding fact that *the theological approach has not directly given rise to or elicited a single new pedagogical practice for religious instruction in the many centuries of the existence of this approach. Surely this fact is one of the most damning indictments of the theological approach.* Every single advance in structural content, whether this advance be the age-old lecture/telling technique or the modern action-reflection technique has been imported into religion teaching from other areas of instructional endeavor. Why is this so? The answer is obvious: all other areas of instruction have adopted a potent and effective macrotheory. This macrotheory, of course, is the social-science approach. Of all areas of instructional activity, only religious instruction still clings to the outmoded theological approach, and only religious instruction has failed to adopt the social-science approach. It is a sure sign of an inappropriate and sterile macrotheory when the theological approach is unable directly to give rise to any new pedagogical practice, or to adequately explain or verify or predict those pedagogical practices which are already occurring. *It is utterly unimaginable for any field of endeavor to retain as its guiding and governing approach one which has consistently failed over many centuries directly to give rise to any concrete or workable practice within the field or which has consistently proven incapable of explaining or predicting or verifying the basic phenomena and laws operative in the field. Yet the utterly unimaginable holds true for much of Christian religious instruction insofar as it adheres to the theological approach.* This patently preposterous state of affairs could never obtain in a respectable field of endeavor; indeed, I am unaware of any field in which such ridiculousness obtains. It is small wonder, then, that religious instruction is such a noncredible field, one brimming over with all sorts of bizarre gratuitous statements and wild, unsupported claims.

Consistency

Another major test of the adequacy and validity of a theory is the degree to which its various interlocking principles and components are consistent with one another. Lack of consistency is a sure sign of a defect in theory because when principles or components which are supposed to be interlocking and coherent are instead disjointed, the structure and operation of the theory is significantly weakened. The greater the inconsistency, the less adequate and valid the theory.

The theological macrotheory of religious instruction is woefully lacking in consistency. Thus, for example, it claims that religion teaching is a mysterious and an unfathomable activity of the Holy Spirit while simultaneously advocating one or another specific pedagogical procedure like the action-reflection technique as a particularly effective pedagogical device, or by stating that a religious educator must possess certain qualities such as holiness or theological knowledge in order to successfully facilitate desired learning outcomes.

Without a doubt, the grossest inconsistency with respect to theory occurs when the most basic principle upon which virtually all elaborations of the theory are derived stands in direct contradiction to the fundamental form and thrust of that theory. No theory or macrotheory can survive such a tremendous inconsistency for the obvious reason that an inconsistency of this magnitude means that the theory or macrotheory is worthless. Yet, amazing to say, such a shocking inconsistency is actually advocated by at least two of the proponents of the theological macrotheory of religious instruction, namely John Westerhoff and Berard Marthaler. Both of these persons consciously take socialization as their major and overarching principle for explaining, predicting, and verifying religious instruction endeavor.[34] Socialization is first and foremost a social-science construct in nature and in theoretical elaboration. A theological approach with a social-science foundation is as self-contradictory

---

34. John H. Westerhoff III and Gwen Kennedy Neville, *Generation to Generation,* 2d edition (New York: Pilgrim, 1979); Berard L. Marthaler, "Socialization as a Model for Catechetics."

conceptually as it is impossible existentially. By making socialization the foundation of religious instruction, Westerhoff and Marthaler automatically, though perhaps unwittingly, abandon the theological approach and concomitantly assert that the social-science approach constitutes the adequate and valid macrotheory for religious instruction. After all, one cannot take a social-science construct as one's basic foundation and then claim that the endeavor which is built on this foundation and through which the structural/substantive process of this foundation flows is theology. If the theological macrotheory were indeed adequate and valid as the foundation of religious instruction, then Westerhoff and Marthaler would obviously use it as a foundation rather than jettisoning it and adopting a social-science foundation.

A Theology of Religious Instruction—The Proper Use of Theological Theory in Religious Instruction

It is important to bear in mind that theological reflection on[35] the religious instruction act is of a fundamentally different genre than the religious instruction act itself. Consequently, the basic theory of and competencies required for the fruitful exercise of theological reflection are fundamentally different in most respects from those required for the fruitful exercise of religious instruction. Religious instruction may utilize theological reflection in such ways as to further the work of religious instruction, but this is far different from asserting that theological reflection is the same or equivalent to the pedagogical dynamic of teaching religion.

If the theological macrotheory is indeed inadequate, invalid, and inappropriate to explain/predict/verify the concepts/facts/laws of religious instruction, then what is the proper function of the theological macrotheory with respect to the religious instruction endeavor? *The proper function of theological theory with respect to the religious instruction endeavor is that of a theological theory which reflects on the theological meaning of the nontheological reality called religious instruction, and not*

---

35. The word here is "on," not "in."

that of a theological macrotheory attempting to explain, predict, and verify religious instruction concepts, facts, and laws.

The theological meaning of a biological reality, for example, is *eo ipso* of a fundamentally different genre than the biological meaning of that reality. Theological theory states what this or that biological concept, fact, or law *means to theology;* theological theory cannot state what this or that biological concept, fact, or law *means to biology.* Similarly, theological theory can only state what this or that religious instructional concept, fact, or law *means to theology;* theological theory cannot state what this or that religious instructional concept, fact, or law *means to religious instruction.*

What I have just written does not suggest or imply that theological theory lacks an authentic or valid function with respect to nontheological reality such as the biological world or the religious instruction world. Rather, what I have written teases apart the valid from the invalid functions of theology with respect to nontheological reality. The proper function of theology with respect to nontheological reality is to explore the *theological meaning* of the nature and operations of one or another reality. For example, theological theory examines the *theological ramifications* of producing a human embryo in vitro. And theological theory furnishes a *theological perspective* on the use of role-playing to teach the learners attitudes toward sinners. To examine the theological meaning of in vitro embryos and of role-playing pedagogy is, of course, far different from explaining, predicting, and verifying the nature and operation of in vitro fertilization or role-playing pedagogy. Rather, to theologically explore these realities is to make more clear the theological dimensions of these diverse realities—dimensions and ramifications which, while not revealing the autonomous ontic nature and operations of these realities, nonetheless do reveal their theological import.

There are instances in which theological theory gives external aid to the work of nontheological realities such as biology and religious instruction; in other instances, theological theory is of marginal or no benefit. When theological theory is of help to biology, to religious instruction, and so on, then these nontheological activities can and should incorporate the fruits of theological reflection into their work *sub specie that work.* Thus the general rule is that *religious instruction makes use of a theology of religious instruction only to the extent that this theology in some way furthers and advances the work of religious instruction.*

Theological Imperialism

Theological imperialism is the attempt to bring under direct theological jurisdiction and control all areas of reality, especially those which in one way or another may be related to theology. Contemporary theological imperialism represents a modern elaboration and hardening of the old "theology is the queen of the sciences" position taken by many theologians during the Middle Ages.

Contemporary theological imperialism regards theology as queen of the sciences and of all reality in three major respects: (1) it is theology which stands both objectively and subjectively as the single most important of the sciences and areas of reality; (2) it is theology alone which has the power, comprehensiveness, and coherence to place all other sciences and all areas of reality into the proper hierarchy, order, arrangement, and sequences; (3) it is a major responsibility of theology to determine the validity of all other sciences and areas of reality not solely in terms of theological validity but also in terms of the very internal validity of those other sciences and areas of reality themselves.

The most drastic form of theological imperialism is theological positivism. Theological positivism is an attitude characterized by an anti-scientific bias, an anti-empirical and anti-experimental stance, and a pro-rationalist posture. *The term "theological positivism" indicates that only theology is capable of providing positive knowledge, namely, sure information and certain interpretation about reality.* Theology gains its surety and certainty from its transcendent objectivity, an objectivity rooted in an eternal God and not in any man-made theory or human experience. Thus the only possible source of fundamental and true knowledge lies in theology or in conclusions derived in one way or another from theology. All reality is basically the mystery of God's gift of creation, and theology alone possesses the power to unlock this mystery, however minimal such unlocking might be. All nontheological assertions are at best only probable and relative. Hence theological positivism expresses an outright denial of or at least strong skepticism toward explanations and forces which lie outside those concepts, facts, and laws determined and verified by theology. Theological positivism exhibits a distinct tendency to prescribe knowledge and circumscribe reality on the basis of what can be known and validated by theology. Only two types of fundamentally meaningful statements and truths exist: those derived directly from theology, and those which can be squared with theology on theology's own terms. All reality can thus be ultimately reduced to theological propositions and truths. The traditional problems and solutions of philosophy, education, history, biology, and so forth, are all theological in their most basic and fundamental sense; hence the traditional problems and solutions of philosophy, education, history, biology, and so forth, can only be genuinely understood and faithfully interpreted in a theological manner. Theology thus is rightly seen as both the starting point for and the final judge of all science, art, technology, and human living. All cognition, affect, and lifestyle must be consciously erected on a theological base and kept firmly tethered to this base by continual theologizing. The only satisfactory foundation for society and human activity is that of theology, not that of religion; after all, religion can only be perceived and lived on theological terms. Religion is not ultimately based on objective and subjective revelation by God. Rather, religion is based on theology and is expressed only in theological terms. All reality is created by God and hence is basically theological; hence the principal task of the other sciences and of all human activity is to constantly relate and subjugate their efforts to theology. Consequently theology is the norm and determiner of all other areas of science and human endeavor. Every kind of valid knowledge must in one way or another be included within or circumscribed by theology. Philosophy, education, history, biology and so forth, are then just handmaids of theology. Reversing the familiar Comtian formula, theological positivism avows three levels of knowledge: scientific, philosophical, and theological. In the lowest or scientific level, one has knowledge only about the external, observable, and often concrete or physical aspects of reality. At the second or metaphysical level, one has knowledge of the inner, abstract, essential nature of reality insofar as these can be learned by unaided human reason. At the highest and positive level, one has knowledge both of the essential nature and outward characteristics of all reality as all reality participates in God's existence in the way(s) positively deduced by theology. A major task of theology is to locate, elaborate, and determine the general principles which are common to and ultimately govern all science and all human activity. One of the prime benefits of such a task is that theology can fruitfully arrange all the sciences and all human activity into a theologically-determined hierarchical order. The social, physical, and other nontheological sciences are useful for external purposes, such as producing technology or making correlations between observable phenomena. Only theology can provide the ultimate truth and basic understanding of reality. Nontheological sciences are not bad or false if they remain subject to theology. There can be no ultimate conflict between theology and the nontheological sciences because in the final analysis there are no nontheological propositions or data which assert anything fundamentally meaningful about foundational realities such as God, grace, revelation, and religion. The surest way to personal fulfillment and perfection is to constantly engage in theological reflection. The intellectual, moral, educational, and political leadership of society ideally should be in the hands of theologians or at least in the hands of persons who are continually theologizing.

Examples of theological imperialism and even of theological positivism are rife in the writings and speeches of the proponents of the theological approach to religious instruction. Indeed it is probably accurate to state that a *certain strain of theological imperialism necessarily courses not only through the heart but even through the remotest blood vessels of the theological approach to religious instruction.* A few representative examples will illustrate this point. James Smart asserts that theology acts as the primary and supreme norm for all areas of religious instruction, including the very learning process itself. Before a teaching method can be used, the teacher must first judge its validity on theological grounds. Before a psychological finding on the nature and texture of learning can be accepted in Christian education, the teacher must first ascertain how and if this finding is theologically acceptable.[36] Campbell Wyckoff declares that "questions of [instructional] objective, scope, context, process, personnel, and timing, I am convinced, are theological questions."[37] Randolph Crump Miller states that religious instruction is not only a theological discipline but a theological method. Thus for Miller, to teach religion is primarily to teach relevant theology. Furthermore, pedagogical methods are both properly judged and directly generated by theology.[38] In John Westerhoff's view, "theological presuppositions provide the screen for our understanding of both [religious instruction] theory and practice." Furthermore, religious instruction is "always dependent upon the theological disciplines for both purpose and practice." Professors of religious instruction in institutions of higher learning "are properly ordained clergy."[39] Berard Marthaler claims that "faith is always and only expressed in some theological idiom."[40] Françoise Darcy-Bérubé, while forced to concede that there are no teaching techniques which are distinctively Christian, nonetheless insists that there are teaching techniques which are opposed to a Christian vision of the person, such as those used "by Billy Graham in his crusades."[41]

The theologically imperialistic claims cited in the previous para-

36. James D. Smart, *The Teaching Ministry of the Church* (Philadelphia: Westminster, 1954), pp. 24–45, 68–83.

37. D. Campbell Wyckoff, "Religious Education as a Discipline: Toward a Definition of Religious Education as a Discipline," in *Religious Education* LXII (September-October, 1967), p. 393.

38. Randolph Crump Miller, *The Theory of Christian Education Practice,* pp. 153–165.

39. John Westerhoff, "A Discipline in Crisis," pp. 11, 13, Westerhoff uses the term "catechesis" instead of "religious instruction."

40. Berard L. Marthaler, "Review," in *National Catholic Reporter* XI (September 12, 1975), p. 13.

41. Françoise Darcy-Bérubé, "The Challenge Ahead of Us," p. 118.

graph are without theoretical or logical foundation. In some cases, these theologically imperialistic claims are preposterous and ridiculous. James Smart's assertion is theologically imperialistic because *theological methodology no more possesses the capability of judging the pedagogical or the religious instructional worth of a particular teaching technique than it possesses the capability of judging the fiscal worth of a particular banking practice. All that theology can do is to render a judgment on what a particular teaching technique or banking practice means to theology*—this is essentially different from stating that theology has the ability to render a judgment on what a particular teaching technique means to religious instruction or what a particular banking practice means to a financial institution. Campbell Wyckoff's statement is theologically imperialistic because the questions of instructional timing and personnel are *eis ipsis* questions of pedagogical competence and not theology; the question of instructional context is obviously one of sociopsychological and physical functioning, and not a question of theology; the question of scope and objective is manifestly determined by both the learner's developmental self and by religious substantive content, and is not determined by theology. If one were to take Wyckoff's theological imperialism seriously, then there would scarcely be any reality in the world which is not primarily theological and hence under the direct seigniory of theology. Randolph Crump Miller's claims are theologically imperialistic because theology does not possess the capacity to judge pedagogical methods on religious instructional grounds. Only religious instruction has this capacity. Nor has theology ever directly generated any pedagogical practice. Furthermore, to teach religion (lifestyle domain) is of a fundamentally different existential order than to teach theology (cognitive domain). John Westerhoff's declaration of his personal convictions constitutes theological imperialism because theology provides only *one* screen for religious instruction, and not *the* screen Westerhoff claims. I should also like to emphasize that this screen as screen is external to religious instruction, and indeed may not be an important screen in many individual situations. To assert that professors of religious instruction are properly ordained clergy exponentially accelerates Westerhoff's theological imperialism for obvious reasons. Berard Marthaler's preposterous claim constitutes theological positivism because it reduces to theology all the myriad and diverse ways in which persons actualize and do their faith. To say that religious dance, cooking supper for one's spouse as an act of religious faith, or feeding a starving child for faith's sake are theological idioms surely represents a clear-cut case of theological positivism. Françoise Darcy-Bérubé's theologically positivistic statement lays bare *an important and almost unavoidable consequence of theological imperialism, namely the firm conviction that all religious truth and all religious life-standards can only be validly judged on the basis of one's own personally held theological stance.* To assert that Billy Graham's teaching methods are opposed to a Christian vision of man because these methods disagree with Darcy-Bérubé's own particular Roman Catholic theological position is contrary to the clear and undeniable evidence given by countless persons in different countries who have been helped to live deeper Christian lives through Graham's pedagogical procedures. It is precisely because Darcy-Bérubé's stance is so unabashedly imperialistic that she can arrogantly make her own personal theological position the measure of all religious standards. And it is precisely because Darcy-Bérubé's stance is so unabashedly imperialistic that she can gratuitously establish her own personal theological position as the sole judge of the validity of pedagogical procedure in religious instruction when, in fact, theology simply lacks this capacity. Theological imperialism, especially in its positivistic form, tends to be absolutistic and tyrannical in nature. Hence it is no small wonder that when they are logically consistent, theological imperialists, especially those of the positivistic stripe, have made life difficult for those who hold contrary views, such as by banning their writings, calumniating their personal lives and motivations, using political pressure so that their voices are not heard, exiling them, and so forth.

Paradoxically, the nature of theology and its wholly unique subject matter (God) present an alluring temptation to imperialism for those religious educationists and theologians who are structurally careless or substantively superficial. James Logan puts it well: "Because theology deals with 'first principles' or 'ultimates,' it is easy for the theologian to conclude that theology is omnicompetent. When theologians have been so tempted, their work loses the force of credibility which it should have."[42] Expressing the same view as Logan, though from a vastly different disciplinary and geographical perspective, Carl Jung writes that "theological thinkers are so used to dealing with eternal truths that they know no other kinds. When the physicist says that the atom is of such and such a composition, and when he sketches a model of it, he too [like I, Jung] does not intend to express anything like an eternal truth. But theologians do not understand the natural sciences and, particularly, psychological thinking. The material of analytical psychology [a form of social science], its principal facts, consist of statements—of statements that occur frequently in consistent form at various places and at various times."[43]

One fatal error of theological imperialism is its cherished assumption that theology proximately as well as ultimately explains all reality not solely in theological terms but in terms of each and every discrete reality itself. *Theological imperialists typically fail to realize that the fact that the world is the creation of God can in no way be tantamount to asserting that the world operates according to theological principles.* It is common sense, as well as the experience of any parent or religious educator, that theology has something to say about the learner's supernatural dimension, but little if anything to say about how an individual specifically behaves and learns. A theological manual is no substitute for a guide to child care.

It is procedurally and substantively invalid for a religious educationist or theologian to prefer or reject this or that social-science law or theory (e.g., humanistic as opposed to behavioristic psychology) simply because a particular social-science law or theory agrees or disagrees with his own theological

42. James C. Logan, *Theology as a Source in Shaping the Church's Educational Work* (Nashville, Tennesee: United Methodist Church Board of Discipleship, 1974), p. 41.

43. C. G. Jung, *Memories, Dreams, and Reflections,* recorded and edited by Aniela Jaffé, translated by Richard and Clara Winston (New York: Pantheon, 1963), p. 217, italics deleted.

speculation. Theology only possesses the capacity to discern the theological meaning of social-science facts, laws, or theories. Theology lacks the potency to validate social-science facts, laws, or theories. Phrased somewhat differently, a social-science law or theory is valid because it adequately explains social-science phenomena, not because it agrees with one or another theological position. To be sure, there is a sense in which theology is subject to social-science facts/laws/theories, to physical-science facts/laws/theories, and so on. After all, sound theology must not only be grounded in the Bible and in ecclesial tradition (and for Catholics in the official magisterium), but also in facts and laws and fruitful theories of the social-science and physical-science world. One's theology might say that the world will end tomorrow; but this theological speculation does not make the world end tomorrow.

An observation made once by Peter Berger might be instructive at this juncture. Toward the end of his volume *The Sacred Canopy,* Berger wrote: "The argument in this book has moved strictly within the frame of reference of sociological theory. No theological or, for that matter, antitheological implications are to be sought anywhere in the argument—if anyone should believe such implications are present *sub rosa,* I can only assure him that he is mistaken. Nor is there an intrinsic necessity for sociological theory, as here understood, to engage in a 'dialogue' with theology. The notion, still prevalent among some theologians, that the sociologist simply raises certain questions, which must then be answered by the theological partner in the 'dialogue,' must be rejected on very simple methodological grounds. Questions raised within the frame of an empirical discipline (and I would emphatically consider sociological theory to be within such a frame of reference) are not susceptible to answers coming out of the frame of reference of a nonempirical and normative discipline, just as the reverse procedure is inadmissible. Questions raised by sociological theory must be answered in terms falling within the latter's universe of discourse. This methodological platitude, however, does not preclude the fact that certain sociological perspectives may be *relevant* for the theologian, though in that case he will be well advised to keep the afore-mentioned discrepancy in mind when he tries to articulate that relevance within *his* universe of discourse. In sum, the argument of this book stands or falls as an enterprise of sociological theorizing and, as such, is not amenable to either theological support or theological critique."[44]

A theologically imperialistic assertion which has caused untold damage to religious instruction is the erroneous claim that theology constitutes *the* theory of religion. The fact of the matter is that *theology constitutes only one theory of religion. Theology is the theory of God; it is not the theory of religion.* God has no religion; certainly he has no need of being instructed in religion. Theological theory, then, examines religious activity only from the viewpoint of God and his proper activities as deduced from revelation. Theology, then, is only one theoretical way of looking at religion. There are other theoretical ways of looking at religion, ways which are just as objectively valid in terms of explaining and predicting and verifying religious activity. Religion necessarily involves persons; hence psychological theory of religion and of the religious individual are as valid for the genuine understanding of religion as theological theory of religion. Religion frequently involves persons in groups; hence sociological theory of religion is as valid for the genuine understanding of religion as theological theory of religion. I could provide numerous other examples, but I think the issue has been sufficiently illustrated. The major point is that theology is not *the* theory of religion; it is only *one* theory of religion. The proper theory of religion is that which I like to term religionology. Religionology is quite different in focus and in extension than religious studies, for obvious reasons. Religionology is an autonomous composite theory drawn from different fields and disciplines which take religion as their subject matter and focus.

Theological imperialism eventually results in consequences which are deleterious for theology as well as for religious instruction. Theological imperialism leads to the dissipation of theology. To be vigorous and valid, theology must remain true to itself, that is, true to its nature and to its

44. Peter L. Berger, *The Sacred Canopy* (Garden City, New York: Doubleday, 1967), p. 179.

parameters. Theology only ruins itself when it attempts to do the work of nontheological areas of reality. By attempting to be all explanations to all reality, theological imperialism becomes no explanation to all reality, and loses its own reality in the process. To operate church finances on theological theory, for example, is not only to result in fiscal disaster but also to seriously erode theological integrity itself. From theological imperialism there remains only one short step to *theologicism,* namely the conviction that theology alone and in itself is capable of solving all problems and providing all meaning whether scientific or literary or technological because the basic meaning of everything can be reduced to theology. With theologicism comes theological despotism and the arrogance characteristically associated with all forms of despotism. In the end, theological imperialism becomes self-defeating. By attempting to rule over areas in which it has no competence, theology becomes a laughing stock and receives the ultimate humiliation by being judged basically irrelevant. Theological imperialism ruins religious instruction by deliberately keeping religious educators in bondage by giving them watered-down theology and little else. Authentic religious instruction theory and practice are not provided because theological imperialists deny the very existence of such theory and practice. *No field can flourish in the absence of a theory and a practice which is authentic and indigenous to it. Nor can any field flourish if its main sustenance comes from watered-down material belonging to an essentially different field or discipline.*

What I have written in the last few pages is not intended to disparage the science of theology or diminish its importance in the work of religious instruction. Rather, what I have written in intended to show that theological imperialism is a manifestly improper and blatantly ineffective way of using theology in religious instruction endeavor. Theology plays a valuable internal and external role in religious instruction activity. Theology's internal role is properly enacted when it becomes a dimension of religious instruction's substantive content (religion) not on theology's terms but on the terms of religious instruction's own substantive content. Theology's external role is properly enacted when it reflects on the theological meaning of religious instruction—not on the religious instruction meaning, but on the theological meaning.

Religious Instruction as Messenger Boy for Theology

The "queen and norm of the sciences" mentality espoused by many advocates of the theological approach to religious instruction, especially when such a mentality is coupled with theological imperialism, has led to religion teaching being regarded as simply a messenger boy or a translator of theology.

Advocates of the theological approach have for centuries treated religious instruction as a sort of messenger boy by whom the knowledges and understandings acquired by theological science are delivered to the learners. Josef Goldbrunner, for example, forthrightly declares that religious instruction is properly considered as the servant of the theological message. All aspects of religion teaching are therefore explicitly subservient to theology.[45] Johannes Hofinger also regards religious instruction practice as consisting of the way in which theological content is transported to learners. Thus religious instruction procedures are ever the handmaid of the theological message to be delivered.[46] James Smart maintains that every aspect of religious instruc-

45. For Goldbrunner, this explicit subservience flows from his contention that religious instruction is essentially and hence implicitly in subjugation to theology. In Goldbrunner's view, the correct theology takes the form of Roman Catholic kerygmatic theology. Josef Goldbrunner, "Catechetical Method as Handmaid of Kerygma," in Johannes Hofinger, editor, *Teaching All Nations,* revised and partly translated by Clifford Howell (New York: Herder and Herder, 1961), pp. 108, 112.

46. Johannes Hofinger, *The Art of Teaching Christian Doctrine: The Good News and Its Proclamation,* 2d edition (Notre Dame, Indiana: University of Notre Dame Press, 1962), pp. 62–73; Johannes Hofinger, *Our Message is Christ* (Notre Dame, Indiana: Fides/Claretian, 1974), pp. ix-x, 1–11. In an extended and intensive *Meinungsaustausch* which I had with the saintly Hofinger for two straight days and nights in May 1981, the Austrian-born Jesuit gladly conceded that pedagogical procedure does indeed constitute structural content and thus forms an authentic co-content with substantive content in the religious instruction act. Hofinger explicitly told me that he regards the conceptualization of structural content as a major advance over the previous notion of method as a handmaid or vehicle for substantive content. My citation of Hofinger in this passage represents what now

tion arises from and flows through theology. Indeed, religious instruction is not just a messenger boy for theology, but more importantly a messenger boy for *the correct* theology. A good messenger boy is one who gives no thought to himself but only to the message he has to deliver. So too, religious instruction (messenger boy) gives no thought to itself but keeps its eyes unswervingly fixed on the message (the correct theology) which it has to deliver in as undiluted a fashion as possible.[47]

The core of the messenger-boy viewpoint is that the soul and goal of religious instruction is to transmit theological knowledges and understandings to the learner in as faithful and undiluted a manner as possible under the circumstances. Thus Alfred McBride identifies religious instruction as "a theology of recital" in which the religious educator endeavors to hand over to the learner as purely as possible the theological doctrine and authoritative interpretation of God's revelation.[48] To insure that the purity of the theological content remains as undiluted as possible in its shipment to the learner, some advocates of the posture of undilutedness regard pedagogical procedures involving active overt learner participation such as discussion and projects and experience-oriented strategies as preludes or postludes to authentic religious instruction rather than as the religious instruction act itself. Thus Josef Jungmann is avowedly skeptical of teacher-learner discussions, to say nothing of learner-learner discussions.[49] In Jungmann's view, it should be the religious educator

---

appears to be the earlier Hofinger. I eagerly await to see how Hofinger incorporates the conceptualization of structural content in his future written works in the field of religious instruction.

47. James Smart, *The Teaching Ministry of the Church,* pp. 24–67, especially pp. 41, 66–67. Smart's somewhat fundamentalist emphasis on the *correct* theology is similar to that of Françoise Darcy-Bérubé, though they greatly differ on what is *the* correct theology.

48. Alfred McBride, *Catechetics: A Theology of Proclamation* (Milwaukee: Bruce, 1967), p. 147. McBride uses the insular Catholic word "catechetics" rather than the ecumenical term "religious instruction."

49. Josef Andreas Jungmann, *Handing on the Faith: A Manual of Catechetics,* translated and revised by A. N. Fuerst (New York: Herder and Herder, 1959), pp. 174–283.

alone who is speaking during the core religious instruction act.[50] In
the same vein, Josef Goldbrunner states that the content of religious
instruction must be transmitted with authority. The theological
message "cannot be grasped through the 'learning by doing' principle. It must be proclaimed and heard."[51] Preparatory to the religious instruction act proper, the religious educator as messenger of
God has "the duty to woo the recipients" [the learners] into undi-
vided attention to the message. Then, during the religious instruction act itself, the learners must sit absolutely quiet while the
educator-messenger proclaims the content in the presentation.[52] In
Goldbrunner's opinion, experience-oriented pedagogical strategies
in religious instruction must have their origin and enactment and
completion in the learner's personal encounter with life-giving
theological content as he receives the substance and form of this
encounter from the mouth of the religious educator. For Goldbrunner, this is the proper theological position on experience-oriented
pedagogical strategies, a position which clearly shows that such
strategies are simply a new dimension of a fruitful oral presentation
by the educator of religious kerygma.[53] Advocates of the messenger-
boy position more often than not use radio transmission as their
model for religious instruction practice. In such a model, the
teacher transmits pure and undefiled theological content to the
learner via a verbal channel.

Some thoughtful advocates of the theological approach to religious instruction are dissatisfied with the nondialogical and noncrit-
ical texture of the messenger-boy viewpoint, to say nothing of its
tendency to a low level of personal theological activity on the part of

50. Ibid., p. 202.
51. Josef Goldbrunner, "Catechetical Method as Handmaid of Kerygma," pp.
112–113.
52. Goldbrunner's view is still held in varying degrees of intensity and direct-
ness. See, for example, Lawrence S. Cunningham, "The Long Search: Resources
and Reflections," in *Living Light* XVI (Spring, 1979), p. 77.
53. Josef Goldbrunner, "Catechesis and Encounter Catechetical Method," in
Josef Goldbrunner, editor, *New Catechetical Methods* (Notre Dame, Indiana: University of Notre Dame Press, 1965), pp. 17–38; Josef Goldbrunner, "The Cor-
poral Works of Mercy," in ibid., pp. 105–114.

the learner. Yet at the same time these advocates of the theological approach wish to retain the dominating character of theology and the subservient role of religious instruction which typifies the messenger-boy stance. To bring a critically processive theological emphasis to religious instruction while still retaining the fundamental form and axis of theology as undisputed queen of religious instruction activity, *some of the more sophisticated advocates of the theological approach have devised a position which places religious instruction in the role of translator for theology. In this perspective, the work of religious instruction is twofold: (1) to translate theological understandings and knowledges for the learner in terms of what the learners can grasp in the light of their own existential situation; (2) to have the learners reflect on these theological translations (theologize) so that they can continuously retranslate their life events back into theology in theological terms. Like the messenger-boy posture, the translation stance regards religious instruction both as a branch of theology and as a way of "getting theological content across to the learner."* In the messenger-boy stage, the content to be gotten across is a specific set of substantive product contents of theology. In the translation stage, the content to be gotten across is the substantive process content of theology. The translation stage also represents an advance in sophistication over the messenger-boy stage in that the translation position regards the relationship of theology as a two-way street (the learner critically dialoguing with theology in the process of theologizing) as contrasted to the one-way street (the learner simply receiving the correct theology) posited by the messenger-boy viewpoint.

The core of the translator viewpoint is that the soul and goal of religious instruction is the translation of theological knowledges and understandings into the learner's Christian existence in such a way that the broad integrity of the objective theological content is not compromised but instead is given an integral subjective and processive dimension. Thus Randolph Crump Miller sees the task of religious instruction as that of translating pure processive theological content into the life of the learner in such a way that this content is joined to his graced life of faith, whereupon the learner translates his graced life of faith back into increasingly higher forms of processive theological content. Thus Miller's motto has consistently been: "Theology in the background; faith and grace in the foregound." Because religious instruction is basically a translator of theology, it follows that theology determines every aspect of religious instruction from aim to curriculum to teaching procedures.[54] For Matthew Hayes, the task of religious instruction is to help the learner translate his personal and communal religious experiences into theological terms in a theological way. Such a translation of the experiential into the theological is essential if the learner's faith is to become living, conscious, and active. The work of religious instruction is to enable learners to articulate their experiences of God in theological terms and to recognize their faith experiences in the theological doctrines and beliefs of the community.[55]

From the standpoint of theory as developed in this essay, there are quite a few fatal flaws in both the messenger-boy and the translator conceptualizations of religious instruction.

First, the messenger-boy and the translator conceptualizations inherently claim that the goal and the method of religious instruction are theological. Yet such a claim clearly runs counter to the name and nature of religious instruction. Religious instruction is manifestly *religious* instruction, not *theological* instruction. Furthermore, religious instruction is manifestly religious *instruction,* not religious *theologizing.* Religion is ontically different from theology, and the instructional process is ontically different from the theologizing process.

Second, the messenger-boy and the translator conceptualizations inherently claim that theology is superior to religion in the religious instruction act. There is no evidence to support this claim. From the Christian perspective, religion is more important than theology

54. Randolph Crump Miller, *The Clue to Christian Education* (New York: Scribner's, 1950), pp. 1–11; Randolph Crump Miller, "Christian Education as Theological Discipline and Method," pp. 153–164.

55. Matthew J. Hayes, "How Much Theology Should Coordinators and DRE's Know?" in *Living Light* XIV (Fall, 1977), pp. 360–365; Norma H. Thompson, "Current Issues in Religious Education," in *Religious Education* LXXIII (November–December, 1978), pp. 617–618.

because religious activity directly leads to a person's salvation while theological activity does not directly lead to a person's salvation. Theology is simply a cognitive reflection on religion; it can never and therefore ought never to pretend to be a substitute for religion. *The importance of theology for religion (and hence for religious instruction) stems from the degree to which theology cognitively illumines and makes more meaningful a person's religious activity.*[56] *In this connection it is instructive to remember that Jesus was primarily a religious educator and redeemer, and not primarily a theologian. It is also instructive to remember that the Bible is primarily a religious instruction document rather than primarily a theological treatise.*

Third, the messenger-boy and translator conceptualizations inherently claim that theology is superior to religious instruction in the work of religious instruction. In the messenger-boy and translator positions, virtually all the emphasis is placed on one and only one dimension of substantive content, namely theology; concomitantly the essential four-variable nature of structural content is reduced to one variable (the teacher as messenger) or to two variables (the teacher and learner as mutual translators). But even here the breadth and integrity of the teacher variable and the learner variable are largely ignored and severely compromised by the messenger-boy and translator positions because both positions intrinsically disvalue structural content or deny its existence as an authentic co-content.[57] Consequently, structural content is not a central and inextricable feature of either the messenger-boy or the translator position.[58]

---

56. On this point, see Mary K. Cove and Mary Louise Mueller, *Regarding Religious Education* (Birmingham, Alabama: Religious Education Press, 1977), pp. 81–98.

57. Seldom, if ever, have advocates of the messenger-boy or translator positions conducted or even made use of careful empirical and formal theoretical research on the actual functions of the teacher and learner during the religious instruction dynamic.

58. Goldbrunner and Jungmann are openly distrustful of structural content. Hofinger, Miller, and Smart imagine that structural content can somehow be deduced from theological substantive content. Hayes's list of competencies required of a religious educator is entirely theological, with no mention made of proficiency in structural content. McBride's writings are so lacking in logical

There is solid theoretical and historical evidence which suggests that the
messenger-boy and the translator positions are fatally flawed by virtue of
their disvaluation and molar neglect of structural content. From the
perspective of theory, there can be no such entity as religious instruction without structural content in the fullness of its four-
variable form because, as noted earlier in this essay, religious instruction by nature is an existential fusion of substantive content
and structural content. From the perspective of history, those religious instruction movements of the past which attempted to operate
primarily or solely on the theological dimension of substantive content ended in failure precisely because they disvalued and neglected
structural content in its four-variable form. Thus, for example,
Mary Boys's scholarly investigation concluded that the Catholic
kerygmatic salvation-history movement in religious instruction
seems to have disappeared from prominence not because of its
theological inadequacies but because of a constellation of cultural
and educational factors including a disvaluation and neglect of
structural content.[59]

Fourth, the messenger-boy and translator conceptualizations are
necessarily rooted in theological particularism. Religious-instruction-
as-messenger-boy is good only when it delivers in pure and undiluted
form that which the religious educator regards as the correct theological product content. Religious-instruction-as-translator is good
only when the educator and the learner make their translations in
what the religious educator regards as the proper theological process
content, namely "sound theologizing."[60] *From the vantage point of*

---

cohesiveness and theoretical consistency that it is virtually impossible to come to
any coherent overview of his constantly fluctuating position.

59. Mary C. Boys, *Biblical Interpretation in Religious Education* (Birmingham,
Alabama: Religious Education Press, 1980), pp. 203–252, 279.

60. Many advocates of the translation position also emphasize correct theological product content. This particularistic emphasis might not be as absolutistic as
is the case with the messenger-boy posture, but it is certainly highly preferential
in terms of *a* correct kind of theologizing (process content) and *a* correct kind of
theological message (product content). Thus Randolph Crump Miller states that
translation may be accomplished with any theology insofar as such a theology is

religious instruction theory qua theory, any kind of theological particularism is untenable because by definition and by adequacy, a theory of religious instruction must possess the power to satisfactorily explain and predict and verify the entire range of religious instruction phenomena no matter what divergent theological viewpoints or processes are incorproated into these phenomena. Any theory which restricts its attention to only one class within the entire range of those product and process phenomena with which it purports to deal is doomed at the outset not only with respect to adequacy for the whole field but also with respect to its own vitality. From the vantage point of religious instruction practice qua practice, any kind of theological particularism is untenable because no adequate theory can be built exclusively upon a certain set of particularities which themselves drastically change from year to year and from era to era. In this vein, Iris Cully, concurring with Sara Little, persuasively argues that theology as such cannot be pivotal for religious instruction theory because there is no consensus among theologians about correct theological product or process contents. Indeed, each new theological particularity "has its day of popularity (heralded by an article in one of the newsweeklies), only to be succeeded by the next wave" of theological particularities. Cully concludes that there is little possibility for religious instruction theory to develop around such short-lived theological particularities.[61]

Fifth, *the messenger-boy and the translator positions both assume that theology directly generates religion. However, both theoretical evidence and historical evidence suggest that this assumption is false.* From the theoret-

---

true and relevant. But Miller himself in a wide variety of writings has set forth criteria for what kind of theology is true and relevant—criteria which evangelical Protestants would by and large reject. Furthermore, Miller forthrightly declares that the specific theological product contents which he espouses are probably the soundest from the theological standpoint. Randolph Crump Miller, *The Clue to Christian Education,* p. 19, and also pp. 15–17.

61. Iris V. Cully, "The Problem and the Clue," in Iris V. Cully and Kendig Brubaker Cully, editors, *Process and Relationship: Issues in Theology, Philosophy, and Religious Education* (Birmingham, Alabama: Religious Education Press, 1978), p. 3; Sara Little, "The 'Clue' to Christian Education: A Historical Comment," in Marvin J. Taylor, editor, *Foundations of Christian Education in an Era of Change* (Nashville, Tennessee: Abingdon, 1976), pp. 30–40.

ical perspective, it must be remembered that theology and religion
are two ontically distinct orders of being. Theology belongs to the
cognitive domain, while religion lies in the lifestyle domain. It is
manifestly impossible for a reality belonging to one ontic order to
directly generate a reality belonging to another ontic order. Just as a
daisy cannot directly generate an elephant, so also theology cannot
directly generate religion. From the historical perspective, it is
virtually impossible to find a single instance in the long history of
Christianity in which theology has directly generated religion. Such
a historical finding is hardly surprising since by its nature theology
is simply a cognitive reflection upon religion rather than religion
itself.

Sixth, the messenger-boy and translation positions tend to rob
religious instruction of its prophetic role. Religious instruction has
as one of its cardinal tasks that of hastening the future, of directly
generating advances in the cognitive and affective and lifestyle activities of persons and of societies. *As a highly significant yeasting and
progressive force, religious instruction possesses the power to directly bring
about productive religious changes in people and in societies, including the
ecclesial and ecclesiastical societies.*[62] *Religious instruction loses its unique
prophetic character and force when persons attempt to transmogrify it into
theology. One would be hard put to locate a single instance in which theology
directly produced a single major advance in nontheological sectors of reality
during the entire history of Christianity. This fact is hardly surprising,
since the task of theology is to make advances within its own sphere of
existence and then offer these advances to other areas of reality for possible
incorporation by those other areas on their own ontic and functional terms.*
But even here theology has by and large failed. Most of the advances
for humanity made in the last thousand years typically came not
from theology but from the so-called "secular" or "profane" sectors.
In the twentieth century, the valiant struggles for social justice,
human rights, racial equality, political freedom, and the like, all
originated in "secular" and "profane" quarters. Only later, and

62. On this point, see James Michael Lee, "Introduction," in James Michael
Lee, editor, *The Religous Education We Need,* pp. 1–3, 7–8.

often belatedly, did theology on a large scale begin to investigate and plunge into these areas. Liberation theology, so fashionable in certain post-1970 theological circles, arose as a theological reaction, and not as a proaction, to the sociology of Marx, the political activity of Latin American revolutionaries, and the instructional practices of Paulo Freire.

Mediator—A New Stage

From the analysis made in the preceding pages, it is obvious that neither the messenger-boy stage nor the translation stage constitute adequate theoretical explanations of the relationship between religious instruction and theology. What is needed is a new stage which explains how and why theology relates to religious instruction in such a way that the integrity of religious instruction is preserved and that theology plays its proper role rather than an imperialistic role. Such a stage must be capable of theoretically explaining the structure of religious instruction as the dynamic combination of substantive content and structural content in a single new ontic entity.

There is a new and higher stage which performs the explanatory tasks delineated in the previous two sentences. I call this stage that of mediator, a conceptualization which I first proposed in the early 1970s.[63] I am not referring to a mediator as an arbitrator between two opposing parties, or as an intercessor between a party of lesser power and one of greater power. Religious instruction is not an arbitrator between religion and theology or between pedagogy and theology. Nor does religious instruction serve as theology's intercessor, or vice versa. The mediatorship to which I refer is mediatorship in its highest, most authentic, and most effective form, namely mediatorship in which two or more realities become united in a new reality. This new reality is of such a nature that it not only unites its

63. Mediatorship stands as a central element in my overall theory of religious instruction. For an early formulation of my concept of mediatorship, see James Michael Lee, *The Flow of Religious Instruction*, pp. 18–19.

components, but unites them in such a fashion that the components are no longer separate entities but rather are subsumed into a new reality. This new reality simultaneously (1) incorporates and retains the essential features of its original components, and (2) puts the essential features of the original components into a new fused relationship with each other so that they are no longer separate but become inextricably combined in the new reality—so inextricably combined, in fact, that in this new reality the components are no longer separate and distinct ontic entities but exist in the new reality only in their united state.[64] *Mediatorship means that substantive content and structural content are so united in the religious instruction act that religion no longer exists as religion* in se *but now exists under the form of religious instruction, and that instruction does not exist as instruction* in se *but now exists under the form of religious instruction.*

The full and authentic kind of mediatorship which I am discussing has at least two fundamental properties, namely (1) subsumption[65] into a new ontic reality and (2) unity. A mediator subsumes

64. It is tempting to make my position completely analogous to that which happens in a chemical compound, especially in a covalent chemical compound. A chemical compound is a pure substance with its own distinct identity. It is formed by the chemical union of its components in such a manner that the components lose their own separate identities. The constituents of a compound cannot be separated by physical means. Thus a compound differs significantly from a mixture. A mixture is a substance in which the components keep their own separate identities and are simply joined together in a conglomerate substance. The components of a mixture can be separated by physical means. Unlike an ionic compound which is formed by the loss and gain of electrons, a covalent compound is formed between like and unlike atoms because they are able to share pairs of electrons. However, I am not using a chemical compound as a perfect analogy with mediatorship for several reasons, among the most important of which is the fact that the composition of a pure chemical compound is always the same—the law of constant proportions. The dynamic character of religious instruction as mediator suggests that the ingredients involved in the religious and in the instructional dimensionalities of the religious instruction act are constantly shifting as the exigencies of the concrete here-and-now religious instruction dynamic demand; hence in religious instruction there can be no such thing as a law of constant proportions.

65. I am using the term "subsumption" in the sense of ontic synthesis and not in the sense in which this term is used in formal logic or in Scottish law. Furthermore, my position is not identical to nor has ever been identical to

into a new reality those entities of which it is composed. A mediator is thus not the sum total of its components, but rather a new entity formed by the new ontic and configurational and functional *relationship* in which these subsumed components now find themselves. The core properties of each component remain, but not in the same ontic

---

dialectic as originally conceptualized by Georg Hegel or as subsequently used with modification by Karl Marx. My position on mediatorship differs from Hegel's conceptualization of the dialectic on several counts. First, Hegel places far more emphasis on the total supremacy of reason and cognition than I am willing to do. Thus in a celebrated statement in his *Grundlinien der Philosophie des Rechts* (*Philosophy of Right*), Hegel forthrightly asserts "*Was vernünftig ist, das ist wirklich; und was wirklich ist, das ist vernünftig,*" that is to say rationality is reality and reality is rationality. Second, Hegel tends to broaden the extensions of dialectic more than I possibly would—though in fairness to Hegel it must be said that this monumental German philosopher himself seems to waffle somewhat on this point. Thus in *Enzyklopädie der philosophischen Wissenschaften* (*Encyclopedia of the Philosophical Sciences*) Hegel states that every entity can overcome itself and therefore is inherently dialectical, while in his *Phänomenologie des Geistes* (*Phenomenology of Spirit*) he asserts that only human reality is dialectical. Still, Alexandre Kojève might not be far off the mark when he accuses Hegel of a somewhat simplistic form of ontological monism in regarding all reality as dialectical. Third, Hegel emphasizes necessity far form than I. For Hegel, both the fact and the procession of the dialectic are fundamental necessities in existence. Thus Hegel's conception of reality has a certain deterministic flavor to it. My theorizing, on the other hand, has always stressed possibility, probability, contingency, and exigency. Fourth, Hegel gives negation a far more global, powerful, and quintessential role in reality than I do. For Hegel every reality is simultaneously identical to itself and different from (in negation to) all other reality; this inner negation which characterizes each reality enables it to overcome its own limitations and so be inherently enabled to grow and to change. My thought assigns less of a place to instrinsic molar negation, stressing instead the reality and the concept of complementarity and the special kind of negation which complementarity suggests. Fifth, Hegel tends to virtually ontologize nothingness (not-being), whereas I view nothingness in a more relational fashion.

There are many dimensions of both Hegelian doctrine strictly interpreted and Hegelian spirit more loosely appropriated which, since the mid-1950s, have held considerable attraction and relevance for the development and sustenance of my own theoretical position. First, Hegel's recurring predeliction for triads seems to have the Trinity as its speculative source and personal inspiration. Because the Trinity is the central revealed reality in Christianity, it should in a cardinal way be central for all reality. But to maintain that all reality participates in some way in the Trinity or even has a trinitarian structure is, to my mind, not identical to asserting that all reality is either dialectical *in se* or dialectical in the way Hegel

or functional fashion as was the case when they existed as separate
independent entities outside the mediational reality. In the mediational reality, the core properties of each component are altered
ontically and functionally by virtue of and in the degree to which
each component now substantively and structurally relates to the

---

claims it is. Second, Hegel has a deep appreciation for the fundamental unity of
reality and fights dualism at every turn. The theological process of Hegel's
dialectic is aimed at first overcoming and then reconciling the separation of
subject and object, person and world, so as to obliterate alienation and lead each
human being to a harmonious integrated life. Though I cannot concur that the
dialectic is the only way of overcoming and reconciling separation, still Hegel's
creative use of negation to bring about genuine rather than phony wholeness is
attractive to my theorizing. Third, Hegel attaches great importance to the organic theory of reality and truth. In this conceptualization, each reality and each
truth is dependent upon, and in turn helps determine, every other reality and
truth. Everything is intrinsically determined by its relations to everything else.
Though I reject determinism in all its forms, still Hegel's perception of the
intertwining of reality is a fruitful conceptualization, one which John Dewey
subsequently uses seminally in his own theory of education. Fourth, Hegel regards negation as an authentic reality rather than viewing it as simply nothing at
all or as a privative "reality." Whereas in most non-Hegelian conceptualizations
a reality simultaneously *is* and is *not*, for Hegel a reality simultaneously *is* and *is
not*. Each reality is at once itself and its complete ontic opposite. (Some
philosophers contend that Hegel is here denying the age-old logical principle of
contradiction). Though I do not concur with the way in which he reifies not-
being, still I find it helpful to note that some creative persons working in the
theory and practice of the arts regard the whole notion of negative space, for
example, theoretically fruitful and practically useful. Fifth, Hegel recognizes the
processive and inherently negational dimensions of every reality as prophetic in
the sense of hastening the future by at once destroying and preserving the past
and present. In dialectical negation Hegel sees a fundamental way in which
primal oppositions, conflicts, tensions, and refutations are courted and treasured
rather than avoided or shunned. Hegel views dialectical negation not as Absolute
Idea completely swallowing up or totally liquidating earlier realities, but of
enabling these realities to play their appropriate part in continuing its life and
stability. For Hegel, skepticism about present reality is the forerunner and essential ingredient of the dialectical process. For Hegel, all knowledge isolates; but
then comes reason's negation-moment of criticism and conflict, after which a
sublation of the dipolar elements necessarily ensues. Negation or primal opposition is thus the essence and the key to successful completion of the dialectic.
Though I cannot concur with Hegel's insistence on either the necessity or the
texture of sublation, still I find it extremely important that in Hegel's theory

other(s). Each component is still recognizable. This recognizability does not inhere in the original component, but rather inheres in this component as it is ontically and functionally altered in the new subsumptional reality. Thus in religious instruction, religion is still recognizable; however it is recognizable as it exists in religious instruction and not as it exists in itself. The subsumptional process

---

reality advances *because* of primal opposition and negation, not *despite* these basic features.

Since 1958 I have frequently mentioned in my classes that education in general and religious instruction in particular must come to grips with Hegel. In the religious instruction sector, such a fundamental encounter with Hegel did not take place in a major way until 1980 when an Irish-born American priest, Thomas Groome, published an important theoretical treatise entitled *Christian Religious Education*. Though the pure waters of Hegelian thought are significantly tempered and filtered by Groome's derivative neo-Marxian tack which he seems to have by and large adopted from his major professor Dwayne Huebner, nonetheless his book is an important attempt to breathe a left-wing Hegelian soul into religious instruction. Indeed it is refreshing to see a Christian religious educationist engage in theory, as contrasted to all the tracts and speculative works which abound in the field. To enter into a fruitful dialogue with Groome, religious educationists must not only explore the internal validity of his left-wing Hegelian theory, but even more importantly examine whether his Huebner-inherited version of this seminal theory is fruitful and adequate for our field, namely whether it can generate more than the single pedagogical procedure he proposes as *the* objectification of his theory, and whether his theory is adequate to explain and predict and verify the many empirically verified effective pedagogical procedures which are substantially different from his shared-praxis instructional method.

For a more complete understanding of Hegel's position on the dialectic, I find the following books (in addition to the works of Hegel which were mentioned in this footnote) to be especially helpful: W. T. Stace, *The Philosophy of Hegel* (New York: Dover, 1955), pp. 88–115; J. N. Findlay, *Hegel: A Re-examination* (London: Allen and Unwin, 1958), pp. 58–82; Émile Brehier, *The Nineteenth Century: Period of Systems,* translated by Wade Baskin (Chicago: University of Chicago Press, 1968), pp. 162–203; Alexandre Kojève, *Introduction to the Reading of Hegel: Lectures on the Phenomenology of Spirit,* assembled by Raymond Queneau, edited by Allen Bloom, translated by James H. Nichols, Jr. (New York: Basic, 1969), pp. 169–259; Raymond Plant, *Hegel* (Bloomington, Indiana: Indiana University Press, 1973), pp. 124–146; Stanley Rosen, *G. W. F. Hegel* (New Haven, Connecticut: Yale University Press, 1974), pp. 47–150; Howard P. Kainz, *Hegel's Pheonomenology, Part I: Analysis and Commentary* (University, Alabama: University of Alabama Press, 1976), pp. 27–37.

creates a new unity. Whereas previously the components existed separately and autonomously, now in mediatorship they are subsumed to form a wholly new unity forged from a new ontic relationship between components. In full mediatorship, the ultimate unity is accomplished, namely the unity whereby the components unite into a new entity in which they become aspects or dimensions of a new reality. This unity brought about by subsumption is one of wholeness in which the original components are not obliterated but rather are brought into new ontic fullness and wider functional power. Because the original components are fused into a new ontic and functional reality, no one component dominates the other(s) or puts the other(s) into servitude. A dynamic equilibrium reigns. The mediator sustains its components within the ontic and functional unity of its mediatorship. Owing to its property of unity, all the efforts of the action of the mediator are efforts of the whole mediator and not the efforts solely of any one or more of its components.[66]

Religious instruction is a mediator of religion and instruction, that is, of substantive content and structural content. This mediatorship is forged through the dynamic subsumption of the distinctly separate realities of religion and instruction, a subsumption which eventuates in that new reality called religious instruction. In the mediational reality called religious instruction, the core properties of religion and instruction are altered functionally and ontically in that religion takes on the form and nature of religious instruction while instruction takes on the form and nature of religious instruc-

---

66. There is an important strand in modern Christology which uses one or another conceptualization of mediator. The major and most seminal of the treatments of Jesus as mediator is Emil Brunner, *The Mediator,* translated by Olive Wyon (Philadelphia: Westminster, 1967). Other significant treatments include Edward Schillebeeckx, *Jesus: An Experiment in Christology,* translated by Hubert Hoskins (New York: Seabury, 1979), pp. 597–612; Karl Rahner, *Foundations of Christian Faith,* translated by William V. Dych (New York: Seabury, 1978), pp. 176–228, 292, Wolfhart Pannenberg, *Jesus—God and Man,* translated by Lewis L. Wilkins and Duane A. Priebe (Philadelphia: Westminster, 1968), pp. 166–169, 390–397; Paul Tillich, *Systematic Theology,* vol. II (Chicago: University of Chicago Press, 1957), pp. 165–180.

tion. Thus we have the united mediated entity of religious instruction rather than the mixed entities of religion and instruction.[67]
As mediator, religious instruction does not stand between substantive content and structural content, but rather ontically reconciles
them in the fundamental new reality called religious instruction.
Religion as it exists in religious instruction is different from the way
it exists in religious dance *per se* or in religious meditation *per se*[68] In
the full mediatorship of religious instruction, religion and instruction cease to be separate entities but become aspects or dimensions
of the new subsumptional reality known as religious instruction. In
this new reality, neither religion nor instruction is obliterated;
rather, each is brought into a new ontic fullness and functional
power insofar as religion and instruction are both changed and
broadened and deepened by the merger with one another. Through
the ontic merging of religion and instruction in the subsumptional
process there emerges the mediation stage of religious instruction.
In the mediated stage of religious instruction, neither religion nor
instruction are imperialistic to one another. Instead, a dynamic

67. Padraic O'Hare's shrill vituperation fails abysmally to grasp even minimally my major thesis about mediatorship and religious instruction as a new ontic
entity. Since a clear and unmistakable delineation of this thesis was set forth in at
least two of my books published prior to his diatribe, one is forced to conclude
that O'Hare failed to read that which he purports to criticize. My thesis of
mediatorship and of religious instruction as a new ontic entity clearly indicates
that I do not have an educational theory, as O'Hare mistakenly claims. I have a
religious instruction theory, which is vastly different from having an educational
theory. In contrast to O'Hare's confused drivel, Mary Boys has correctly interpreted my position on this matter. Padraic O'Hare, "The Image of Theology in
the Educational Theory of James Michael Lee," in *Living Light* XI (Fall, 1974),
pp. 452–458; Mary C. Boys, *Biblical Interpretation in Religious Education,* pp.
231–239.

68. Thomas Aquinas holds that the soul (form) is *in se* equal in all persons, but
that an individual's total human functioning (soul-fullness) is determined by the
potential and real attributes of the body (matter) to which it is joined. Aquinas's
position on soul (form) and body (matter) seems at first notice to be fruitfully
analogous to my position on instruction (form) and religion (matter). Still, for
several reasons, I am presently hesitant and even a bit intellectually uneasy in
advancing such an analogy; hence I will refrain from doing so until I theorize
further on this point at some later time.

equilibrium reigns. This equilibrium is that of two complementary dimensions of one ontic reality rather than of two separate ontic realities thrown into a single functional grab-bag.

The place of theology in terms of the mediated entity called religious instruction is determined not by criteria external to the mediated entity (such as theological criteria in se), *but rather by internal criteria, namely how theology fits into religious instruction on religious instruction's own distinctive ontic and functional terms as religious instruction is being enacted in the here-and-now.* Since the dynamics of the here-and-now are in constant flux, so too will the role of theology be in constant flux. Hence in some instances the place of theology in religious instruction endeavor will be considerable, at other times minimal, and so on. What I have written in this paragraph in no way suggests that theology is a handmaid to religious instruction. Rather, my analysis suggests that the proper role of theology in religious instruction is determined by the manner and degree to which it relates to religious instruction endeavor at any one particular time or phase of that endeavor. Because religious instruction is a mediated reality, theology is not incorporated into religion in the religious instruction endeavor, but rather is incorporated into the whole of the new subsumptional reality of religious instruction on religious instruction's own ontic and functional terms. In the religious instruction act, theology no longer exists as theology's theology but instead as religious instruction's theology. Because the fruits of a mediated reality come through the mediator as a whole, any theological fruits which may and do eventuate from religious instruction activity come directly from religious instruction activity and not from theology *in se.*

A mediator reconciles, brings to wholeness. In so doing, a mediator brings a re-novation and re-newal to each of the realities which are subsumed into it. Thus religious instruction as mediator brings a renewal both to religion and to instruction. This renewal constitutes a major vital force for the prophetic nature and function of religious instruction not only to the dimensions of religion and instruction which are intrinsic to religious instruction, but also for every reality which religious instruction endeavor touches.

Method-Content Duality

One of the many advantages accruing to the mediator stage is that it satisfactorily resolves the problem of the method-content duality in religious instruction.

The fundamental postulate of the method-content duality is that method and content constitute two ontically distinct and actually separate realities. Usually this postulate is extended in such a way as to assert that method is simply a way of "transmitting" content, that method is external and instrumental to the content which is being taught. To be sure, both the messenger-boy and the translation stage conceptualize the relation between method and content in basically this manner. In the messenger-boy stage, method is dichotomous from content. Thus method is ever the faithful hand-maid of the theological content to be delivered to the learner. In the translation stage, method still remains dichotomous from content, though perhaps less blatantly so. In this stage, method is that extrinsic instrumentality which enables the learner to dialogically translate theological truths into his own life as well as translate his own life into theological truths.

The claim of a method-content duality should be obviously fallacious. Properly considered, method is structural content. Properly considered, content is substantive content. Consequently, method and content cannot be considered dichotomous because both are contents in their own right. It is patently absurd to posit a content-content duality. But how can we explain the fallaciousness of the method-content duality from the extremely important vantage point of theory? The mediator stage permits us to make an adequate theoretical explanation. In mediation, the religious instruction act serves as the mediator which subsumes method[69] and content. In

69. I am using the word "method" only because this is how structural content is globally referred to in the field of religious instruction, especially when contrasted with [substantive] content. I have shown in my previous books that it is inaccurate and misleading to use the term "method" to denote the entire typology of pedagogical procedure. Empirical analysis and subsequent theoretical reflection of the structural content of religious instruction has led me to devise a *taxonomy of*

the subsumptional process, structural content and substantive content are reconciled in the new ontic entity called religious instruction. To be sure, the religious instruction act itself is a new ontic entity born of the subsumption of method (structural content) and substantive content. Structural content and substantive content, when considered *sub specie* the religious instruction act, do not possess any ontic existence of their own. *Sub specie* the religious instruction act, these two contents by themselves are simply logical beings, mental constructs which are conceptually devised primarily for the purpose of intellectual analysis.

Because religious instruction is a mediator, there is no such thing in the real order of the here-and-now religious instruction act as a pedagogical procedure which is ontically separate from the substantive content being taught. Pedagogical procedure does not exist in a vacuum. One cannot teach nothing; one can only teach something (substantive content) in some way (structural content). As mediator, the religious instruction act does not stand between pedagogical procedure and substantive content (including the theological ingredient), but rather ontically reconciles them in the fundamentally new reality called religious instruction. In this ontic reconciliation, method and content are complementary dimensions of one single reality rather than two opposing entities. Because method and content are complementary essential dimensions of the same mediational reality, neither dominates the other nor is either in servitude to the other.

ONTIC AUTONOMY

Step by step since the very first page of this essay, the evidence has been progressively mounting and the logic has been inexorably

---

pedagogical procedure. This taxonomy enumerates six discrete classes of pedagogical procedure, beginning with the most general and ending with the most specific: approach, style, strategy, method, technique, and step. For an elaboration of these taxonomic classes, see James Michael Lee, *The Flow of Religious Instruction,* pp. 31–38.

closing in on the inescapable conclusion that religious instruction enjoys ontic autonomy. *By ontic autonomy I mean that religious instruction is not subject to theology, but is rather a separate and independent field. Religious instruction and theology are basically different ontic entities and operate on different levels of reality.*

The ontic autonomy of religious instruction from theology stems from two fundamental and converging vectors, namely fact and theory. In terms of fact, religious instruction is ontically autonomous from theology because each is and does fundamentally different things. Religious instruction is the pedagogical activity in which religious outcomes are facilitated, while theology is the cognitive investigation of the nature and the activities of God. In terms of theory, two points are especially worthy of mention, one negative and the other positive. Negatively, theology fails the six-component test required of any theoretical base claiming to validly serve as an adequate explainer and predictor and verifier of religious instruction activity. Positively, theology's claim to seigniory is smashed by the mediator conceptualization of religious instruction. As a mediator entity, religious instruction is formed by uniting structural content and substantive content in such a fashion that these two contents are no longer separate entities but rather are subsumed into a new reality. Thus theology, which usually but not necessarily is an ingredient in substantive content disappears *qua theology* when substantive content is essentially transformed in the subsumptional process of mediation. Thus any theology which might have been present in substantive content prior to mediation, now, having been mediated, exists under the form of religious instruction. Theology as a distinct science *external* to the religious instruction act can and usually does see a *theological* significance in religious instruction endeavor. In other words, theology can ascertain what religious instruction *means for theology.* Also, theology can externally present this theological meaning to religious instruction (1) for possible reflection by religious instruction itself on what religious instruction is doing and ought to do, and (2) for possible incorporation into religious instruction on religious instruction's own autonomously ontic terms.

Every ontic entity has its own ground and its own medium. Religious instruction endeavor is no exception. If a field is to be coherent and fruitful, its fundamental ground and basic medium must be congruent. The proper ground and medium of religious instruction is social science. As the ground of religious instruction, social science is that which religious instruction *works out of*. As the medium of religious instruction, social science is that which religious instruction *works through*.

The proper ground of religious instruction is social science precisely because the essential nature *of religious instruction is the facilitation of desired religious outcomes.* The only valid theoretical ground for adequately explaining, predicting, and verifying the facilitation of these outcomes is social science. Only social science possesses the theoretical tools and capability to serve as an adequate ground for religious instruction. Theology, by definition and nature and operation, simply lacks the requisite theoretical tools and capability. The only practical ground for enabling religious instruction to successfully accomplish its task of actually facilitating desired outcomes is social science. Theology's practice *eo ipso* lies in quite different directions.

The proper medium of religious instruction is social science precisely because religious instruction in all its activity functions *essentially along facilitational lines.* Religious instruction is a process of facilitation; hence its specific medium is the bring*ing* about of desired learning outcomes. Social science is the sole overall medium in which this special kind of activity takes place. Thus social science and only social science has the capability of empowering the effective deployment of religious instruction activity. In and through the way it functions, theology simply lacks this capability.

The assertion that social science rather than theology is the proper ground and medium of religious instruction does not mean that one imperialism (theology) is overthrown so that another imperialism may take its place. Theology is imperialistic when it attempts to exert absolute domination over an area of reality which is not properly its own. Such improper domination is what constitutes an empire, after all, as for example the Roman Empire, the British

Empire, the Soviet Empire, and so on. Theological imperialism consists in the absorption by theology of sectors of reality inappropriate to it, which is exactly what happens when theology tries to rule over religious instruction. Theological imperialism is the attempt to dictate the very nature and operations of areas which are foreign to it, such as "Christian teaching methods," "Christian learning theory," "Christian dental techniques," "Christian engineering theory," and the like. Social science is not imperialistic with respect to religious instruction because religious instruction genuinely belongs in what is properly social-science territory. Theology is imperialistic when it tries to impose norms and procedures from a source extrinsic to the religious instruction act itself, namely from theology. Social science is not imperialistic with regard to religious instruction because social science merely clarifies and operationalizes those existential norms and procedures which underlie and flow through religious instruction activity itself. The foundation of a nonimperialistic ground and medium of religious instruction is the religious instruction act itself, especially the developmental nature of the learner and the actual functioning of the pedagogical dynamic. Religious instruction simply uses social science as ground and medium (1) in order to theoretically explain and predict and verify *from its own nature* what it is doing, and (2) in order to practically augment the effectiveness of its operation. This is not domination: it is enlightenment and enhancement. *Advocates of the theological approach to religious instruction must learn to accept the fact that each nontheological sector of reality operates according to its own essential and developmental laws, and not according to theological laws.*

Religious Instruction and General Instruction: Scope and Norms

Because its ground and medium lie in the social sciences in general and in the field of instruction in particular, *it is only natural for religious instruction to be intrinsically related to general instruction.*

From the perspective of scope, all instruction may be classified as general and specialized. General instruction consists in the facilitation of learnings which are or should be common to all human beings by virtue of their being human. Examples of general instruction include basic language skills, arithmetic competence, history knowledge, logical reasoning, artistic appreciation, and so forth. Specialized instruction consists in the facilitation of those learnings which for one reason or another are reserved for a particular group of persons engaged in a series of specialized tasks in society. A clearcut example of specialized instruction is vocational instruction, a broad category which ranges from instruction in the trades to seminary preparation to teacher training, and so forth. In most societies throughout the world, religious instruction in one form or another has been and still is regarded as an integral part of general instruction. To be sure, church leaders and religious educators are especially insistent that each human being, by the very fact of that individual's humanity, needs religious instruction to bring out and fulfill his human nature. Religious instruction is for all, and should not be restricted to a select group of persons. In a word, religious instruction is and must be an intrinsic and inseparable part of general instruction.

Though the point I discussed in the preceding paragraph is obvious, it is nonetheless heatedly denied by many advocates of the theological approach to religious instruction.[70] These individuals typically warn religious educators of the inherent dangers involved in "importing" pedagogical procedures from what they label "secular" or general instruction. Thus Johannes Hofinger warns religious educators of the grave danger involved in appropriating pedagogical procedures "which are fully in accord with profane subjects, but meaningless or even harmful in religious formation."[71] Many Evangelical and especially fundamentalist Protestant religious educationists and church leaders are outspoken in criticizing "godless"

70. Not all advocates make such denials. Randolph Crump Miller, for example, concedes that religious education "in most ways is like secular education," and then goes on to provide numerous illustrations to support his contention. Randolph Crump Miller, *The Theory of Christian Education Practice*, pp. 179–180.

71. Johannes Hofinger, *The Art of Teaching Christian Doctrine*, p. 63.

principles and procedures of general instruction. These persons warn their readers and listeners to resist the alluring temptation of importing or applying these principles and procedures into Christian instruction lest contamination ensue.

Theological imperialism lies at the root of the claim that the principles and procedures of general instruction do not apply to and might well contaminate religious instruction. In advancing their claim, the advocates of the theological approach are basically asserting that theology is not simply *an* extrinsic norm for general instruction and religious instruction, but also is *the* intrinsic norm. Hofinger puts it directly when he asserts that theology provides the norm for determining the inherent pedagogical qualities of every teaching procedure.[72] The fundamental fallacy in this imperialistic claim is that *theology simply lacks the power or the competence to serve as the intrinsic norm for any reality other than itself. The only thing theology has the potency to accomplish is to ascertain whether general instructional activity or religious instructional activity squares with the norms of theology. In other words, theology can only gauge what general instruction activity or religious instruction activity mean to theology.* Theology lacks the capability to determine both *what* general instruction means to religious instruction and *how* general instruction means to religious instruction. Theology is simply not competent to determine the intrinsic norms of any nontheological reality or to determine how nontheological reality works. Theology can no more provide the intrinsic norms for the principles and practices of general instruction and religious instruction than it can provide the intrinsic norms for the principles and practices of sculpting, dentistry, engineering, creative writing, and so on. Theology can no more provide religious instruction with principles and procedures of effective teaching than it can provide engineering with the principles and procedures of building a bridge.

Every class of reality has its own set of intrinsic norms. These norms arise from the distinct nature of any given class of reality, and these intrinsic norms flow through the distinct functioning of any

72. Ibid.

given class of reality. But these norms are theological only when the class of reality for which they are intrinsically normative is theology itself. *To assert that theology is intrinsically normative for all classes of reality is to transform all classes of reality into theology.* Hence the assertion that theology is intrinsically normative for all classes of reality is patently absurd.

The operational dynamic by which a reality functions and actualizes itself tends to enflesh the intrinsic norm(s) governing that reality. Thus Bernard Lonergan can characterize the basic operational dynamic of all reality ranging from natural science to theology as being "a normative pattern of recurrent and related operations yielding cumulative and progressive results."[73] Lonergan goes on to state that theological norms are distinct from the norms of other classes of reality, including religion. Furthermore, "the normativeness of any theological conclusion is distinct from and dependent on the normativeness attributed to divine revelation, inspired scripture, or church doctrine."[74] Indeed, Lonergan declares, "theology is neither a source of divine revelation nor an addition to inspired scripture nor an authority that promulgates church doctrines."[75] Religious instruction is ontically autonomous from theology. Its fundamental operational dynamic is substantially different from that of theology. Consequently the intrinsic norms for religious instruction are not theological nor are they directly derived from theology.[76]

73. Bernard J. F. Lonergan, *Method in Theology,* pp. 3–20.

74. Ibid., p. 299.

75. Ibid., p. 331.

76. Berard Marthaler grossly misinterprets Lonergan's position when he erroneously claims that religious instruction ("cathechesis" in Marthaler's terminology) represents the eighth of Lonergan's functional specialities, namely communications. Even the most cursory, once-over-very-lightly examination of Lonergan's book reveals that Lonergan explicitly states that (1) religion and theology are ontically distinct entities, and that (2) communications as a functional speciality of theology refers exclusively to the communication of the process and product contents of theological reflection. See Bernard J. F. Lonergan, *Method in Theology,* pp. 101–145 (especially pp. 138–144), 170, 267–268, 331, 355–368. See also Berard L. Marthaler, "Catechesis and Theology," in *Proceedings of The Catholic Theological Society of America* XXVIII (June, 1973), pp. 263–267.

Any attempt to remove intrinsic religious instruction norms from the work of religious instruction and to subsequently replace these intrinsic norms with theological norms not only results in the extinction of religious instruction as a separate ontic entity but also eventuates in the noxiously straight-jacketed effects of *theological particularism*. Thus Michael Warren can openly declare that all religious instruction practice "must be based on adequate theology."[77] But what is "adequate theology"? In the end, the norm of "adequate theology" comes down to "my denomination's particular theology" and even to "my own personal particular theology." Religious instruction is no less destroyed by such theological particularism than religious psychology would be liquidated if theology were to serve as the intrinsic norm governing the practice of religious counseling. Randolph Crump Miller can assert that the view of revelation with its theory of knowledge "determines" the choice of religious instruction procedures and substantive content.[78] But whose view of revelation is the authentic one? And who will determine which is the correct theory of revelational knowledge? In the end, the norm of one's view of revelation and its knowledge comes down to "my denomination's particular theology" or "my own personal particular theology." Religious instruction is no less destroyed by such theological particularism than religious literature would be destroyed were theology to serve as the intrinsic norm governing the practice of writing a religious novel. Perhaps nowhere is the inevitable result of making theology intrinsically normative for religious instruction more graphically illustrated than in Françoise Darcy-Bérubé's particularistic statement cited earlier in my essay to the effect that certain religious instruction practices used by Billy Graham are *for her* "unacceptable from a theological standpoint because they are manipulative."[79]

Do theology's norms have any place in religious instruction qua religious instruction? My answer to this question is "yes." Theology

77. Michael Warren, "All Contributions Cheerfully Accepted," in *Living Light* VII (Winter, 1970), p. 31.
78. Randolph Crump Miller, *Education for Christian Living,* 2d edition (Englewood Cliffs, New Jersey: Prentice-Hall, 1963), p. 5.
79. Françoise Darcy-Bérubé, "The Challenge Ahead of Us," p. 118.

presents—not imposes—its norms to religious instruction in two important ways. First, as a recurring dimension of the substantive content of religious instruction, theological norms enter into religious instruction activity from the outset. To be sure, religious instruction as mediator changes these theological norms into religious instruction norms; but still, the theological norms do exert an influence in the mediational formation of religious instruction norms. Second, theology presents relevant theological norms to religious instruction from outside religious instruction activity. Religious instruction is then free to utilize these theological norms on religious instruction's own terms in whatever way is helpful for enriching religious instruction activity.

Efforts at bifurcating reality into "religious" on the one hand and "secular" on the other represents attempts to establish one theological position as the norm for the interpretation of reality. There is a second theological position which asserts that such a bifurcation is theologically incorrect, and that "religious" and "secular" are simply logical constructs which may not legitimately be reified. In this more expansive view, all reality is religious because all reality was created by God and is in the process of being continuously renewed in this creation by God. Viewed from this perspective, some realities are more focused and/or freighted with God's participatory with-dwelling than others. Such realities are labeled "religious" because of the prominence and salience of their religious dimension. There is a body of social-scientific evidence which externally supports the second theological position. *Thus there is no empirical evidence which suggests that religious learning is founded on different psychological principles and proceeds according to different psychological axes than the principles and axes of all other kinds of learning. There is no empirical evidence which suggests that religious instruction is founded on different pedagogical principles and proceeds according to different pedagogical axes than the principles and axes of all other kinds of instruction. There is no empirical evidence which suggests that the basic causes of the effectiveness or ineffectiveness of a pedagogical procedure in religious instruction are any different from the basic causes of the effectiveness or ineffectiveness of pedagogical practice in general instruction.*

Flowing from what was just adduced in the previous paragraph, it may be legitimately asserted that the claim that general instruction is "secular" and that only Christian instruction is "religious" is just as ridiculous as the claim that general dentistry is "secular" and that only dentistry performed in a Christian spirit by a Christian dentist on a Christian patient is "religious."

If one can legitimately warn religious instruction against the grave dangers of using the principles and procedures of general or "secular" instruction, then should not one also be able to legitimately warn theology against the grave dangers of using general or "secular" principles and practices of logic and philosophy and linguistics in the work of theology itself?

I find it self-contradictory and indeed comical that among those Christian church leaders and religious educators who stoutly insist that every Christian should experience religious instruction as a necessary part of one's general instruction there are some individuals who simultaneously denounce the fact that Christian religious educators typically employ the pedagogical procedures and theories of general instruction. It is well known that those highly successful church leaders and religious educators who are the most strident in their condemnation of the dependence of Christian religious instruction on other forms of general instruction are the very same individuals who make the most conscious and extensive use of the pedagogical procedures and theories of that general instruction which they so vehemently denounce.[80] What I am asserting, then,

---

80. While this statement holds especially true for evangelical and fundamentalist preachers and religious educationists, it is also valid for certain Catholic and mainline Protestant religious educationists. Thus, for example, John Westerhoff denounces the dependence of religious instruction on general instruction, developmental psychology, and social science. Yet the religious instruction programs he devises and the pedagogical procedures he advocates are typically based on or taken from general instruction, developmental psychology, and social science. To be sure, Westerhoff uses the social-science construct of socialization as the fundamental theoretical matrix out of which he devises programs and practices in religious instruction. See, for example, John H. Westerhoff III, *Tomorrow's Church* (Waco, Texas: Word, 1976), pp. 97–128 (in this selection Westerhoff also staunchly advocates launching a religious instruction program which incor-

is that *religious instruction uses the same theories, laws, concepts, and procedures which apply to all general instruction precisely because it is an indispensable and inextricable aspect of general instruction.* For a long time now, the entire field of general instruction, with the solitary exception of religious instruction, has been governed by the social-science approach. Is it not time for religious instruction to catch up with the rest of general instruction, and to adopt that approach which lies at the bottom of the advances made in other areas of general instruction—advances which religious instruction often ends up borrowing anyway? Why must religious instruction always be left behind? Why must religious instruction be isolated from its ecological source and wellspring? Simple observation of any religious instruction endeavor will confirm the fact that effective religion teachers are those who consciously or unconsciously use the theories and the procedures of the social-science approach. Therefore why not wholeheartedly and consciously embrace the social-science approach with its theories and laws and procedures so that the entire field of religious instruction of a broad front may take a major step forward?

The Language of Religious Instruction

Because religious instruction is a mediated reality and enjoys ontic autonomy from theology, its proper language must be that of religious instruction and not that of theology. Indeed, the proper language of

porates behavioral objectives, though he elsewhere denounces behavioral objectives); John H. Westerhoff III, *Will Our Children Have Faith?*, pp. 104–126; John H. Westerhoff III, "How Can We Teach Values?" in John H. Westerhoff III, editor, *How Can We Teach Values?* (Philadelphia: United Church Board for Homeland Ministries, 1969), pp. 1–5; John H. Westerhoff III, "The Visionary: Planning for the Future," in John H. Westerhoff III, editor, *A Colloquy on Christian Education* (Philadelphia: United Church Press, 1972), pp. 236–245; John H. Westerhoff III and Joseph C. Williamson, *Learning to be Free* (Philadelphia: United Church Press, 1972); John Westerhoff III, *Difference: Planning for the Future* (student workbook and teacher's manual) (Washington DC: National Education Association, 1976); John H. Westerhoff III, *Values for Tommorrow's Children* (Philadelphia: Pilgrim, 1970), pp. 80–99.

religious instruction must necessarily reflect (1) the substantive content and the structural content of religious instruction as mediator, and (2) the ground and medium of religious instruction. Hence the proper language of religious instruction is not theological language, but rather that kind of religious instruction language which is religious, instructional, and social-scientific in denotation, connotation, tone, and overall reference.

Religious language is basically different and distinct from theological language. Unhappily this distinction is insufficiently recognized by Christian religious educationists. Religious language is that set of linguistic symbols used in man's verbal encounters with God in his manifestations, or in linguistically reliving, refeeling, or reflecting upon these encounters. Theological language is that set of linguistic symbols employed in the cognitive, scientific reflection about God and his workings in the world. As Valerio Tonini perceptively states, "religious language and theological language are a complementary duality resembling the duality between 'communication' and 'information.' " Tonini further asserts that "religious language is essentially a normative language while theological language is essentially a predicative language."[81] Religious language sometimes makes use of theological language in its own way and for its own purposes, but theological language draws upon and receives considerable sustenance from religious language. Religious language is verbal behavior *to or with* God as he is in one or more of his manifestations. Theological language is verbal behavior *about* God. Because of its existential character, there is a strong tendency for religious language to be intensely subjective and personalistic. Due to its cognitive and scientific character, there is the strong tendency for theological language to be objective and impersonal. Religious language is often deeply affective, sensuous, metaphoric, and allegoric. Theological language, on the contrary, tends to eschew

81. Valerio Tonini, "Commentaire," dans Stanilas Breton, redacteur, "Langage religieux, langage théologique," dans Enrico Castelli, redacteur, *Débats sur le langage théologique* (Paris: Aubier, 1969), pp. 127–128, translation mine. I regard the Tonini article as one of the finest contributions available on the relationship between religious language and theological language.

affect, sensuousness, and allegory because these forms of language are ill-suited to the precision necessary for a careful cognitive science like theology.[82] Religious language, like religion itself, is basically personal. Theological language, like theology itself, is basically propositional. *Because religious instruction, as its name suggests, is first and foremost both religious and instructional, the language used by the educator and the learners in the religious instruction act as well as by religious instruction scholars examining this act ought to be first and foremost religious language and instructional language.*[83] Theological language, sports language, political language, ecclesiastical language, and the like should be employed only in a manner and to the extent that they broaden and deepen the religious language and the instructional language used in the pedagogical situation.

82. Some Christian interpreters of the Bible, notably those who take a literalist and/or fundamentalist hermeneutical stance, make the basic error of failing to appreciate that the Bible for the most part was written in religious language and not in theological language. These well-intentioned but poorly-informed individuals try to make a literal propositional theological interpretation of a biblical language which for the most part is existentially religious. For example, metaphor and allegory lose much of their deep religious meaning and significance when a person attempts to directly cast these linguistic forms into a ratiocinative, lexical theological language. Adequate biblical interpretation demands that religious language be approached and interpreted from within the framework of religious language. Only in this way will the authentic meaning of the text be made accessible to subsequent and derivative theological interpretation.

83. For a nice illustration of how persons in religious instruction can make fruitful use of religious language and instructional language in the work of religious instruction, see Maria Harris, "Word, Sacrament, Prophecy," in Padraic O'Hare, editor, *Tradition and Transformation in Religious Education* (Birmingham, Alabama: Religious Education Press, 1979), pp. 35–57. *Religious educationists and other kinds of commentators on religious instruction often are so cemented in their presumption that the language of religious instruction must be theological that they frequently fail to appreciate and even brand as alien any attempt to bring the language of religion into the center of religious instruction discourse.* Dwayne Huebner's negative comments on the religious, nontheological language of Harris's essay amply illustrate this point. See Dwayne Huebner, "The Language of Religious Education," in ibid., pp. 107–109. Huebner is probably correct, though, when he states that Harris's religious language would not resonate well with other religious educationists, educationists whose language of religious instruction is usually theological. Predictably, Huebner sides with the theological camp in this matter.

The language of instruction is basically different from the language of theology. The language of instruction describes the pedagogical interaction which takes place in religious instruction endeavor, and prescribes pedagogical practice on the basis of how the interactions represent instances of instructional laws. The language of theology describes the activities of God and prescribes theological propositions on the basis of how God's activities represent instances of theological laws.[84] Instructional language and theological language, then, are rooted in two entirely different perspectives on reality and reflect two entirely different sets of theories, laws, facts, and concepts. Theological language is competent and appropriate to adequately describe a theological view of reality and to prescribe theological propositions on the basis of this view. But theological language is incompetent and inappropriate to adequately describe an instructional view of reality, as, for example, the instructional effectiveness of teaching technique x or the instructional impact of pedagogical environment y.

The language of social science is essentially different from the language of theology for basically the same reasons that instructional language differs from theological language. Social science and theology look at reality from quite different perspectives; their respective languages reflect this fundamental difference. Also, social-scientific theories, laws. facts, and concepts are of a fundamentally different genre than theological theories, laws, facts, and concepts.

The basic issue which I am highlighting in this section is not so much the language of religious instruction simply qua language, but more significantly the language of religious instruction as indicative of the proper source and proper control of the field. Language is a verbal symbol which points to some particular reality. Furthermore, language is an authentic content in its own right and not simply the bearer of some other content. Thus language serves as a

---

84. These theological laws are grounded in the Bible, in general revelation, in tradition, and in official ecclesiastical pronouncements as all these are interpreted by theological theory. *Theological theory thus belongs to a different order of reality than do ecclesiastical pronouncements of prescribed propositions and doctrines. It is for this reason and in this sense that theology enjoys autonomy from official ecclesiastical mandates.*

double source of control because it both points to and embodies a particular content. If the language of religious instruction is theological, then it both points to theology as the proper controlling ecology of religious instruction and also to a certain extent forces religious instruction to be conceptualized in theological terms. But if, on the other hand, the language of religious instruction is religious instructional, then such a language points to religious instruction as the proper controlling ecology of religious instruction and also to a certain extent forces religious instruction to be conceptualized in religious instructional terms. Thus it is quite understandable that theological imperialists, especially those of a positivistic cast, vigorously reject the specific language of religious instruction used by others[85] and by myself.[86] Theological imperialists, of course, insist on using theological language to describe and prescribe religious instruction endeavor because they wish

85. See, for example, Marie McIntyre, "Review," in *Review of Books and Religion* V (Mid-March, 1976), p. 6. In this review of Harold William Burgess's *An Invitation to Religious Education*, McIntyre stated that she could readily understand Burgess's chapters on various theological approaches to religious instruction but could in no way understand his chapter on the social-science approach. McIntyre's ease with theological language and her difficulty with religious instructional language can probably be accounted for largely because she regards religious instruction as a form and branch of theology rather than as an ontically autonomous entity. Hence McIntyre is at home and conversant with theological language but neither at home nor conversant with religious instructional language.

86. Françoise Darcy-Bérubé, for example, states that she and many other religious educators are not accustomed to my religious instruction vocabulary, do not understand it fully, and therefore may feel vaguely threatened by it. She rejects my religious instruction language because it is religious instructional and social-scientific rather than theological. To be sure, my linguistic failure is even worse from Darcy-Bérubé's perspective because I do not use her own particularistic Roman Catholic brand of theological language in place of religious instruction language. (I pass over Darcy-Bérubé's signal error in labeling my language "behaviorist." Anyone even vaguely familiar with behaviorism or with my religious instruction language and theory will instantly recognize that I certainly am not a behaviorist. That Darcy-Bérubé would commit so elemental an error is interesting since she represents herself as a psychologist of religious development.) Françoise Darcy-Bérubé, "The Challenge Ahead of Us," p. 112.

theology to control religious instruction at every turn. Theological imperialists are typically unwilling to concede that theology looks at reality from only one perspective, and that theological language is therefore restricted to verbalizing that one perspective.[87] For these individuals, every single reality is ultimately determined by theology because they contend that everything is quintessentially freighted with theological content and theological meaning. In this view, theology is fundamentally descriptive and prescriptive and normative for each and every kind of reality. Darcy-Bérubé champions this position. Consequently in her mind theology "inspires and shapes" both the learning outcomes and indeed the very pedagogical processes used in religious instruction. She probably would assert the same thing about dentistry, engineering, farming, and the like.[88] The fatal flaw in the imperialistic claim for theology's total and intrinsic seigniory over all areas of reality is this claim's abject failure to realize that *theology provides only a theological description of any particular reality and not a description of the nature and workings of that particular reality as it is in itself. Theology only provides valid knowledge from its own perspective, and not from other perspectives.*[89] Theological imperialists throughout history seem to have been especially prone to equate the theological perspective with all perspectives, and to use theological language to describe and prescribe the

87. Helmut Thielicke's pregnant words further remind us of the severe limitations inherent even in the one perspective that is theological language when he observes that "theology is always an undertaking of fallen man. The sinfulness of man finds expression in the given structural realities of his functions of thought. This does not mean, of course, that it is better not to attempt a theological examination of faith, thereby safeguarding faith against [conceptual and linguistic] refraction. Faith's claim to the whole man entails a claim to his acts of thought. The only point is that *theology is not a sacred affair. It needs forgiveness in the same way as all else that man does.*" Helmut Thielicke, *The Evangelical Faith*, volume II, p. 4, italics added.

88. Françoise Darcy-Bérubé, "The Challenge Ahead of Us," p. 118.

89. *The distinguished Protestant theologian Emil Brunner declares that even within its own perspective, theological knowledge is essentially reactive rather than proactive. For Brunner, "the function of theology is to criticize and eliminate; it is not positively creative."* Emil Brunner, *The Mediator*, pp. 14–15, italics added.

nature and workings of every single kind of reality. The Galileo fiasco is a graphic illustration of my point.[90]

When religious instruction is clothed in theological language rather than in religious instructional language, there is a marked tendency for religious instruction to be conceptualized and operationalized in theologically particularistic terms. Now, most of theological particularism directly arises from and directly flows back into a particular ecclesiastical system, that is to say a particular church institution. To be sure, theological particularists in the field of religious instruction typically conceptualize theology exclusively from within the parameters of their own particular denomination. Françoise Darcy-Bérubé, for example, explicitly defines theology for her purposes as "a critical reflection on the Tradition of the Church." There is no doubt that by "the Church" Darcy-Bérubé unequivocally means the Roman Catholic Church.[91] Berard Marthaler reflects the imperialism inherent in theological particularism when he unflinchingly declares that in all of religious education, theology serves as the "systematic and critical reflection on the experience of a particular religious tradition or church community."[92]

Theological particularism as both the conceptualization and the language of religious instruction results in three noxious consequences for the theory and the practice of religious instruction. First, it imperialistically destroys the ontic autonomy of religious instruction. Second, it precludes any real possibility for genuine ecumenical religious instruction. If religious instruction is ontically defined and linguistically described solely in terms of one particular denomination's stance, then such a definition and description inherently forbids the infusion of nonparticularistic views from entering the theory or practice of religious instruction. Nor can members of

90. It is interesting to note that as of the date in which this present essay was written (1981), the Roman Catholic Church still has not officially retracted its theological judgment of Galileo's writings on natural science.

91. Françoise Darcy-Bérubé, "The Challenge Ahead of Us," p. 117.

92. Berard L. Marthaler, "A Discipline in Quest of an Identity: Religious Education," in *Horizons* III (Fall, 1976), p. 212.

one denomination teach or be otherwise involved in the religious instruction work of another denomination. What necessarily ensues from such a sorry state of affairs is stultification of religious instruction theory and asphyxiation of religious instruction practice all along the line.

Theological particularism almost inevitably introduces external political control over religious instruction, namely political control by the ecclesiasticum.[93] The logic of theological particularists such as Berard Marthaler is simple, clear, and inexorable. For him, faith is validly experienced, authentically lived, and properly interpreted only in and through theology. In his view, theology does not operate either in a vacuum or in general, but only in some particular ecclesiastical community. Therefore, faith and the way it is communicated must flow from and must be validated by a particular ecclesiastical community. A perusal of Marthaler's writings clearly shows that he unambiguously regards genuine theology and therefore genuine religious instruction[94] as that which is authentically proposed and interpreted by the official Catholic magisterium in its formal documents.

The conceptualization and language of religious instruction becomes hopelessly politicized when the field is determined by theology as this theology is interpreted authoritatively by the ecclesiastical officials of a particular denomination. *Ecclesiastical control and concomitant politicization is destructive of genuine theory and practice in religious instruction.* In ecclesiastical politicization, the supreme criterion for the acceptance of one or another religious instruction theory or practice does not flow from the nature and function of religious instruction activity itself, but rather on the degree to

93. The *ecclesiasticum* is the denomination's institutional form and political apparatus, while the *ecclesia* is the worshiping and praying and fellowshiping community.

94. "Catechesis" and "catechetics" comprise his preferred teminology—a terminology which emphasizes the point I am making here. Catechesis/catechetics is, of course, that branch of religious education whose foundations, goals, content, personnel, and legitimacy are authoritatively determined by and are politically controlled by the official Roman Catholic *ecclesiasticum*.

which the theory and practice reflect overall official ecclesiastical policy and are couched in ecclesiastical language. The ecclesiastical politicization of religious instruction inevitably leads to the enthronement of officially-sanctioned religious instruction theories and practices, and the concomitant condemnation of those theories and practices falling outside official policy.[95] Those religious instruction theorists and practitioners inside the denomination whose views and activities do not concur with the official ecclesiastical line are isolated, ostracized, banned, or exiled. Those religious instruction theorists and practitioners outside the denomination are automatically denied a hearing unless their views coincidentally conform to official ecclesiastical policy or unless their views have been sufficiently laundered so as to be rendered acceptable to official policy. Ecclesiastical control of religious instruction leads to the punishment of those theorists and practitioners who look to the intrinsic nature and functioning of religious instruction activity itself as the source and baseline of their theories and practice. Conversely, ecclesiastical control of religious instruction leads to the rewarding of those theorists and practitioners who become sycophants and toadies of the ecclesiastical establishment.

THE HOLY SPIRIT

No essay or book on religious instruction seems to be complete without some express mention made of the Holy Spirit. The issue of the role of the Holy Spirit in religious instruction is essentially a simple one, though it has been rendered unnecessarily complicated by the obfuscatory and mystificational comments made by many contemporary writers in the field.

95. In a particularly insightful article, Gabriel Moran notes that the ecclesiasticalization of the church typically leads dissidents from within and opponents from without to frequently employ anti-ecclesiastical language in linguistically framing their positions. Gabriel Moran, "Two Languages of Religious Education," in *Living Light* XIV (Spring, 1977), pp. 7–15.

Most proponents of the theological approach to religious instruction needlessly befog religious instruction endeavor by claiming that the Holy Spirit is not only the ultimate cause of religious instruction activity but the single proximate cause as well. In this hypothesis, religious instruction is regarded as basically a mysterious affair in which the Holy Spirit proximately brings about religious learning single-handed. The best the religious educator can do is lead the learner to the threshold of learning, whereupon the Holy Spirit will take over and do the real job of teaching—or not do it, depending on the Spirit's pleasure.

It is quite easy to remand this hypothesis to the logical rubbish heap from whence it originates. After all, this hypothesis is nothing more than a gratuitous statement. Any statement which is gratuitously asserted can be gratuitously denied just as easily and just as validly. To be sure, the very nature of the Spirit hypothesis intrinsically prevents its proponents from adducing any logical support for it. After all, if the Holy Spirit's activity is wholly mysterious and unfathomable, then there is absolutely no way for the advocates of the Spirit hypothesis to ascertain even in the slightest degree whether or how the Spirit is acting in (or not acting in, or even involved with) religious instruction activity.[96]

Even though the Spirit hypothesis is logically untenable and existentially unworkable, I will briefly deal with it because it is so widely invoked in the field and because it directly bears on a primary axis of my essay.

In the final analysis, *the Spirit hypothesis represents the ultimate breakdown of the theological macrotheory of religious instruction.* The

---

96. An appeal to the knowledge born of religious faith fails to resolve this problem because this kind of faith itself is not indiscriminate. Religious faith deals only with trust in and assent to realities authentically revealed by God in the Bible, and for some Christian denominations in tradition, in sacrament, and in everyday human experience. There is no clear evidence that either scripture or tradition or sacrament or everyday human experience specifies that the Holy Spirit is the sole or even the primary proximate cause of effective religious instruction. If religious faith were indiscriminate, then every sort of hokum would be able to be declared factually true because one has religious faith in that hokum.

prime purpose of any macrotheory or theory is to explain and predict and verify the phenomena under its purview. But the advocates of the theological macrotheory claim that their theory is unable to explain or predict of verify religious teaching-learning activity because this kind of activity is the mysterious and unfathomable work of the Holy Spirit. In effect, the advocates of the theological macrotheory are forced to drag the Holy Spirit in by the heels in order to provide that explanation and prediction and verification which the theological macrotheory itself should be able to provide were this macrotheory adequate and valid.

The consequences of the Spirit hypothesis are destructive of virtually all phases and dimensions of religious instruction theory and practice. The Spirit hypothesis renders religious instruction activity totally unworkable because this hypothesis posits such activity to be utterly mysterious and unfathomable.[97] It is, of course, manifestly impossible to plan or implement an activity whose foundations and operations are utterly mysterious and unfathomable. The Spirit hypothesis also leads to a radical distrust of the Spirit's continuous working in the world. Advocates of the theological macrotheory seem to drag the Holy Spirit into religious instruction endeavor by the heels because they apparently do not really trust him to effectively do his work from the withinness of the world which he has made and pervades in his immanence. Finally, the Spirit hypothesis leads to patently ridiculous consequences. For example, if it is indeed the Holy Spirit and not the teaching-learning process which proximately brings about desired instructional outcomes, then the religious educator is really grading the Holy Spirit when he assigns marks to the learners at school or makes rough evaluations of the learner at home.

A clear indication that no one—including the advocates of the theological approach to religious instruction—really believes in the Spirit hypothesis is the fact that no one actually seems to operate on this hypothesis. Proponents

---

97. For an adamant advocacy of religious instruction endeavor as basically unexplainable and totally unpredictable in its foundations and processes, see Françoise Darby-Bérubé, "The Challenge Ahead of Us," pp. 116–119, 153.

of the theological approach verbalize their wholehearted belief in the Spirit hypothesis and then proceed to devise programs and propose pedagogical procedures which are totally at variance with the Spirit hypothesis. There almost seems to be an unwritten law that the more loudly and passionately a religious educationist or educator proclaims adherence to the Spirit hypothesis, the more carefully and systematically that person consciously structures the religion program or lesson to deliberatively facilitate the desired outcomes. [98]

A fundamental weakness of the Spirit hypothesis is its implicit and explicit reliance on the Spirit-as-variable fallacy.[99] This fallacy states that religious instruction can in no way be adequately explained, predicted, or verified by any human theory because the Holy Spirit is a fundamental *variable* in all religious instruction activity. The reason why the Spirit-as-variable fallacy is a fallacy, and indeed a fallacy of major proportions, is twofold. First, God is God; therefore he is the ground of all reality and not simply a variable operating in or on reality. This last statement is not only good philosophical theology, but also has been affirmed again and

98. Françoise Darcy-Bérubé is an example of this. Though she is an uncompromising proponent of the utter unexplainability and absolute unpredictability of religious instruction due to the totally free action of the completely unfathomable Spirit, the religious instruction curricula she has authored are carefully and systematically structured in such a way as to make religious instruction as explainable and as predictable as possible. The careful sequencing of concepts, the systematic employment of language to match the age-level and concepts involved, the deliberate use of judiciously selected examples, the ordered selection of pictorial representations—all these and more show that Bérubé is trying hard to make religious instruction activity optimally explainable and predictable. She has even prepared both a parent's guide and a director's guide to her curricula. These guides provide specific cognitive, affective, psychomotor, and conduct instructions to the parents and directors so that these religious educators will be able to deliberately heighten the effectiveness of the instruction they furnish when using Darcy-Bérubé's curricula. Reviewing curricula such as these, one can only wonder whatever happened to Darcy-Bérubé's pivotal hypothesis that the Spirit works in a totally unexplainable and unpredictable way in religious instruction endeavor.

99. Few religious educationists have more clearly articulated and more ardently advocated this fallacy than Françoise Darcy-Bérubé. See Françoise Darcy-Bérubé, "The Challenge Ahead of Us," p. 116.

again throughout the entire Christian tradition. Second, if the Spirit is indeed simply a variable, then there is absolutely no way in which anyone can ascertain *whether* this variable is present or *how* this variable is present unless this variable is somehow made observable. Once the fact and the manner of this variable's presence is ascertained, then the Spirit hypothesis itself vanishes because social science by definition and comprehension is able to explain and predict and verify the relevant observables in religious instruction activity.

The Spirit-as-variable fallacy represents a flat rejection of the natural law in any form, and ultimately reduces all human activity including religious instruction to a nihilistic and spooky affair. Yet all science (including theological science) and all human activity (including religious instruction activity) is heavily dependent upon the natural law.[100] The natural law bids religious educationists and educators to look to the inherently explainable and predictable and verifiable workings of the world as a fruitful source and benchmark for understanding and operationalizing our activities here on earth. An inference which may be legitimately drawn from the natural law is that if God truly exists and is operative in the world, then his existence and operations here on earth occur in conjunction with the natural law and not against it. It would seem repugnant to God's nature and intelligence to suppose that he works against rather than in and with the nature he created and continues to create through his presence and power and existence in all reality. Teaching and learning are not inexplicable miracles magically wrought by

100. By "natural law" I do not mean highly specific absolutized imperatives emanating mechanistically from the nature of a reality, but rather a definite course of growth and development which tends to ensue from the inherent structure and flow of a particular reality as this reality interacts with other realities. Natural law thus describes the basic structure and processive unfolding of a particular reality according to the dynamics of that reality's own exigencies and interactive functioning. Necessarily implied by natural law is that reality can be explained and predicted and verified by ascertaining its nature and interactions, charting its functions, and then devising a theory on the basis of what was ascertained and charted.

proximate zaps of the Holy Spirit.[101] If there is any miracle involved in the teaching-learning process, it is that God has magnificently designed the nature and functioning of all reality in such a way that reality is inherently amenable to human explanation, prediction, and verification on its own terms. One of the quintessential miracles in the universe is the way in which God has deliberately chosen to work in the world so that by explaining and predicting and verifying reality, we are equipped to fulfill the biblical mandate of mastering the world (Gn. 1:28).

101. For a brief treatment of the zap "theory" in religious instruction, see James Michael Lee, "Toward a New Era: A Blueprint for Positive Action," in James Michael Lee, editor, *The Religious Education We Need,* pp. 130–131.

Chapter 6

Experiencing Reality Together: Toward the Impossible Dream

LAWRENCE O. RICHARDS

The Man of LaMancha portrays Don Quixote as something more than a madman who tilts with windmills. He is a man possessed by an impossible dream. Rejecting the values of his day, he sets out to create a separate reality. In the process he confronts issues that are basic to Christian theology. He meets an unnamed woman, who describes herself as

> born on a dung heap,
> to die on a dung heap,
> a strumpet men use
> and forget.

But Don Quixote rejects this perception, even though it is brutally demonstrated by her history, and in her rape and ridicule as "little bird." Don Quixote calls her by a new name, Dulcinaea. His gentle madness ultimately robs her of her one defense: hatred.

But then Don Quixote is confronted with the forgotten reality about himself, reflected in a mirror held up to him by priests engaged by his embarrassed family. Crushed by what he sees, Quixote falls into despair. But before he dies he is snatched back from that despair by the appearance of Dulcinaea, who has come to accept Don Quixote's image of her, and who calls him back to his impossible dream.

Like Don Quixote, we Christians are called to a reality which is at odds with the values and perceptions of our society. It is even in painful conflict with our own experience. We know too well the dark tangled shapes of individuals and society, but still affirm the worth of every person, the hope of justice, and the love of God. We persist in inviting others to surrender their old self-perceptions and, in Christ, to take on a fresh identity—to be reconciled, redeemed, and renewed. In spite of disappointments, and the failures that mirror our own imperfection, we continue to affirm the impossible dream of a community of faith which expresses Christ's own kingdom: the enfleshing of Jesus in man's world.

The task of religious education is no less and no different than this basic calling of the church: to facilitate, in the context of community, the experience of a reality revealed by God.

REALITY REVEALED

Christianity, rooted deeply in the Old as well as New Testament, is a revealed religion. God, as the Christian understands him, is the One who made himself known to Abraham and entered into covenant relationship with him and his descendants. God is the one who further showed himself as Jahweh ("the one present with us"), and in the mighty acts of Exodus proved faithful to his covenant promises. God is the one who continued to speak through the prophets and finally, in the great unveiling, expressed himself in the person of Jesus of Nazareth. God, in Christ, sealed by death the prophesied New Covenant, extending to all the hope of redemption and release.

Looking back across the milleniums-long unveiling, the Apostle Paul quotes a pagan poet[1] and affirms that

> "No eye has seen,
> No ear has heard,

1. Traditionally this quote has been seen as a reference to Isaiah 64:6. However the quote itself, and its use by Paul in the argument of Corinthians, seem to correspond too well to a passage from Empedocles (5th century B.C.). The quote

No mind has conceived
what God has prepared for those who love him."

Yet this hidden knowledge "God has revealed to us by his Spirit"
(1 Cor. 2:10).

Paul's argument continues. While an individual's acts can be
observed, and thus we make our interpretations, what we see can
never be truly understood until the hidden thoughts and motives are
communicated by the individual himself. How much more so with
God. We can observe, and dream we know, but the shape of the
whole lies hidden from us. But now Paul affirms that the Spirit of
God, who knows him intimately, has revealed the inner workings of
his mind in words, and that Spirit has come to us as interpreter (1
Cor. 2:10–14). Thus the shape of the whole, over which Empedocles despaired, has been unveiled at last!

In this context "revelation" is neither exclusively personal [God's
revelation is self-revelation] nor is it exclusively propositional
[God's revelation is information]. Here revelation is the communication, through the medium of words, of a framework for perception of ourselves and the world.

Some years ago I took my sons fishing before dawn on a familiar
Arizona lake. We motored slowly along a black shoreline swallowed
up in the dark before a desert dawn. Then, unexpectedly, we were
lost! A strange bulking shadow loomed up on our right; a dark I
knew was not supposed to be there. Suddenly all sense of familiarity
was gone, and the shrouded lands and water were alien and frighten-
ing. Finally dawn spilled over the western cliffs, and I saw at last
where we were. I had missed a point of land, turned at the wrong
time, and completely lost my orientation. But with light every-

---

in its context reads: "Weak and narrow are the powers implanted in the limbs of
man; many the woes that fall on them and blunt the edges of thought; short is the
measure of the life in death through which they toil. Then are they borne away;
like smoke they vanish into air; and what they dream they know is but a little
that each hath stumbled upon in wandering about the world. Yet boast they all
that they have learned the whole. Vain fools! For what that is, no eye hath seen,
no ear hath heard, nor can it be conceived by the mind of man."

thing fell into place again. I recognized the landmarks, and with a cleared perspective on the whole, not only knew my way but found release from the fears that the dark strangeness of the lake had caused.

This is the picture Paul gives us of revelation. Man lives in a shrouded universe, cluttered with distorted shapes that men and cultures imagine as they struggle to make sense of life in their "wandering about the world." Scripture is God's light, brushing away the shadows of misunderstanding, and establishing the land-marks by which we are to order our lives.

This concept is in unique harmony with an affirmation both Old and New Testaments make about God's word. In both, Scripture is viewed as "truth."

Theologians, philosophers, and common man alike may debate the nature of truth. But the Hebrew and Greek terms are not that difficult to interpret.[2] The OT word, אֱמֶת, is regularly translated in the LXX by ἀλήθια ("truth"), while English versions sometimes render it "faithfulness." In the context of the OT we often would lean toward a rendering of faithfulness, in the sense of reliability. Whether used of God or man, a word of אֱמֶת is something on which others can rely. In the wisdom literature אֱמֶת tends to stand in contrast to deception or illusion. That which is true can be relied on, because it portrays reality in a reliable and not illusory way.

The New Testament term, ἀλήθεια, is not found in the NT in a philosophical as much as theological sense. There is in its common use in the gospels a strong contrast between truth and falsehood. In Paul there is a tendency to identify truth and revelation. John regularly uses ἀλήθεια to contrast with appearance or illusion. Yet in each there is a common element. Like the OT, the NT affirms that in the words of Scripture and the person of Jesus, God has given us a reliable and trustworthy portrait of reality. Here, the illusions

---

2. For an excellent discussion, see A. C. Thiselton's discussion in *Theologisches Begriffslexikon zum Neuen Testament,* edited by Lothar Coenen, Erich Beyreuther, and Hans Bietenhrd, published in 1971 by Theologischer Verlag Rolf Brock-haus. A 1979 English translation is available from Zondervan Publishers.

and the dark uncertainties under which humans labor are dissolved by dawning light.

By revelation we are at last able to discern who we are, and the true shape of the universe around us.

Implications for Christian Education

The understanding of Scripture as a revelation of reality gives direction to Christian education on several levels. On the level explored here it has an impact on the design of the teaching process and on the construction of curriculum.

We can illustrate the impact easily. If the Bible is seen primarily as a book of personal revelation, a contact point at which an individual may encounter God, then educational processes will be designed to faciliate contemporary revelational experiences. And the Bible will be used in ways which educators believe will help achieve that goal.

If the Bible is seen primarily as a book of propositional revelation, a source from which the individual may assemble and organize information about God, then educational processes will stress cognition. And the church will become the guardian of an orthodox belief system, transmitting in frozen creedal formulations ideas locked in seventeenth century categories.[3]

---

3. I do not intend here to deny essential harmony of creeds with Scripture. My point is simply that creeds, which attempt to arrive at truth by verbal definition, are less in harmony with the nature of Scripture than confessions, which affirm the great landmarks of historic faith without assuming to explain them once for all. A good example of a confessional expression of faith comes from Irenaeus around A.D. 190. It reads,

"The Church, though dispersed throughout the whole world, even to the ends of the earth, has received from the apostles and their disciples this faith: (She believes) in one God, the Father Almighty, maker of heaven, and earth, and the sea, and all things that are in them; and in one Christ Jesus, the Son of God, who became incarnate for our salvation; and in the Holy Spirit, who proclaimed through the prophets the dispensations of God, and the advents, and the birth from a virgin, and the passion, and the resurrection from the dead, and the ascension into heaven in the flesh of the beloved Christ Jesus, our Lord, and his (future) manifestation from heaven in the glory of the Father 'to gather all things

But if the Bible is perceived as a revelation of reality, an unveiling of the landmarks by which we can map our universe and chart our course in life, then educational processes must be designed to help persons orient themselves and commit themselves to the kind of world that God portrays.

The impact of our understanding of the nature of Scripture on educational process is matched by its impact on curriculum construction. We now ask: What are the great landmark themes which are to orient human experience? Here a confessional approach is significant. We do not define truth by focusing on differences or on details of biblical interpretation. Instead we seek to identify the great affirmations about God, and man, and life in the world, which recur in Scripture and which have been held in common by the church across the ages.

Landmark themes are not difficult to identify. A very short list, which all can easily expand, would include such affirmations as: God is forgiving. God is creator. God is just. God is faithful. And with these affirmations come others. Human beings are special, each created in the image of God. Sin has twisted individuals and society. And we might go on and on.

The point is that a Christian educator whose theology leads him to understand Scripture as a revelation of reality, will find in that theology direction both for the educational process he will shape,

---

in one,' and to raise up anew all flesh of the whole human race, in order that to Christ Jesus, our Lord, and God, and Savior, and King, according to the will of the invisible Father, 'every knee should bow, of things in heaven, and things in earth, and things under the earth, and that every tongue should confess' to him, and that he should execute just judgment towards all, that he may send 'spiritual wickedness' and the angels who transgressed and became apostates, together with the ungodly, and unrighteous, and wicked, and profane among men, into everlasting fire; but may, in the exercise of his grace, confer immortality on the righteous, and holy, and those who have kept his commandments, and have persevered in his love, some from the beginning (of their Christian course), and others from the date of their repentance, and may surround them with everlasting glory."

This translation can be found in *Against Herecies* I, XXVII, 1, and is quoted by Robert E. Webber in *Common Roots* (Zondervan, 1978), p. 123.

and for the curriculum he designs. The content, method, and goal of the educational enterprise will all be theologically determined.[4]

REALITY EXPERIENCED

For many, "truth" is something to be believed and faith is assent to orthodox formulations. But when we take "truth" in its biblical sense as reliable portrayal of reality, the notion that mere belief is an adequate response to truth is totally inadequate. Jesus expresses this clearly in a saying recorded by John, often snatched out of context and used on the masthead of one newspaper to imply that information can guarantee freedom. "If you continue in my words," John reports our Lord's saying, "you are really my disciples. Then you will know the truth, and the truth will set you free" (John 8:32).

The revelatory word is not to be merely heard, but "continued in." The truth is not to be learned, but "known." And in some way, knowing truth sets Jesus' disciples free.

The phrase "continue in my words" is μείνητε ἐν τῷ λογῷ τῷ ἐμῷ. The word "continue" (μένω) literally means "stay," in the sense of dwell or lodge. μένω is also used often in the NT in a figurative sense, of a realm or sphere of life in which one remains.

---

4. I might note that the way the Bible is used in the learning setting will also be dramatically affected by approaching it as a revelation of reality. Traditionally Scripture has been used in educational process as if it were simply the source of information to be taught. But the Bible does more than "teach," in a propositional sense, its landmark truths. Scripture also illustrates, as when a historical passage shows how a landmark theme has found expression in the life of an individual or community of God's people (cf. James 5:11). There is exemplary use, where historical passages demonstrate what happens when the landmarks are ignored and God's people wander off into illusion (cf. 1 Cor 10:6). And there is empathetic use of Scripture, where poetic or other passages invite us to share the inner experience of God or one of his people, to help us match emotions and responses to landmark revelations.

If we begin with a reality orientation to biblical revelation, we discover that these and other uses of Scripture in our learning settings move toward much greater freedom and creativity in teaching.

Thus a believer "remains in the teaching of Christ" (2 John 9) and "continues in what has been learned" (2 Tim. 3:14). The point here is not that disciples keep the words in mind, but that the words keep disciples within the borders of the sphere of life they mark out. The words are landmarks, to orient the one who abides among them to life.

The phrase "you shall know the truth" is γινώσεσθε τὴν ἀλήθειαν. It is commonly recognized that γιυώσκωas used in the NT shares the OT emphasis on intimate and personal acquaintance, gained through personal experience. While there are infrequent NT passages that use γιυώσκω and imply abstract theoretical knowledge (cf. Matt. 13:11; Luke 9:10), this is not typical. And γιυώσκω is used by John in a deeply relational sense, which stresses personal touch with reality.

The freedom promised by Jesus, then, can only be found through personal commitment to live the life marked out in his words, and thus experience the reality they portray.

The same theme is often stressed in gospels and epistles, and nowhere stated more clearly than in Jesus' story of wise and foolish builders:

> Therefore everyone who hears these words of mine and puts them into practice is like a wise man who built his house on the rock. The rain came down, and the streams rose, and the winds blew and beat against that house; yet it did not fall, because it had its foundation upon the rock. But everyone who hears these words of mine and does not put them into practice is like a foolish builder who builds his house on sand. The rain came down, the streams rose, and the winds blew and beat against the house, and it fell with a great crash (Matthew 7:24–27).

Implications for Christian Education

Christianity is a revealed religion. But its revelation makes unique claims, contending that it involves a divine unveiling, in human language, of essential reality. In living and written Word all illusory images of our universe are stripped away, and a perspective available nowhere else is provided.

Educational ministries must thus be designed which are in harmony with the essential nature of revelation. It is inadequate to see Christian education's task either in terms of stimulating encounter or transmitting information, although each of these may play a part in educational ministry. The overriding challenge to Christian education is to orient to reality, and call believers to a disciple's commitment to experience revealed truth.

I have already noted that this understanding of educational ministry has an impact on our choice of what we concentrate our teaching on (landmark themes), and on the way we use the Bible in teaching, as well as on the design of process. But as we move on to note that revealed reality must be experienced to be freeing, we see that theology has even greater implications for educational ministry. If the appropriate response to revelation is not assent, but action, educational processes must be designed to encourage action. If the Scriptures' words of revelation are to be dwelt among, to be practiced, and to be done, educational ministry must do more than simply make the words known. We are not called to show reality once removed, like a photograph or painting. We are called to lead learners to walk the broad land Scripture unveils.

One of the most serious difficulties in Christian education is to shift the level at which persons relate to Scripture from the cognitive to the personal and experiential. Even the multiplied illustrations and applications provided in preaching and teaching usually evoke little more than casual note, as though we had settled back for a time to watch with light interest some characters from a book or play before returning to our own real lives. Even when dealing with landmark themes, they all too soon seem hollowly isolated from life.

We are helped to break through the barriers when we realize that if Scripture *does* portray reality, then its landmark truths will impact on the life of every individual, and at every age. Even a child, who lacks the capacity to comprehend a biblical concept, will have the capacity to experience the reality revealed, on his or her own level.[5] The educator, then, has the task of understanding how the biblical reality touches the life of the learner, and of designing learning processes that help him or her explore the "lived meaning" of that truth.

We are familiar with the idea of a cognitive map. At this point I'd like to introduce the concept of a "life map," or perhaps more accurately, an "emotional map."

We are all bombarded daily by thousands of bits of information from many sources: radio, TV, books, magazines, newspapers, conversations, etc. Most of these data we ignore. Many of them we do not even "hear." But there are some we attend to, a few of those we attend to that we file, and even fewer still of those we file we are able to retrieve. Very seldom, unless we're engaged in some academic persuit, is this attending, filing, and retrieval keyed to the cognitive map. This is one reason why subjects taught in a school setting are so difficult to transfer to life situations. We can recall them when we are in the academic setting or being tested. But

---

5. This seems to me to suggest a practical answer to the dilemma posed by the work of Piaget and Kohlberg, which correctly demonstrates that many religious and moral ideas simply cannot be comprehended by those at lower levels of cognitive development. If Christian education were in fact an enterprise concerned with communicating concepts Ronald Goldman might be right: perhaps we should refrain from providing Christian teaching until learners are old enough not to misunderstand the ideas with which they are asked to deal. But Christian education, taking its direction from theology, is concerned with communicating reality. Since landmark truths of Scripture are in essence revelations of reality, then they should be open to the experience of individuals at every age.

While, for instance, no children (and few adults?) can fully grasp what a passage like Hebrews 9–10 shares about God's perception of forgiveness, still even very young children can experience the reality that forgiveness portrays, and begin to develop freedom to approach God confidently when pangs of guilt cry out "Hide!"

In essence, the Christian educator's task is to identify the life impact of the great realities revealed in Scripture, and then design learning experiences for those of every age that help him or her to experience the truth portrayed, always linking it to the biblical terminology. As the child grows his grasp of concepts will shift many times. Yet the reality expressed and experienced at every stage of development will be an anchor for both faith and life.

because there is no real link between the information and our life situations, the information is unavailable beyond the classroom setting. It's no wonder then that when Christian truths are taught with the trappings of the school that, no matter how solidly the map be inked on the individuals cognitive map, the truths are unavailable for, or perceived as irrelvant to, real life. This is true even when part of the data filed on that cognitive map includes specific behavior patterns!

The solution seems to demand recognition that, outside the classroom, a different mapping process is used. In that process, data is rejected or selected, filed or forgotten, retrieved or lost, on the basis of a different coding system. Thus the challenge, when dealing with Scripture as reality, is to link landmark truths to the life map in such a way that a truth is no longer perceived simply as information, but is integrated as a basic element of the individual's perception of and response to his life situations.

What I suggest is that the coding system by which items are filed on one's life map is essentially emotional; that emotions are not only critical in selecting what we attend to, but also provide the "pigeonholes" in which data is stored; and further that the experience of emotions is the key by which data is recalled.[6]

---

6. The argument might be made that no two individuals share a common life map. This is a strong argument if we assume that the map is formed by unique experiences. Then the orphan and the child from a happy home, the drunkard and the successful businessman, would have nothing in common. But the fact that the topography on one's life map is essentially emotional makes a great difference.

Two notes from Scripture are appropriate here. "No temptation has seized you except what is common to man," Paul notes in 1 Corinthians 10:13. And the writer to the Hebrews says of Jesus that he "has been tempted in every way, just as we are" (4:15). The point is not that Jesus has experienced every possible life situation. Our Lord was never a mother, watching her child die. Or an invalid, stretched out for years on a helpless bed. But the agonizing sense of loss the mother knows, the frustrating sense of helplessness known by the invalid, the pull of desire, the sudden surge of joy, are known to some extent by all of us. The experiences that tap these emotions will vary. But the range of response will be common, for these are common to all humankind.

Thus when biblical realities are located on the life map they are not related to *situations*, but to the emotional topography on which various situations rest. Thus

Thus the Christian educator, in designing learning situations, must use processes which help learners locate the landmark themes of Christian faith on their own life maps, believing that when one finds himself in a situation to which that reality applies, the emotions stimulated will trigger recall of truth and make possible a disciple's response.

An illustration may be appropriate here. In teaching a unit on justice, rooted in the landmark truth that "God is just," our sessions with primary and junior age children began with a game. The boys and girls were divided into two teams, and organized in lines. A long word was written twice on a chalkboard, and the children invited to have an eraser race. The first team was instructed to run to the board, erase one letter from the word on the left, run back and give the eraser to the next child in line, and "see who wins." The other team was instructed to run to the board and erase *two* letters from the word on the right.

The first pair dashed to the board, and immediately cries were heard from the first team. "He did two letters!" "That's no fair!"

After talking briefly and letting the children express their anger, the game was begun again, with each team allowed to erase two letters. But now the second team was lined up several feet closer to the chalkboard than the first! After a very few minutes we had a group of children who were intensely concerned with justice!

Working through the rest of that unit, and exploring justice in our relationships with God, home, school, and community, it was possible to deal in a vital way with what the Bible means when it affirms that God is just, and that his people are to share his own commitment to "do justice." It was possible, because the justice landmark truth had been firmly located on the emotional, and thus the experience, map of the boys and girls.

---

too the importance of helping believers build their perception of biblical realities on the slopes and valleys marked on the emotional map that is to some extent common to all. Anchored there, God's truths do serve as landmarks. The details of the individual's life will differ. But the basic challenges that face each of us, and the guidance found in unveiled reality, are common to us all.

For younger learners it is often necessary to design an actual experience to enable them to locate on their own emotional maps the reality with which a landmark Bible truth deals. With older learners, it is possible to use recall. But it is vital that the process not halt with the discussion of personal experiences or situations, but probe beneath them to seat the foundation of the learning to take place on the common emotional location even those with different situations will recognize.

It should be clear by now that theology holds even greater implications for Christian education than we observed in the first section of this chapter. There we saw that theology points us to the landmark truths that are to be taught, warns us against a transmissive approach that would treat Scripture as information, and suggests that learning processes must be found to communicate the Christian revelation as an unveiling of reality.

In this section we've noted that the reality which Scripture unveils must be experienced to be known. Thus Christian education is called to the making of disciples, who will live the reality the words unveil. But linking words with life is a very different enterprise than constructing a belief system. In fact, the very schoolized approaches associated with secular and religious education may be counterproductive, when our goal is viewed in terms of life. It is theology, and not educational philosophy, which must rule Christian education, and if permitted to rule will force us to develop distinctive educational processes which shift our concentration from the cognitive mapping of verbalized truths to the emotional mapping of revealed realities, which must be linked to our personal perception of reality if they are to transform our lives.

REALITY EXPERIENCED TOGETHER

The Christian educator who views revelation as an unveiling of reality will find his approach to educational ministry dramatically affected. Several areas of impact have been noted in earlier sections. But one impact of this theological supposition has not yet been examined. The issue can be expressed this way: If Scripture is a source of landmark truths, which orient us to reality and give us a frame of reference by which to order our actions,[7] then we should seriously explore the Bible for landmarks which will shape our understanding of educational process.

We should not rely on traditional educational philosophy, or the latest approaches taken in the public schools, to guide us. We should not assume that because such approaches may be functional for the kind of teaching/learning the schools do that they will also be functional for the kind of teaching/learning the church is to do.

If we do explore Scripture for relevant landmark truths, we are immediately confronted by one theme which will serve to illustrate the impact of taking theology seriously in Christian education. That landmark can be summed up by affirming that revealed reality is to be experienced in community.

The NT is especially rich in the images and language of community. We can find many illustrations by turning to a single book, such as Ephesians, and noting its expressions of this dimension of revealed reality.

•Believers can find their shared identity, Ephesians 3:14 suggests, by seeing themselves as part of an extended family, founded on personal relationship with God as Father (cf. 2:19, 5:1). This image is the source of the extensive "brother/sister" terminology of the NT.

•Believers are linked in an intimate relationship, pictured by the human body and its members. In this new organic unity, old barriers of hostility are broken down and relationships of peace are

---

7. I might note that just this kind of reorientation of perceptions, involving values, attitudes, behaviors as well as beliefs, is what is meant in Romans when the Apostle says "do not conform any longer to the pattern of the world, but be transformed by the renewing of your mind (12:2). The phrase "renewing of your mind" (ἀυακαινώσει τοῦ νοῦδ) does not refer to the cognitive map or new information. The word νοῦδ (mind) is, as Arndt and Gingrich point out in *A Greek-English Lexicon of the New Testament,* University of Chicago Press, 1952, p. 456), a "way of thinking, as the sum total of the whole mental and moral state of being."

established (2:14–16). Within the body, which does have an essential unity (4:1–6), each individual is called to the service of other members (4:12). Through participation in mutual ministry by each member, the body of Christ is built up, leading to greater unity and to maturity (4:13). This growth is said to depend on the functioning of each part in the whole, as the community members nurture one another in a climate marked by love (4:15–16).

•Believers are a holy temple, being "built up together" to become the dwelling place of God (2:20–22).

•Much emphasis is placed on the lifestyle of members of the community (Ch. 4:17 - 6:9 particularly). Bitterness, rage, anger, and malice are to be replaced by a completely different set of responses to others, which are characterized as kindness, compassion, and a willingness to forgive that is modeled on the forgiveness extended to us in Christ (4:31–32). This reorientation of life and the specific behaviors which will express it is characterized in Ephesians, as in Romans, as "adopting a new attitude of mind" (4:23, cf. Rom. 12:2). That new attitude is in fact the shared perspective of the whole community, and transforms the individuals life in this world.

The Greek text of Ephesians 4:23 reads, "ἀνανεοῦσθαι δὲ τῷ πνεύματι τοῦ νοὸς ὑμῶν." Ἀνανεοῦσθαι is either a future passive or future middle (reflexive): "be renewed" or "renew yourselves." It is not used here to call back to what we once had, but to shape something new to replace the old. Τῷ πνεύματι, "the spirit," is used in a common sense of one's inner personality, while νοὸς, as in Romans 12, speaks of basic perception—that faculty by which one's world view and all related elements are laid, as a grid, over our experiences to interpret them. We might paraphrase the verse as does the NIV, or lay a slightly different stress which preserves shades of meaning: "Together, reorient your perception of your world." This paraphrase is awkward, but it does lift up one dimension seen in the Greek but lost in English. The verb, ἀνανεοῦσθαι, is distinctively plural, as are the nouns and adjectives. Paul is not speaking to individuals, nor is he speaking to an aggregation of individuals. His message is to a community of believers—to a family, a body, a building under construction. He calls them, together, to experience in community a transformation of outlook which will impact every dimension of their lives, touching and reshaping attitudes, values, feelings, beliefs, and behaviors.

In context, the images, teachings, and the very words used to explore Christian transformation, demand a community as context for renewal.

The emphasis on community as the context of transformation is not isolated to Ephesians, nor is it unique to the New Testament. Each NT report of the church gathering stresses an interpersonal, interactive process, in which teaching and learning are participated in by all, as life and gifts are generously shared. Hebrews portrays the gathered church "spurring one another on to love and good deeds," and describes the process as "encouraging one another" (10:24,25). Corinthians reports an assembly to be marked with ordered sharing, where "everyone has a hymn, or a word of instruction, a revelation, a tongue or an interpretation" which is offered "for the strengthening of the church" (14:26). Acts tells of the assembly of small groups that meet in homes to worship, fellowship, explore the meaning of the apostles' doctrine, pray and meet one another's needs (2:42–47; 4:32–35).

The OT emphasis on community is even more clear and striking. The law organized all of society to communicate a common vision of God and a common experience of covenant life. Annual festivals reenacted salvation history; ritual and liturgy affirmed a common faith; a single law informed social, religious, and political life, gently shaping the nation toward becoming a holy community. Within the broader community children were to be nurtured by parents who had taken God's words into their own hearts and who thus would be able to teach the words diligently, not as an isolated belief system, but as that which gave meaning to all of life while "sitting at home, walking along the road, lying down, and rising up" (Deut. 6:6–8; cf. 11:19–21).

Implications for Christian Education

It is compelling to see the wide range of biblical evidence which supports the concept that Christian education is intended to take place in community. There is no hint in OT or NT of reliance on school-like settings to communicate a faith which is not so much a system of belief as it is a framework within which to understand and experience reality. In the Scripture, communication of faith is a natural process; the socialization of children, and of adults introduced by conversion into the believing community. In the context of community the words of faith are lived, and the life of the community is understood in terms of the words of faith.

While the biblical evidence is compelling to one who views Scripture as unveiling God's perspective of reality, it is also valuable to note confirming data from the behavioral sciences. In an excellent text,[8] Berger and Luckman argue that reality is socially constructed. In one significant passage exploring that process, they argue that "the individual not only takes on the roles and attitudes of others, but in the same process takes on their world. Indeed, identity is objectively defined as location in a certain world and can be subjectively appropriated only *along with* that world" (p. 132). To "be" a Christian involves taking on a new identity which can only be found by subjectively entering a new world. Entry is not made by intellectual acceptance of a set of abstract beliefs about reality; it is made by personal identification with the roles and attitudes of others, who actually live in that unique social world.

A survey of behavioral science literature suggests the characteristics of a social setting in which this kind of identification is facilitated. These are[9]

1. Frequent, long term contact
2. Warm, loving relationships

8. Peter L. Berger, and Thomas Luckmann, *The Social Construction of Reality* (Garden City, New York: Doubleday & Company, 1967).
9. Adapted from Lawrence O. Richards, *A Theology of Christian Education* (Grand Rapids, Michigan: Zondervan, 1975), pp. 84, 85.

3. Exposure to the inner states of others
4. Models who can be observed in a variety of life settings and situations
5. Consistency and clarity in others' behaviors, values, etc.
6. Correspondence between behavior and beliefs (ideals, standards) espoused
7. Explanation of the lifestyle conceptually, with instruction accompanying shared experiences

The implications of the biblical and behavioral science data are far-reaching. For a person to "be" Christian, in the fullest biblical sense, his identity and perceptions of reality need to be rooted in participation in a community which is committed to give living expression to God's revealed perception of reality. It is simply impossible to communicate a biblical faith in a schoolized way, with stress on cognitive structures, unless that setting is simply one facet of the life of a committed community in which the learner participates fully.

At the same time, if Christian education is to be understood as a process of socialization, which takes place as one participates in the life of the believing community, our understanding of educational ministry is greatly expanded. The Christian educator is not simply the writer of lessons and trainer of teachers. The Christian educator is a facilitator of community, and requires a mastery not of formal education but of nonformal education—a discipline closer to sociology and anthropology than to education.

Perhaps even more important is the realization that Christian education must be rooted in theology, and that the Christian educator must find his guidance for care of the community of faith in the disciplines of a living theology, that grows out of a perception of Scripture as God's reality revelation. Strikingly, the challenge of guiding the community of faith toward shared experience of re-revealed reality is not the province solely of the Christian educator. It is instead the heart of an adequate concept of ministry, and thus a mission shared by all congregational leaders.

SUMMARY OF FINDINGS

Theological Presuppositions	Some Education Implications	Some Education Issues Raised
Revelation is an unveiling of reality. אֱמֶת, αλήθεια	• neither transmissive or encounter processes are indicated • creedal formulation and numinous experience are both inadequate learning outcomes • landmark truths that put "the whole" into perspective must be identified	• what are Scripture's landmark themes? • what methods are appropriate to communicating truth as reality? • what learning goals are required, and how can achievement be measured? • how will the Bible be used in teaching/learning reality?
Revealed reality is to be experienced. μείνητε ἐν τῷ λόγῳ τῷ ἐμῷ	• response to truths taught must involve personal commitment and action • biblical landmark themes must be linked to each learner's personal experiences • landmark truths may be experienced by persons who are unable to comprehend them • schooling provides an inadequate model for reality teaching	• what keys attending, filing, and recall of reality data? • what kind of educational processes encourage emotional mapping of Bible truths? • what ways will learning processes and structures differ from those currently relied on in CE? in what ways will they be the same?
Revealed reality is to be experienced in community. ἀνανεοῦσθαι δὲ τῷ πνεύματι τοῦ νοὸς ὑμῶν	• the community of faith constructs the reality experienced by its members • processes facilitating identification with the community are our most powerful educational tools	• what role if any can formal education play in community nurture? • what are the nonformal processes by which reality is constructed • how do we guide local churches toward becoming transforming communities?

THE IMPOSSIBLE DREAM

And so we at last return to Don Quixote, the comic-tragic figure of a man gripped by an impossible dream. He rejected the values and the perceptions of the society of which he was a part, and hungered for something new and pure. Captured by his vision, he set out, essentially alone, to live as if what he saw was actually real. He often struggled. And all too often he was seen by those around him as merely foolish or mad. But his impossible dream had a unique redemptive power. Convinced in spite of herself, at least one oppressed person, Dulcinaea, found a new identity and a new life, breaking free of the bonds that had held her captive.

The music of LaMancha has always moved me deeply. For the story to me is nothing less than a powerful call to the church to recover its identity and its mission.

Like Don Quixote, we *can* deny the reality which culture and society construct around us. We too can be gripped by the vision of an impossible dream; a dream unveiled by revelation, calling us to enter its vision by faith, and prove its reality together. Unlike the aging man of LaMancha, we are not forced to quest alone. Instead, we are called to quest in community, linked to others who will support us as we struggle to enflesh that which is ever old and yet ever new. Holding one another's hand we can explore God's ideal world; that world that philosophers describe, but only faith can ever truly *know*.

It is as God's own community, and only so, that we will communicate to a lost world the possibility of hope. And, as Quixote touched the life of Dulcinaea, redeemingly affect the individuals and the society in which we live.

Chapter 7

A Catechetical Way of Doing Theology

JOHN H. WESTERHOFF III

Theology, literally talking rationally about God, emerges from the human quest for meaning and understanding; it is a speculative science, an intellectual activity to explain, comprehend, and defend one's experience of ultimate reality from the point of view of a particular perceptual field. Christian theology, therefore, is a systematic reflection on every aspect of human life from the perspective of the gospel. To do theology is to rationally explore every dealing between God and humanity. Insofar as theologians are Christians, their thinking is an activity of faith carried out within a Christian community of faith. As such, theological reflection is rooted in and founded upon the Christian heritage as witnessed to in the Holy Scriptures of the Old and New Testaments and upon common human religious experience, as both are continuously interpreted and reinterpreted by the church; thereby Scripture/tradition, human experience and reason are brought into a dynamic, dialectical relationship and become the threefold authority for theologizing in every age.

Historical theology (historia) attempts to understand and explain past efforts at doing theology in particular historical, social, cultural settings. Systematic theology (theoria) attempts to do theology in the present within a particular historical, social, cultural setting. Practical theology (praxis) reflects on the dialectical relationship between historical and systematic theology and the activities of a

faith community within the liturgical, catechetical, pastoral, asceti-
cal, moral, missional, and ecclesiastical dimensions of its life and
work as they relate to the future.

As such, practical theology is neither philosophical nor apologet-
ical. Written from faith to faith, it assumes a historical community of faith and its concern to transmit and sustain those eternal yet
ever reforming understandings and ways which decisively aid in the
living and interpreting of human individual and corporate life.
Practical theology begins with present-day reality within a particular existential situation. It encourages a hermeneutic which both
explores present action interpreting the heritage from this individual and social perspective *and* which explores the heritage applying it to present day experience and action. Thus, practical theology
is inductive; that is, rather than beginning with philosophical first
principles or universals and deducing conclusions, it emerges from
personal and communal action within a particular historical, social,
cultural context as it relates to contemporary experiences of a living
God and the gospel tradition. It is, therefore, a process of seeking
out amidst present activity questions to be asked and trying out in
the light of past experience various answers to these questions. Its
purpose is praxis or reflection on the activities of a community of
Christian faith which leads to new actions and reflection.

Just as liturgics and theology are closely related, so is the relationship between catechetics and theology. Because liturgics and
catechetics are functions of practical theology, we need to engage in
theological reflection from those perspectives. Geoffrey Wain-
wright's new book *Doxology* has provided us with a liturgical way of
doing theology. The intention of this essay is to suggest a catechetical way of doing theology.

Practical theology in its catechetical expression is two-
dimensional. It looks to historical, foundational, and systematic
theology and to the process of catechesis. It is bi-polar: one pole is
the Christian heritage as it is continuously reshaped and the other
pole is the experience of catechesis within a community of faith. A
catechetical way of doing theology is the art of relating these two
poles creatively in ways that maintain the particular integrity and

inherent value of each. Therefore, before we can proceed, we need to illumine the activity of catechesis, for it is this activity which will frame the questions that need to be addressed in what I have identified as a catechetical way of doing theology, or one dimension of a holistic practical theology.

Catechesis, best understood as intentional socialization in a community of Christian faith refers to every activity engaged in by the church which celebrates and illuminates the word or activity of God. As such, catechesis includes evangelization and assimilation.

Evangelization refers to encounters with the gospel through deeds and words which aid conversions or human transformations in the realms of thought, feeling, and behaviors. Its concern is new beginnings or births. As such, it aims to introduce persons to Christian understanding and ways through experience, and it summons persons and the community to Christian understandings and ways through consciousness raising.

Assimilation refers to incorporation into the gospel tradition through deeds and words which aids nurture or growing-up in the realms of thought, feeling, and behavior. Its concern is actualization and maturation. As such, it aims to aid persons in the adoption and internalization of Christian understanding and ways through participation in community life, and it encourages persons to interpret and apply Christian understandings and ways to individual and social life through reflective action.

Catechesis is a symbolic, interactive, dialectical process within a living, learning, worshiping, witnessing community of faith. Catechesis, understood as process, is best defined as deliberate, systematic, and sustained interpersonal helping relationships of acknowledged value which aid persons and their communities to know God intimately, to live in relationship to God, and to act with God in the world.

Catechesis implies (1) intentional, mindful, responsible, faithful activities; (2) lifelong sustained efforts; (3) open, mutually helpful interpersonal relationships and interactions of persons within a community; (4) a concern for every aspect of life, the political, the social, and the economic; (5) involvement of the entire person in all of that person's relationships with God, self, neighbor, and the natural world.

Catechesis aims to provide persons with a context for experiencing the converting and nurturing presence of Christ day by day as they gather in the Lord's name with other baptized persons to confront and be confronted by God's word and gospel, to respond to the gift of grace, to pray for the world and church, to share God's peace, to present the offerings and oblations of their life and labor, to make thanksgiving for God's grace, break bread and share the gifts of God and thereby be nourished to love and serve the Lord. Catechesis aims to provide persons with a context for falling in love with Christ and thereby having their eyes and ears opened to perceive and hence experience personally the gospel of God's kingdom come. It further aims to provide a context for persons to live in a growing and developing relationship with Christ so that they might be a sign of God's kingdom come. And last, it aims to provide a context for persons to reflect and act with Christ on behalf of God's kingdom.

Catechesis assumes life in a community of Christian faith, the church, the family of God, a visible, historical, human community called to convert and nurture people in the gospel tradition so that they might live under its merciful judgment and inspiration, to the end that God's will is done and God's kingdom (community or government) comes. As such, Christians have always regarded the church as that community through which we experience the reality of the gospel and mediate it to others. Catechesis addresses the processes for that task.

Catechesis implies the need for (1) a knowledge and understanding of the church's living tradition and the reflective cognitive abilities to use that tradition in responsible decision making, (2) a deepened authentic piety unifying attitudes, sensibilities, motivations, commitments, and values into an exemplary style of life in community, and (3) a clear vision of God's will for individual and corporate human life and concomitant skills for its realization in the political, social, and economic world. Thereby is believing, being, and behaving united in the lives of persons who in community have a relationship to Christ and a commitment to the gospel.

Catechesis is a ministry of the word in which the faith is proclaimed and interpreted in verbal and nonverbal ways for the formation and transformation of persons and the community whose end is a lived loved relationship with God and neighbor. Catechesis occurs within a community of faith where persons strive to be Christian together uniting all deliberate, systematic, and sustained efforts to discover the vision and will of God, to evaluate the community's interior and exterior life, and to equip and stimulate the community for greater faithfulness.

Catechesis, as a pastoral activity of intentional Christian socialization, includes every aspect of the church's life which incorporates persons into the life of an ever-changing (reforming), tradition-bearing (catholic) community of Christian faith. It is a process intended to both recall and reconstruct the church's tradition so that it might become conscious and active in the lives of maturing persons and communities. It is the process by which persons learn to know, internalize, and apply the gospel to daily individual and corporate life. As such, catechesis aims to enable the faithful to meet the twofold responsibility which Christian faith asks of them: community with God and neighbor. Catechesis, therefore, is a life's work shared by all those who participate in the mission and ministry of the Christian church. It values the interaction of faithing souls in community, striving to be faithful in-but-not-of-the world. The fundamental question which catechesis asks is this: What is it to be Christian together in community and in the world? To answer this question is to understand the means by which persons actualize their baptism within a community of faith. Catechesis, therefore intends to aid persons understand the implications of Christian faith for life and their lives, to critically evaluate every aspect of their individual and corporate understandings and ways, and to be equipped and inspired for faithful activity in church and society.

Importantly, catechesis acknowledges that we are enculturated or socialized within a community of memory and vision. Baptism incorporates us into a family with a story, a living tradition. This adoption into a new family creates a change intrinsic to the self. We are historical beings, implicitly and explicitly influenced and formed by the communities in which we live and grow. Catechesis acknowledges this influence and challenges all persons to be morally responsible for both the ways in which they live in community and for the ways by which they influence the lives of others. While catechesis affirms that persons are both determined and free, the product and agent of culture, it makes it incumbent upon the community of faith to accept responsibility for disciplined, intentional, faithful, obedient life together. Catechesis, therefore presents us with three foundational questions: How is Christian faith acquired, enhanced, and enlivened? How is divine revelation made known? And how is our human individual and corporate vocation realized? Every generation must reflect afresh on these questions which are at the heart of a catechetical way of doing theology.

Faith

A catechetical way of doing theology begins with a concern for activities related to faith. But how are we to understand faith? Faith can be a troublesome word. Many persons understand faith as synonymous with beliefs or intellectual assertions of truth. Typically, persons in the church use the words faith and doctrine (theological formulations) interchangeably.

I recall going to a class on October 2 and asking my students how they had celebrated that festival day. After an embarrassing silence, one student asked, "What is today"

I responded, "Today is the festival of your guardian angel!"

"You don't believe in angels?" blurted out another.

"Do me a favor," I said, "Write down one sentence expressing something significant that occurred in your life today." They did and shared them. A few were: I had a difficult act to perform today but somehow I found the courage to do it; while reading the New Testament today, I had a flash of insight, I wasn't sure I was going to make it through the day, but I did; and during my morning meditation I was at long last able to discern what I should do about next year.

And then I recall saying, "Have you all forgotten what God promised to our foreparents? It is recorded in Exodus (23:20–21). Listen to what God says, 'See I am sending an angel to accompany you, to enlighten you, to guard you on the way, and to bring you to the place I have prepared for you. Be attentive to your angel and listen for your angel's voice' (translation mine). The problem appears to be that you all lack faith." As you might imagine, that opened an interesting conversation. During that discussion, I discovered that we did not share a common understanding of the word faith. To aid an understanding of my use of the word, I shared a story told by the Sufi's, the prophetic storytellers of Islam: It is a story about a confessed smuggler who each day crosses the border with a donkey loaded with hay. Each day the guards search him and his donkey, but find nothing illegal. At thirty, he retires a wealthy man and throws a party for the border guards. During the festivities, one of the guards asks, "After all these years, please tell us what you have been smuggling." And the man responds, "Donkeys!"

At that point one of my students was illumined: "You are equating faith with perception," he exclaimed.

"Right," I responded, "Since you do not expect to 'see' angels you don't." If God or miracles are not within our perceptual field, it is impossible to experience either. If we do believe in God, it is because any data that might be interpreted to indicate the presence or activity of God is either ignored (filtered out) or labeled without malicious intent to point to something else. Our world is mediated to us by our world view. Faith is a particular way of perceiving life and our lives. Through faith, our perceptions, the world comes to consciousness for us. It is not a case of faith versus no faith; it is only a matter of what faith we hold. Christians share a particular set of perceptions. Those within a community of faith who do not share these perceptions can be said to be persons of unfaith, but not no faith, for everyone functions from some perceptual field or faith.

Faith, therefore, is not one factor in human life alongside others.

It is a basic orientation of our total personality, the centeredness out of which we live. Faith embraces, illumines, and influences all of life and life's experiences. When a person is converted to a new faith, that person perceives life differently. When a person's faith is deepened or given greater clarity, that person's perceptual field is enhanced and enlivened. Further, when we become conscious of our faith, we experience doubt for we realize that we have by necessity bet our very life on a particular set of perceptions, which, since they cannot be proved, could be erroneous.

Of course, we have no choice. Everyone lives out of some faith. Neither is it an issue of whether or not there is *the real*. The issue is that reality and unreality are mediated to us by our perceptions. The only issue is whether or not our perceptions are of the real. An act of faith is the most centered act of the human mind, it is an act of the total personality which necessitates risk, for, if it proves to be a failure, the meaning of one's life is destroyed. Of course, faith is related to community. Our faith is always first a community's faith, and our faith is sustained by a community which holds a similar faith. Yet faith, a central phenomenon in each person's personal life, is an essential aspect of every human life. As such, faith can only be attacked in the name of another faith, for a denial of faith is itself an expression of an alternative faith or perceptual field.

Now faith, understood as perception, expresses itself in-tellectually as believing and manifests itself as doctrine; it expresses itself attitudinally as trusting and manifests itself as centeredness; and it expresses itself behaviorally as worshiping and manifests itself as ritual. Still the activities of believing, trusting, and worshiping and their manifestations in doctrine, centeredness, and ritual can-not be confused with faith.

Beliefs, doctrine, and dogmatic theology are human attempts to express symbolically the cognitive content of faith. Our beliefs are historically influenced and always being reformed and reinterpreted, while faith is constant, prior to, and more basic than beliefs. Faith is that primal and primitive force that preceeds and indeed constructs knowledge itself.

Indeed, the Apostles Creed, the baptismal covenant of Christians, is not so much a rational statement of cognitive beliefs to be analysed and debated as an act of the heart in trust. "Credo ut intelligam" (I give my heart in order that I may believe.) The creed does not therefore begin with the word *opinio*—I make an intellectual assertion that something is true—but with the word *credo*—I give my love or loyalty to. As such it is best understood as an affectional action,

Further, ritual, the repetitive patterns of symbolic behaviors expressive of a community's faith, reminds us that we are more apt to act our way into new ways of thinking than to think our way into new ways of acting. Because this is true, the changing of a people's patterns of worship can result in conversions to new faith and for this reason it is people's rituals which must be reformed if faith is lost, dulled, or confused.

The issue for catechetics, therefore, is what is the historic communal Christian perception of life and our lives and how is that perception acquired, sustained, and deepened within the life of a community which claims Christian faith.

Revelation

Once the issue of faith is resolved, a catechetical way of doing theology turns to a concern for divine revelation. But how are we to understand revelation? Most persons, I find, understand revelation in terms of Scripture and tradition. However, while the Bible surely contains revelation, it is not to be equated with revelation. The Bible is a historical book; the very language of the Scriptures and every image it presents speaks of the culture and time from which it emerges. Only through a literary-historical-critical-analysis of the Scriptures can we even approach the intended meaning of the text. Nevertheless, the Bible is one step removed from revelation and such critical examinations of the text will not bring us into contact with divine revelation.

Revelation is the self-disclosure of God, it is the experience of God, it is shared historical intimacy with God. The Bible is like a diary. When you keep a diary you record your most intimate experiences, relationships, and insights. Your diary represents your experience, but it is never synonymous with it. Many people spend their whole lives as voyeurs, looking in on other people's experiences of God without ever having the experience themselves.

To memorize and quote Scripture or recite the Creed is no guarantee that we are in touch with the saving reality they proclaim for it is one step removed from the reality itself. Indeed, tradition is two steps removed from reality; it is our human attempt to intellectually express and make sense of the story we tell of the experiences we have. Divine revelation is neither these stories nor our expressions of knowledge; it does not make us more learned or well-informed about God. It rather effects our consciousness, it transforms and forms all our relationships and experiences. Faith makes revelation possible, but revelation is a personal encounter with a living, acting God. Revelation is not stories or ideas about God. God does not reveal ideas about God's self. God reveals God's self.

The story of the resurrection is one step removed from reality it tells about, the doctrine of eternal life is two steps removed. Our lives can be shattered by accident, sickness, failure, and death. We are all vulnerable to forces beyond our control, but the good news is that in every experience of death God is present transforming it into life. That experience is divine revelation.

Recently a senior in the Divinity School came for his first session of spiritual direction. I asked him to tell me about his relationship or friendship with God. He was silent and then said, "I'm not sure what you mean." So I expanded my question by saying, "Well, tell me about the quality of your time alone with God, what sort of time do you waste together, how do you express intimacy, how well are you able to share feelings, what common experience do you share, what have you heard God saying recently, and what have you been working on together?"

Once again he was silent and then said, "I read my Bible every day and I pray, but I haven't experienced God and God doesn't say anything." Like many persons, this theological student was intellectually well trained, but had no experience of or intimate relations with God; divine revelation was not known to him.

Divine revelation is that personal, intimate experience of a relationship with God. Divine revelation expresses itself intellectually as narrating or storytelling—our own, the biblical story, and the story of the community of faith—and manifests itself in Scripture and tradition. Divine revelation expresses itself attitudinally as hoping or in open anticipation—listening to God, self, neighbor, and the natural world—and manifests itself as prayer. Divine revelation expresses itself behaviorally as relating or disclosing, and manifests itself in community. God gives God's self to us as lovers give themselves to each other. It takes a lot of being together, of touching and sharing experiences to become intimate with life and God and it is through such relating experiences that the gift of community comes to us.

To focus solely on Scripture and tradition, the record of God's unveiling, is to ignore a concern for revelation. Without present experience we are reduced to passivity and memorization. The Scriptures tell us of a personal God who longs for a relationship with humanity similar to that which lovers have with their beloved. Revelation is a way of knowing. The Hebrew verb for to know is *yada;* it is a word which points more to the heart than the head. Knowing arises not from standing back in disinterested observation but from active, passionate engagement in lived experience. Indeed, the verb *yada* when given a direct personal object is used for lovemaking and the past participle of *yada* is used for intimate friendship. The Hebrew Scriptures talk about "knowing the Lord" as an activity in which God takes the initiative through lived experiences, events, and relationships that call for a response. To know in Greek is *ginoskein,* a word also used for lovemaking. For St. Paul, true knowledge of God is always a dynamic relationship which finds expression in our daily experience.

Thus revelation calls for an open listening attitude which in silence "hears" God speak through symbolic, affectionate, or intuitive images. Revelation calls for us to acknowledge God's presence in us and in the world. As Lamentations (3:25) reminds us, "The

Lord is good to those who wait for him, to the soul that seeks him. It is good that we should wait in silence for the salvation of the Lord." Revelation requires that we affirm the world of solitude, silence, and dependent listening, a difficult task in a fast-moving, production-oriented, rational, independent-minded world. Still, hopeful waiting and seeking are the principle means of relating to God.

Revelation stresses the incomprehensible mystery of God and the provisional, tentative, functional character of all theological statements. It expresses itself in the apprehension of truth through narrating, hoping, and relating and stresses the contingent and dependent existence of the universe and ourselves in relationship to the activity of God who can be known directly through encounter and participation. Still, revelation can not be confused with its experiences or manifestations; it is the experience of God in the present.

While revelation, understood as the relational experience of God, is dependent upon our faith, the issue for catechetics is what has been the historical communal Christian experience of God, and how can this ever present divine revelation be made known to us personally in our own day.

Vocation

Typically, in common speech vocation is used to mean occupation. We speak of vocational schools as trade schools. An avocation is considered one's hobby, and religious vocations are the occupations of those who are ordained clergy or members of religious orders. Typically, people confuse daily labor with vocation, some being labeled secular and some sacred. We confuse vocation with work, and commonly with work for economic reward. As a result, parenting and housekeeping are not included among vocations, and some modes of work are considered to be of greater vocational worth. Vocation, in the sense we are using it however, relates to our common human calling to fulfillment or perfection. Our modes and contexts for human activity are not our vocation, but ways and means of fulfilling our vocation. In this sense, all humans share the same vocation.

I recall the day a student came in to see me and said, "I'm very troubled. After three years in divinity school, I have lost my sense of call, my sense of Christian vocation. Ever since I was a small child I had been told and believed that God wanted me to be a minister, and now I'm not sure. I'm very confused, my life is being ripped apart. I guess I could go and be a businessperson, my undergraduate degree is in business, but I feel like I've lost everything that is important to me and no longer will be able to do the one most important thing in the world, be a minister in the church. I no longer have a Christian vocation."

I didn't know where to begin. The problem was deep and was related to this person's understanding of vocation and ministry. I had had this student in a course on spirituality, and I had thought that after three years she had discovered her vocation and had made significant progress in realizing it, but she did not recognize her spiritual pilgrimage as her true vocation. I tried to explain that her vocation was the same now as always—to live a truly human life in community—and that I thought she had come a long way in doing just that. I tried to explain that she was still called to ministry, for our ministry is wherever we live out our vocation, and that, having just birthed a baby, this rearing of her child was a ministry and that perhaps being a businesswoman was also to be her ministry. I tried to explain to her that what she had come to discover was that her ministry was not to be as priest, but that her new sense of ministry seemed to be the place God was calling her to fulfill her vocation. I tried, but I'm not sure I succeeded, for she had a different understanding of vocation. It did not help when in frustration I suggested she reflect on the fact that to continue in her program toward ordination to the priesthood might really become an avocation, a sin that would get in the way of her fulfilling her real vocation.

Vocation has to do with every aspect of personal and social life; it cannot be restricted to the world of work or be divided into material and spiritual, secular and sacred, masculine and feminine, body and soul. It rather is concerned with every aspect of life and our continual quest to be fully human in community. Of course, it is our faith which informs us of what it means to be human and our revelatory experiences which enable us to be so.

Vocation points to communal life lived in the world. Vocation is expressed intellectually as visioning and is expressed as ethical principles and norms for individual and corporate life. Vocation expresses itself attitudinally as loving and manifests itself as sacrificial service or the disposition of the heart toward God and the good of the neighbor. Vocation expresses itself behaviorally as reflective action, and manifests itself as daily personal and social life discerning and doing the will of God.

The issue for catechetics is what does it mean to be fully human in community and how is that vocation to be actualized by each of us during our lifetime. While dependent upon faith and revelation, vocation, when understood as true human communal life lived in the world, makes faith present to others and enhances and enlivens it in our own lives. And so the catechetical circle is completed. Faith as perception, revelation as relational experience, and vocation as true human life in community each influence and make possible the other.

Catechesis is the means by which a community of faith transmits, sustains, and deepens Christian perceptions of life and our lives; the means by which a community of faith encourages and aids persons and the community to experience the presence of God in their lives and within history; and the means by which a community of faith supports and helps persons and the community to actualize their human potential for wholeness of life in community by discerning and doing the will of God in the world.

We need then to reflect on the catechetical life of the church as it relates to the church's ever emerging understanding of Christian faith, divine revelation, and vocation.

Christian Faith, Revelation, and Vocation

As in every age, we engage in catechesis and thereby address the theological issues of faith, revelation, and vocation from within a particular historical, social, and cultural context. Of course, our understanding of that context is influenced by our personal experience of it. As a white, male, Episcopal priest living in the United States my understanding of the context for contemporary theological reflection is tainted, but I hope not distorted.

Briefly, I sense that we live in a period of radical transition. For a long time we have been dominated by a secular, scientific materialistic society in which religious pluralism has provided a relativism and skepticism devoid of historical consciousness and futuristic vision. While searching for community, we celebrate a rugged individualism; while longing for being, we advocate having; while desiring a this-worldly relevance for human life, we lived for an other-worldly salvation; while wishing for a spiritual reality we can know directly by participation and encounter, we acknowledged solely a material reality known only indirectly by sense experience and reason; while affirming a humanitarian commitment, we supported an inhuman social order; while confessing belief in the gospel, we lived as if God has not acted in Jesus Christ to transform human life and history; while defending both the intellectual and intuitional modes of consciousness, we have been both anti-intellectual and anti-intuitional; while confessing a commitment to prophetic judgment and change, we have acted on behalf of conservative institutional and national survival; while conscious of our expanded human choices and seemingly unlimited possibilities, we have become immobilized and escapist; while aware that we are called to be a sign and an advocate of a new world, we have blessed the status quo; while possessing great personal and social resources, we have acted as if we are miserable worms without hope; and while our rhetoric speaks of paradox and integration, we live lives of disintegration, flip-flopping from one heretical extreme to another. Amid these existential realities, we are confronted by a world that is radically changing before our very eyes. Within the context of this challenging reality, I would like to reflect on Christian faith, revelation, and vocation as they relate to the catechetical ministry of the church.

The Christian faith provides us with one possible way to understand our lives and history, makes possible particular experiences, and implies particular ways of living. Christian faith or perception can best be expressed in the language of poetry and story, in the symbolic narrative at the opening of the church's Eucharistic prayer is one version:

God of all power, ruler of the universe, you are worthy of glory and praise.

At your command all things came to be: the vast expanse of the interseller space, galaxies, suns, the planets in their course, and this fragile earth, our island home.

From the primal elements you brought forth the human race, formed us in your image, and blessed us with memory, vision, reason, and skill.

You gave the whole world into our care so that with you, our Creator, we might govern and serve all your creation. But we keep turning against you and each other betraying your trust. Still you did not abandon us but again and again you call us into covenant with you. Through prophets, sages and priests, you reveal to us your will and teach us to hope and work for your rule of salvation.

In the fullness of time you, in your love, came to our aid in Jesus Christ, born of a woman, and transformed all human life and history, opening to us the way of justice and peace, freedom and equity, community and human well-being. Living as one of us, but without sin, he preached the good news of salvation to the broken, freedom to the captive, joy to the sorrowful, and new life to the dying. To fulfill your purpose he gave himself to death and in your raising him from the dead you destroyed the power of evil and gave the whole creation new life.

And that we might live as you intended you sent your Holy Spirit to continue your work in the world to achieve sanctification and bring salvation to all.

Therefore we praise you joining the heavenly chorus together with prophets, apostles, and martyrs and with all who in every generation have looked to you in hope to proclaim your glory. . . .

At our baptism we are made Christians, incorporated into this story and vision, and are bound to an ever renewable covenant:

To devote ourselves to the apostles' instruction and the communal life, to the breaking of bread and the prayers.

To preserve in resisting the power of cosmic, social and personal evil and wherever we fall into sin to repent and return to the Lord.

To proclaim by example and word the good news of God in Christ.

To seek to serve Christ in all persons, loving our neighbors as ourselves.

And to strive for justice and peace among all people, respecting the dignity of every human being.

To help us understand the radical nature of our baptism the *1979 Book of Common Prayer* recommends that baptisms be celebrated within the Eucharist on the Easter Vigil, Pentecost, All Saints Day, the Sunday after Epiphany (Jesus' baptism), and the visitation of the bishop.

The Easter Vigil reminds us that we are to die to our old broken and incomplete self and be born as a new whole, redeemed person.

Pentecost reminds us that we have been reunited with God's spirit and thereby enabled to live and grow in grace.

All Saint's Day reminds us that we are now saints, perfect persons, justified by God's grace and called to sanctification or the actualization of our true human condition.

The Sunday after Epiphany reminds us that we are to live our lives with Christ in ministry to the world as a sign and advocate of salvation that the world might know what is true for them also.

The visitation of the bishop reminds us that we are members incorporate in that mystical body which is the church.

Further in the *1979 Book of Occasional Services* new emphasis is placed on the preparation of adults for Holy Baptism. While still affirming the place of baptism for the children of the faithful, adult baptism is made the norm and a program for the systematic instruction and formation of adult catechumens established. It is described as a period of training and instruction in a Christian understanding of God, human relationships, and the meaning of life; it is marked by three stages.

Stage One is a precatechumenal period in which those who have been initially attracted to the Christian community are guided to examine and test their motives, in order that they may freely commit themselves to pursue a disciplined exploration of the Christian faith's implications for living.

Stage Two, the catechumenate, combines regular participation in the faith community's liturgies, the practice of life in accordance with the gospel, including service to the poor and neglected and action on behalf of justice and peace; encouragement and instruction in the life of prayer; and basic instruction in the history of salvation as revealed in the Holy Scriptures of the Old and New Testaments.

Stage Three, candidacy for baptism, has two parts. First, just prior to baptism, participation in private disciplines of fasting, examination of conscience and prayer in order that the candidate will be spiritually and emotionally ready for baptism, and second, following baptism, being involved in formal and informal activities to experience the fullness of the corporate life of the church and to gain a deeper understanding of the meaning of the sacraments.

Following baptism, it is assumed that the Christians will center their lives in the liturgical expression of the church's life, especially in the nourishing weekly sacrament of the Eucharist, which in the new prayer book has particular characteristics aimed at nurturing Christian faith, experience and life. Governed by the church year and the lectionary, this weekly celebration combines word and sacrament, is communal (as contrasted with individualistic) in nature, necessitates participation (as contrasted with observation) of the total personality, reminds persons and the community of its redeemed (as contrasted with penitential) character, and is apostolic (as contrasted with escapist and other-worldly) or mission oriented.

Behind these radical reforms in the church's liturgical, and therefore catechetical, life is a particular understanding of faith, revelation, and vocation.

The central vision of world history in the Bible is that all creation is in unity and harmony, every creature in community with every other, living in interdependence and security toward the joy and well-being of each other and nature. It is a vision of a social, political, economic world in which all people in their uniqueness are drawn into community around the will of God, that is the care and maintenance of all of God's creation. It is a vision encompassing all of reality under God's governance.

God acted historically to produce this world and subsequently acts in history to develop it according to God's visionary plan.

Humanity is created by God in God's image to enter into community with God, self, neighbor, and the natural world, and to actualize God's vision through creative acts.

Still, we humans experience ourselves as broken and incomplete, we experience our existence as fragmented and distorted, we experience our world as torn and twisted. We share with all humanity longings for freedom and community, but they appear beyond our grasp. It is easy to conclude that human nature is fundamentally evil and/or that we are prisoners to cosmic and social evil.

The Christian faith proclaims that this experienced existential "slavery" and alienation has been overcome. While not eliminated—the battle between good and evil within each of us and the world continues—a dramatic change has occurred and life can be different.

Whatever our propensities to do evil, the mystery of salvation announces that, granted the eyes of faith and the experience of revelation, the propensity to do good is now stronger. In Jesus Christ a new sacred humanity has been created. Where there once appeared to be only a slavery to sin, we humans are free to live lives of grace. We are truly a redeemed people. We may still sin and live in sin, but we need not do so. A new possibility exists.

Through Jesus Christ, God has overcome personal and social disorder and reestablished the possibility of creations intention. It is a mystery, of course, not in the sense of that which we do not understand, but in the sense that we are continually surprised by the discovery of that which appears impossible.

God acted in Jesus Christ and set things right, that is, God overcame the essential estrangement which had existed between God and humanity. It is a recognition that human life was despoiled, if not decadent, but is now made new by God's gracious generosity. The restoration of human life to its original intention is now an essential fact and an existential possibility. Humanity has been redeemed through the life, death, and resurrection of Jesus Christ.

Through the mystery of this historic event we are placed in a new relationship to God, self, neighbor, and nature, we are called to a new self-understanding, and we are granted the possibility of a new style of life. By the grace of God we are justified, that is we are given a new life, and we are empowered to be sanctified, that is to actualize our new possibility for human personhood.

Baptism is the sacrament of justification, it announces our new human condition and possibility. The Eucharist is the sacrament of sanctification, it nourishes and nurtures us as we grow into our new human condition, the persons we were created to be and indeed already are.

As such, we are liberated historical beings in process, actualizing through God's help our true humanity by moving from a distant past toward a hidden future of reconciliation with God, self, neighbor, and the natural world.

Humanity experiences both a life of essence—who we truly are by God's grace—and existence—who we are as we live out our lives day by day. Christian faith brings us to a vantage point from which we can grasp our authentic life, and Christian revelation, as the experience of new life lived in relationship to God, aids us in the fulfillment of our vocation to make and keep human life genuinely human.

Further, a new age has dawned, a new creation given birth, a transformed order established. God is sovereign over the world and human affairs. God has changed both the direction of history and the human condition so that God's long-standing historical purposes might come to completion and that God's work begun with the creation of the universe might reach fulfillment.

The gospel is the "good news" of what God has done, is doing, and will do; it is the announcement that something is happening and despite all evidence to the contrary all things have been made new. Each human being and the whole human community are reunited with God. The kingdom or government of God has arrived; God is working in and through the words and deeds of human beings, in the social-political-economic-historical world to actualize this new state that God's will might be done and God's community come.

No matter how problematic or obscure it might be, history is purposeful, directional, and intentional. We are not alone; God, the power of unmerited love, is with us liberating and reconciling all of creation. God is in love with humanity, offering to us not what we deserve, but what we need. The purpose of human life is to respond to God's love and join God in God's history making.

While most of our human efforts go badly and even our accomplishments appear inadequate, we can have hope, for God transforms every failure and death into success and new life. God is at work in the world. The plan of God is moving irresistibly forward. We can dream the impossible dream, envision the wildest hope and be confident. Nothing can ultimately stand in the way of God's plan.

There is no need to live in fear or to amass material possessions, power, or prestige. We can trust and risk to live in freedom. Indeed we can sing and dance in the face of evil for good will ultimately triumph.

In spite of the evening news we can have peace and the unity of the human family. Humankind can live together in justice, friendship, abundance, and tranquility. Surely this will not be achieved without struggle and disappointment. We cannot afford an evolutionary optimism or naive sense of natural progress. The path to the actualization of God's reign will be difficult and filled with setbacks. All we can know is how history will end, not when or how. The kingdom of God is in our midst and yet hidden in the future. We are called to do the planting and leave the harvest to God.

The revelation or experiences of salvation through God's grace confirms our fundamental goodness. Broken, incomplete, fragmented, distorted, twisted, and torn we and our world may appear, but our true condition is whole health, well, unified. We are now capable of becoming who we already are. No longer is a gloomy pessimism appropriate. Neither is a naive optimism, but the battle is won and will eventually, by the action of God, triumph.

The victory that Christ reveals is both the goodness of God and the goodness of humankind, created in the image and likeness of God. Just as the victory of Christ was not easily won, we continue to wrestle with our tendency to sin as we open ourselves to God's transforming power to become what God intends.

Religious experience or revelation is the necessary and natural outcome of Christian faith, just as any interior meeting with God preceeds any exterior expression of Christ's life or vocation. For Christian faith, God is the good news that humanity is possible. Christian faith leads us to a sacramental understanding of human life, and it brings persons into a redemptive encounter and a living relationship with God. While Christian faith transforms our consciousness, revelation transforms our personal and social lives making us aware and desirous of living as God intends and has made possible. Divine revelation, when experienced by us existentially, transforms our relationships to God, self, neighbor, and nature; it reveals to us the possibility of a new way of life. God's revelation recreates us. The good news is that God is always present to human life and creatively involved in human history, creating the conditions by which we might fulfill our true humanity. Thus in the solitary silences of human experience we hear "the still small voice." It is not an echo of our own thoughts and impressions, but the experience of the redemptive encounter with God calling us to fulfill our potential for wholeness of life with God.

Conscious of a new reality through the gift of faith and called by experience to a new self-understanding and style of life we are empowered to work out our salvation, to live into our baptism, to be made holy and whole, to actualize our perfection, to fulfill our vocation.

We are twice born, once in our natural birth and then again at our baptism. At our baptism we celebrate the truth that God has reached into the heart of our being, transformed us, and empowered us to live a life of grace. Through our baptism we die and are reborn, we receive the gift of God's sanctifying Spirit, we are made saints, we are called to ministry and we are incorporated into the body of Christ. So radically altered are we that we can never again think of ourselves as merely natural persons. A permanent change has been announced and reenacted. Our vocation is to live into our baptism, to become fully in community who we already are.

Christian vocation can be characterized individually and corporately as life with God under the lordship of Christ. It is life in the world but not of it, participating in ordinary activities in the social, political, and economic contexts of human community to the end that God's will is done and God's government comes. It is not longing for another world or another place in history. At its deepest level our Christian vocation is simply human life devoted to helping to make and keep all human life genuinely human.

Christian vocation is not simply the fulfillment of "religious duties" such as prayer, the support of the church, reading the Bible, and the like. It is rather to be the agent through which God realizes God's intentions for creation. Our vocation is to actively engage in a witnessing community, the church. Our vocation is to be an advocate and sign of God's rule, to become an historical agency through which God is remaking the human world.

We are called to identify with others, especially those who are denied God's intention for all humanity, and become vulnerable; to serve human need and to bring liberation and reconciliation to those who suffer from oppression and estrangement; and thus to make disciples, that is, others who recognize God's intentions for life and our new human condition.

As a community of faith, the church is called to be an active participant with God in the reformation of all human life. As such, we need to express the good news of our own liberation and reunion by liberating others so that they might recognize and be captured by a vision of what God intends for creation, be open to the transformation of their lives, and be enabled and empowered to act with God for the realization of that vision. We need to help others acquire the eyes of faith, to experience God's transforming grace and to reflectively act with God in the world.

Indeed Christian existence must always be understood as life within community and social-political economic history. Christian vocation assumes a radical community centeredness, the acceptance of ethical norms and the search for faithful decision in the light of the complexities of human individual and social life, and to engage corporately in acts which witnesses to God's will.

Our vocation in the church is to help the community continually reorder its existence in ways that will make it more faithful to its role in history, that is, to be an agent within the wider human society through which God's redemption of the world can be made known.

The church is to be a sign and an advocate of this new reality so that all humanity might know what God has made possible for those who have the eyes of faith and the will to live accordingly. Thereby is the church the body of Christ, a hidden, prophetic creature of God's spirit, an instrument of God's transforming power and a witness to God's continuing revelation in history.

It is one church, a paradox to the mind: sinful, yet holy; immanent yet transcendent; divided yet one; continuously in need of reform, yet the bearer of God's transforming eternal word; a human institution and a holy community; a desperate assembly of baptized sinners living, sometimes unconsciously, by grace, yet also an intentional, obedient, steadfast, faithful company of converted, visible saints; a mystery even to itself, but aware, in often incomprehensible ways, that it has a mission in the world and a ministry both to those who by birth or decision find themselves, not entirely by choice, within that family which bears the name Christian and to all people.

The church's mission, like Christ's, is to live in and for the gospel, to witness to and to be a sign of God's coming kingdom. That is, to become what it already is, only more so, the incarnate body of Christ.

The church is a pilgrim community of memory and vision. The vocation of the church is to hear God speak, to see God act, and to witness in word and deed to these experiences. Christianity from the beginning has been essentially a missionary community: the gospel has been committed to the community. The responsibility of the church is to be a living sign and an advocate of that gospel. As such the church is to be an ambassador of Christ and the gospel, to be of service to all people so that individual and corporate life might be more truly human and enriching.

Such is the framework of a theology which is faithful to the nature of catechesis, the Christian heritage, and our present historical-social-cultural context.

Contributors in Order of Presentation

NORMA H. THOMPSON — New York University

RANDOLPH CRUMP MILLER — Yale University Divinity School

GABRIEL MORAN — New York University

OLIVIA PEARL STOKES — Greater Harlem Comprehensive Guidance Center

JAMES MICHAEL LEE — University of Alabama in Birmingham

LAWRENCE O. RICHARDS — Dynamic Church Ministries

JOHN H. WESTERHOFF III — Duke University Divinity School

Index of Names

Index of Subjects

WESTMAR COLLEGE LIBRARY